What Women Want—
What Men Want

What Women Want—
What Men Want,

Why the Sexes Still See Love and
Commitment So Differently

John Marshall Townsend

OXFORD UNIVERSITY PRESS
New York   Oxford

Oxford University Press

Oxford   New York

Athens   Auckland   Bangkok   Bogotá   Buenos Aires   Calcutta
Cape Town   Chennai   Dar es Salaam   Delhi   Florence   Hong Kong   Istanbul
Karachi   Kuala Lumpur   Madrid   Melbourne   Mexico City   Mumbai
Nairobi   Paris   São Paulo   Singapore   Taipei   Tokyo   Toronto   Warsaw

and associated companies in

Berlin   Ibadan

Copyright © 1998 by John Marshall Townsend

First published by Oxford University Press, Inc., 1998

First issued as an Oxford University Press paperback, 1999

Oxford is a registered trademark of Oxford University Press

Library of Congress Cataloging-in-Publication Data
Townsend, John Marshall.
What women want—what men want:
why the sexes still see love and
commitment so differently / John Marshall Townsend.
p. cm.
Includes bibliographical references and index.
ISBN 0-19-511488-4
ISBN 0-19-513103-7 (Pbk.)
1. Sex differences (Psychology) 2. Man-woman relationships.
3. Men—Psychology. 4. Men—Sexual behavior.
5. Women—Psychology. 6. Women—Sexual behavior. I. Title.
BF692.2.T69   1998
155.3'3—dc21
97-43547

1 3 5 7 9 10 8 6 4 2
Printed in the United States of America

For Munchie, Veeger II, Totus and Beckasoidis,
with Love

Contents

Preface

I FIRST BEGAN to study sex and marriage in 1982 when I received a grant from the National Endowment of the Humanities to investigate marriage, divorce, and child custody among Mexican Americans and anglos in California. My previous work had concerned mental disorders. I wanted to determine how much of the behavior we labeled "mental illness" was actually produced by how we treated the people we called mentally ill, by what opportunities they had or didn't have, and by the institutions we put them in. Over a period of seven years I studied matched samples of mental patients, mental hospital staff, and the general public in Germany and the United States. I concluded that the evidence overwhelmingly favored the view that the major mental disorders are universal and they had a biogenetic basis. On the other hand, social factors—like family supports, social class, and whether patients were in custodial institutions, and if so, for how long—were often more potent determinants of what eventually became of people—whether they could lead relatively normal lives or not—than their diagnosis, symptoms, and medical treatment. I published a book and a series of articles stating this, and, happily, worldwide research sponsored by the World Health Organization later supported my conclusions. I thus began that study by assuming that part of the behavior of the mentally ill could be viewed as socially constructed roles, and my findings supported that view—as well as indicating that some equally valid evidence supported a biomedical view.

My experience in studying heterosexual relationships has been similar. Social factors—like childhood training, religious strictures, income, and occupational status—strongly affect our sexual attitudes and behavior. On the other hand, the evidence I review in this book suggests that there is a biological substratum for our sexuality, and this substratum differs for men and women. In this book I emphasize evolutionary explanations of the differences between men's and women's sexual behavior—not because I believe that cultural explanations are invalid or unimportant—but because most social scientists neglect or deny the importance of biological factors. Controversy is healthy if we are to find truth rather than dogma, and my hope is that this book can make a positive contribution to the controversy. It was certainly written in this spirit.

I would like to thank all the people that helped me with my research. Susan Vogel, M.D. provided crucial assiatance and support in organizing the study of medical students and helped get the entire project going. My friend Jodi Eisenberg-Rubinstein has been unstinting in her encouragement and support. My coauthors Jeff Kline (who helped with data collection and analysis), and Timothy Wasserman (who crunched more numbers than either of us wants to remember), both put a lot of effort into the research that forms the basis of this book. I owe them a debt of gratitude. Bill Jankowiak, who is a good friend and fun to work with, generously allowed his Chinese data from our original article to be reviewed in Chapter 10, and his Milford Manor study in Chapter 7. Thanks are also due Xinyong Liu who supplied and translated the recent research on China reviewed in Chapter 10.

Gary Levy and I coauthored two "costume-status" experiments, and I still view that research as some of the most fun and productive in the whole project. My coauthor Laurence Roberts helped with data collection and analysis in the study of law students. Over the years, numerous friends and colleagues have read manuscripts and offered advice, but I would like to single out the following for a special word of thanks: Bob Baesemann for organizing interviews in southern California and for being a loyal friend; my brother, James Townsend, for his friendship and support; Don Symons for reading earlier versions of some of the chapters; and Alan Mazur and Martin Daly for helpful criticism and encouragement.

The initial part of the research was supported by Grant RO-20296-82 from the National Endowment for the Humanities. This work was also supported by several Appleby-Mosher Grants from the Maxwell School, Syracuse University, which also generously provided me with teaching-relief time to conduct the research. My editor at Oxford, Joan Bossert, has been a real pleasure to work with and I appreciate it. Finally, I want to thank all those people who were interviewed or filled out questionnaires. They gave their time and opened up intimate portions of their lives to scrutiny. This was sometimes intense and even painful. They make up the essence of this book, so they have earned the deepest gratitude of all.

What Women Want—
What Men Want

Introduction

Attractiveness, Sexuality, and Choosing Mates

I am convinced that men and women are intrinsically so different that
nothing we do will obliterate or even reduce the differences. I do not
think men have to worry that women will become unsexed or women,
that men will. In fact, the freer we become in allowing both sexes to be
themselves, the more fundamental and ineradicable differences will
show up.

—Jessie Bernard, *The Future of Marriage*

Why Write a Book Like This?

WHEN I BEGAN the research for this book, I had studied mental disorders for
fifteen years. The major mental disorders do appear cross-culturally, which
suggests that they have some biological basis. Social factors, however, like
income and family support, are often more important determinants of what
happens to mental patients than their symptoms. So, although there is an
underlying biological basis for mental disorders, to some extent they are also
socially constructed roles. I assumed I would explain changes in sexuality,
dating, and marriage in similar terms, and I initially assumed that cultural
influences and socialization were by far the most important determinants of
how we behave sexually. Certainly, the way we were raised and the environment we live in strongly influences how we act—in bed and out. But the more
people I interviewed, and the more I read, convinced me that sexuality and
choosing mates were of a different order than other social behavior. Sexual
behavior and mate selection are at the root of how we as a species came into
being and how we will continue to evolve. Any explanation of these phe-
nomena that ignores biology and evolution is bound to be inadequate.

As a young man I experienced the consciousness of the 1960s and '70s. I
truly believed then that the sexes were going to become more alike as we
sloughed off our confining, outmoded sex roles and became freer, more self-
actualized human beings. Masters' and Johnson's *The Human Sexual
Response* showed that women were capable of having multiple orgasms,
whereas men were not, and with the proper stimulation women could reach

orgasm as quickly as any man. After reading this, I actually thought that it would not be long before millions of women were having daily, multiple orgasms with their multiple lovers. In other words, like many young men in that era, I thought sexual liberation would mean that women would become more like men. I was disappointed when I discovered that many women thought that sexual liberation would involve men becoming more like women, and this meant giving up a lot of the things we young men most wanted to do. I discovered that the ancient process of conflict and negotiation between the sexes had not changed at all; only the rhetoric had changed. The freedoms conferred by effective contraceptives and women's economic independence have made men and women more alike in some ways, but these developments have also allowed the sex differences I discuss to become *more* pronounced rather than less.

During my research I became increasingly convinced of the importance of biology and I encountered a great deal of resistance to my approach. This resistance was strongest among academics and intellectuals—particularly those who had absorbed the notion that sex differences in behavior were purely a product of socialization. I believe I understand some of the reasons for this resistance. First, many misinterpret biosocial explanations. They assume that such explanations are deterministic: that we are saying human beings are like animals, that we are "wired" for certain behaviors, and that these instinctive behaviors will emerge whether we want them to or not. Second, people still tend to think in terms of the nature-nurture dichotomy: a behavior is either caused by biology or by the environment, and it is either learned or innate. Third, many assume that biosocial arguments are fatalistic, cynical, or amoral. If someone argues that men have a greater tendency than women to be physically violent, for example, or to be attracted to a variety of sexual partners, then this person accepts these sex differences as "natural" and therefore feels it is acceptable for men to beat up people or cheat on their wives. All of these assumptions are false. As human beings we have inherited certain predispositions from our evolutionary past, but that does not mean we have to act on them. Obviously, if we gratified every selfish, aggressive, or sexual impulse we had, the world would be a lot more dangerous and chaotic than it already is. How we act involves moral choices. Personally, I do not approve of a great deal of what I describe here, including much of the behavior by men that the average woman would consider sexist and exploitative; after all, I am the father of three daughters, and I love and worry about them a great deal. But anyone who argues that we are born with no predispositions whatsoever, and that men and women would act exactly the same if society did not teach them to act differently, is ignoring a mountain of evidence from the major scientific disciplines.

A great many people do not want to admit the tendencies I describe because they find them depressing. If men and women are as different as I claim, what hope is there for stable relationships and marriages? Given that the traditional economic and procreative bases of marriage have declined in importance in recent decades, what is there to hold people together? My answer to these questions is that knowledge is generally better than ignorance. Sex differences in sexuality and mate selection exist and they are not going away; information about these differences is therefore useful. The cases I analyze in the following chapters yield insights into the problems men and women encounter in relationships and what they do about these problems. This information can enable people to make more informed decisions about their own relationships, and can offer them a greater possibility of negotiating and reconciling these differences in their own lives.

Some may believe that although these sex differences characterize our society, they are totally absent in others. As I explain in Chapter 10, these sex differences appear to exist everywhere. My argument is not anti-feminist. On the contrary, I argue that the changes that gave rise to the women's movement—especially the availability of convenient, effective contraceptives and women's increasing participation in the labor force, have given both sexes unprecedented freedom to express their basic desires. This freedom has allowed basic differences between the sexes to become more visible. Whether a person thinks this development is good or bad is a value judgement, and how people evaluate this development depends on how it has affected their lives. This book is not about sexual equality, or women's rights, or any other political issue. My personal belief in this regard is that discrimination on the basis of sex, race, or religion is against the law and should be punished, but this book has nothing to do with these issues.

A word about my methods: I interviewed over 200 individuals for this book, including 50 medical students and 50 Mexican Americans. All participants were citizens of the United States; most were middle class; about half were divorced; one-third were married or remarried, and the median age range was the early thirties. My instrument for these interviews was a schedule consisting mainly of open-ended questions.[1] The men and women I interviewed were assured of the confidentiality of their responses, so the names that appear in the text are pseudonyms, and certain details have been altered to protect anonymity.

Like the Kinsey researchers, I frequently noticed a blatant discrepancy between what people said and what they did. In college educated circles, for example, denial and repudiation of these sex differences, in speech if not in actual behavior, is the norm. In such circles admitting to these tendencies, or, even worse, believing that they have biological origins, is considered sexist, elitist, or reactionary. I therefore tried to concentrate more on what people did than on their attitudes. Because men and women do differ in fundamental ways, heterosexual relationships require the sexes to compromise some of their basic desires. Consequently, the causes of people's dissatisfactions in relationships, what they would ideally prefer, and their fantasies are more likely to reveal basic sex differences than what women and men actually end up doing with each other. I therefore concentrated my questions not only on what people did, but on their disappointments, the causes of their breakups, and on what they would have preferred to do. It is in their most secret fantasies that men and women differ the most—as most women who has been exposed to male pornography and most men who have tried to read a romance novel know.

In the wake of the women's movement, numerous authors predicted that as women gained power and financial independence, their sexual behavior and standards for choosing partners would become more like those of men. If women were no longer dependent on men for their financial security and lifestyle, these experts reasoned, they would no longer be forced to link sexual relations to love, security, and hopes of marriage, and they could be indifferent to how much money their partners made and what they did for a living. To test these predictions, I reviewed the literature on upwardly mobile women, interviewed women medical students and physicians, surveyed women law students, and talked with numerous women who held high-prestige jobs. The results were striking, as we will see.

In addition to my personal interviews, I collected questionnaires on people's sexual behavior and partner selection from over 160 law students and 2,000 university undergraduates.[2] I believe, however, that the ultimate test of the validity of my methods will come from the reactions of the readers of this book. If my quotations and descriptions ring true, and if women and men can not only identify with the characters that appear in these pages, but can also recognize the behavior of their partners and begin to understand their actions, then I will feel that I have accomplished my purpose in writing this book.

Sex in the 1990s

With the introduction of the pill in the early 1960s, convenient and effective contraception became widely available for the first time in human history. In 1973, the U.S. Supreme Court declared unconstitutional all laws that prohibited or restricted abortions during the first trimester of pregnancy. In the sixties and seventies the number of women working outside the home and entering higher paying occupations increased dramatically. Many experts believed that these changes would radically alter women's sexual behavior.[3] Female sexuality would be liberated from the fear of unwanted pregnancy, and women would no longer have to tie their sexual activities to desires for marriage because they could now be economically independent. There is no doubt that these innovations have changed sexual behavior, but have they altered the basic pattern? Chapter 1 analyzes male-female differences in sexual psychology, reviews studies from Kinsey's landmark research in the 1950s to the most extensive studies of the 1980s and 1990s, and outlines the explanation of these differences offered by evolutionary psychologists. In the following chapters, conflicts and problems will be described that have plagued people for centuries, and we will see how women and men cope with them in the 1990s.

Do women still link sex to love?

Chapter 2 describes the sexual behavior of professional men and women, college students, and people with histories of multiple casual partners. In the following excerpt, one of the women medical students describes her attempt to continue a casual relationship with a man she really liked:

> At first I thought his leaving was an asset. I wanted a romantic and affectionate relationship with a man like this but without long-term commitments. But it became painfully apparent his leaving was not an asset. I wanted him to call me and show he cared. I felt like a split personality. My rational side kept saying, "You can make it work. Enjoy it for what it is. That's the way I've run my career. I decide what I want to do and I think, "I should, I can, and I will." This has always worked for me in the rest of my life but in this situation the gut feeling was saying, "It's unrealistic. It won't work. It's too painful. You can't do it." I was like a split-brain experiment with no corpus callosum to join the two sides. The conflict in my mind was that intense.

In Chapter 2 we also hear from women who have had multiple casual partners. The woman in the following interview was 20 years old and had had sixteen one-night stands and within the past year three different sex partners. She thought that sex without love was totally acceptable and did not feel that she needed to be emotionally involved with a man before having sex. Her emotions, however, eventually overwhelmed her abstract attitudes and led her to reject casual sex.

> If I had sex with a guy and I didn't like him, then I just wouldn't go out with him again. I would date other people. I was very promiscuous when I was younger but within the last six months I have become very picky about who I sleep with. Everyone should have their fun for a while and go crazy once they're away from their parents, but after a while, it isn't fun anymore and you want to start getting serious with someone. . . . I didn't like waking up with strange guys in strange places; it bothered me sometimes. It made me feel sort of used.

The men we interviewed ranged from the most loyal and devoted to the most dedicated womanizers. In Chapter 2 we see that despite their diversity, these men share certain similarities in their fantasies, motivations, what they find attractive in women, and what arouses them sexually.

What do women want?

In traditional societies men's attractiveness to women is based more on men's status, skills, and material resources than on their age or physical appearance. In Western societies, there are now many women whose own earning power and resources could allow them the option of ignoring men's resources in choosing mates. Does higher status and income reduce or eliminate women's desire for men of equal or higher status? Chapter 3 describes the standards of men and women professionals as they select and reject partners for sex and marriage.

Do clothes make the man (or woman)?

Can the right costume, income, and occupation make even unattractive men acceptable for dating, sexual relations, and marriage? Can these trappings do the same for women? In Chapter 3 we dressed homely and good-looking men in different types of costumes—including hamburger-chain uniforms, designer outfits, and silk shirts with gold chains—and described them as having appropriate incomes and occupations. The results were startling.

Do men and women agree on who is attractive?

Chapter 3 describes studies designed to see whether men show more agreement than women in judging who is sexually attractive. Men and women ranked photographs of the opposite sex, including pictures of professional models in bathing suits. People rated the attractiveness of various movie stars and celebrities. People were asked whether they would be willing to have sex, date, or marry various individuals in photographs. In all three experiments men agreed more in their assessments than did women. Chapter 3 explains why.

Do women compete with each other for high-status men?

Men emphasize physical attractiveness when they choose partners, and women emphasize partners' status and earning power. Because men are relatively indifferent to women's status and earning power, women with higher levels of education and income must compete with women from all levels for the relatively small pool of higher-status men. Chapter 4 describes this competition—which can be heated and intense.

Are men threatened by successful women?

In Chapter 4 we see that most women do not want to marry "down" in terms of income and occupation, and they are frustrated and angered by men's willingness to do so. In their frustration these women claim that men are threatened by women who are their equals and prefer women who are ignorant and subordinate. The interviews in this chapter reveal how higher-status women deprecate their lower-status competitors and the men who date them.

What do men want?

Chapter 5 describes men's sexuality and preferences in choosing partners for dating, sex, and marriage. Heterosexual men consider women who exhibit the signs of peak fertility the most sexually attractive, and these criteria operate whether the man expresses a conscious desire for children or not. Some researchers have claimed that standards of beauty have varied so enormously in other societies and eras that no generalization can be made about what constitutes beauty. Chapter 5 shows that the components of beauty are quite definable and consistent around the world—although the components differ depending on whether men or women are the judges.

Do American men like skinny women?

The current obsession with female thinness has resulted in the fact that almost 90 percent of anorexia nervosa and bulimia cases are women, and although the incidence of these disorders appears to be increasing rapidly, the frequency of male cases has decreased or remained the same.[4] Most men, however, continue to prefer the curvaceous busts and hips of *Penthouse* and *Playboy* models to the extreme thinness of high fashion models. In Chapter 5 we learn why.

Is there a shortage of marriageable men?

Chapter 6 explores the dating-mating market. In the last decade the ratio of single women over thirty to single men their age has shown a huge increase. Some authors have tried to explain this increase either in terms of a shortage of men or a "marriage squeeze," and these explanations are misleading. Chapter 6 explains why.

Some women do date or marry down from their own social status, but these women's experiences support rather than contradict our argument. Other women choose to be the mistress of a high-status, married man rather than be the wife of a lower-status man. This pattern is becoming increasingly prevalent among women with successful careers. In evolutionary biology, this phenomenon is termed the "polygyny threshold" and appears in many species. Can its occurrence among human beings be solely a product of sex-role socialization? The case for this view is not convincing.

Are women turned on by dominant men?

In Chapter 7 we see that women are turned off by domineering men, but they are attracted to men who appear confident, self-assured, and capable. Men who appear weak, ineffectual, and easily dominated by others are less able to protect and help a woman and her offspring, and women seldom find such men attractive. The winning combination is a blend of traits: skill, strength, and dominance in dealing with the outside world, and warmth, protectiveness, and nurturance within the family. As a highly successful woman physician phrased it, "I want someone I can respect . . . a man that I can have confidence in...a strong man with one weak spot—me and our family, and we're so dear to him he'll do anything for us. But with everyone outside the family he'll be able to walk over them if he has to."

Women's attraction to male status, and men's tendency to have casual sex with a variety of partners, give rise to the groupie phenomenon. Men with high status tend to have lots of sex partners because many women find them attractive. In Chapter 7 we look at such men and women's attitudes toward them.

What do women and men want in marriage?

In Chapters 8 and 9 men and women describe the qualities they desire in a marriage partner, and they reveal the causes of their marital conflicts, dissatisfactions, and breakups. Although men and women share many of the same goals, when their goals differ, they differ in the predicted directions. Husbands complain much more than wives about sexual relations, and much less about the emotional content of the marriage. When husbands or wives complain about inadequate finances, they almost invariably mean the husband's income—even when the wife's income equals or exceeds her husband's.

Although many women enjoy their incomes and careers in their own right, modern-day costs of living continue to escalate, along with divorce rates, making it a virtual necessity for women to work whether they desire to or not. In our society, domestic services, like food preparation and childcare, can be purchased at relatively low cost. This means that the wife who does not work outside the home is more economically vulnerable than ever before in human history. She is also more vulnerable to her husbands's sexual infidelities and possible abandonment because contraceptives have greatly increased the availability of extramarital sexual relations. Contemporary wives thus face more intense sexual competition for their husbands than women did in previous eras. These different vulnerabilities of the sexes are a major cause of the heated polemics surrounding discussions of contemporary sex roles. In Chapters 8 and 9 we explore these vulnerabilities and how couples cope with them.

Are things different in other cultures?

In Chapter 10 we examine sexuality in the People's Republic of China and the Polynesian culture of Samoa. The Samoa described by Margaret Mead in the 1920s was quite permissive compared to the America of Mead's day.

Nevertheless, a strong sexual double standard was present and the same conflicts between men and women that affect Americans today were dramatically evident. Compared to Samoa, mainland China up until quite recently was almost puritanical, and relationships between the sexes in some ways resembled those in nineteenth-century America. The sexual scene in China is changing now, and the changes reflect the same patterns predicted by evolutionary psychology: increases in the divorce rate and the availability of nonmarital sex; young and old men who enjoy high status having multiple sex partners; older divorced men choosing younger women when they remarry; and divorced women searching for higher-status males and not remarrying if they fail to find them.

Are sex differences disappearing as societies change?
Evolutionary psychology provides a powerful framework for analyzing worldwide changes in marriage patterns and sexuality. Internationally, urbanization and industrialization have caused family systems to converge toward the nuclear type of family. The urban nuclear family is characterized by marriage at later ages, greater freedom of individuals to choose their own mates, greater emphasis on the personal relationship between spouses and less emphasis on ties with other relatives, a decline in the sexual division of labor, and reduced power of family elders. All of these changes undermine the traditional basis of marriage: a contract between two family lines regulating the exchange of male economic investments for female fertility and parental investment. Wherever men possess sexual alternatives to marriage, and women possess economic alternatives, marital dissolution rates are high. In the conclusion I present an overview and explanation of these changes.

The idea that early childhood training determines male-female differences in sexuality so pervades research in social science that it now permeates popular beliefs as well.[5] In fact, no study has shown that differential training produces basic sex differences in sexuality and partner selection. As we will see, these sex differences emerge in many individuals *despite* their egalitarian ideology and rejection of a double standard.

Individuals and groups that have consciously repudiated traditional sex roles also provide test cases for this thesis. If we find that these groups and individuals succeed in changing other aspects of traditional sex roles, but find it difficult or impossible to change the specific sex differences under discussion here, then the evolutionary argument gains additional weight. Such groups include communes, utopian experiments, group marriages, and gay men and lesbians. Studies indicate that these groups invariably end up showing precisely the sex differences in sexuality that evolutionary psychology predicts.

The sex differences we are discussing here are not easily modified, and attempts to eliminate or reverse them usually produce disappointing results. For example, we will see that women who have succeeded in high-status occupations that were previously closed to them have indeed rejected much of what was traditionally considered "feminine." They may place their careers above love and marriage for years or even indefinitely, and in their ambition and assertiveness they are equal or superior to most men in their professions—yet, they continue to show precisely the same preferences in sexuality and mate selection that we see in more traditional women. My goal is to explain why.

1

Women's and Men's Sexualities

Differences in Arousal, Goals, and Selectivity

The possibility of reconciling the different sexual interests and capacities of females and males, the possibility of working out sexual adjustments in marriage, and the possibility of adjusting social concepts to allow for these differences between females and males, will depend upon our willingness to accept the realities which the available data seem to indicate.

—Alfred Kinsey et al., *Sexual Behavior in the Human Female*

JOAN LIVES IN A LARGE CITY in the western United States. She is 24, single, works full-time and has her own apartment. In the last five years she has become painfully aware that men's sexuality is different from women's. Her experiences have certainly been broader than those of most women in her mother's and grandmother's generations. Joan came of age in the 1970s in a relatively sophisticated urban environment, and she absorbed the notion that sexual equality meant that men and women were basically the same—or would be if they were allowed to be. She is thus perplexed as to why men act the way they do, and bitter when they do it. Her philosophy and upbringing did not prepare her for the differences between men's and women's sexuality or for her emotional reactions to them.

Joan

I think a lot of men divorce sex from relationships and feelings. The one thing I am looking for is a relationship with a lot of communication. Real honest talking. Most men don't want to talk. They want to go out, and go to dinner, and screw. I talk openly to them if they want to listen, but they seldom do. I want to be friends, but not many men want to do that. Every man that I've ever gone out with has just wanted to go to bed. They say right on the first date, "I think you're attractive. I want to make love to you. Let's just make love." I don't understand why sex is so important to men. So many of their actions seem to be dominated by a few inches of spongy flesh.

I would like to go out with a man and have a really good time and have him drive me home. I could kiss him on the cheek, or he could kiss me on the cheek, and we could look at each other and say, "I really had a good time. What are you doing tomorrow?" I would love to have a man court me, bring me flowers, all those things. But it just doesn't happen. Sex always comes up first. Many men say jokingly that you're supposed to put out by the third date—at the latest! I think they are only half joking. I would love to have that kind of sexual attraction held in the background for a while. I love it when it's an undercurrent—when you know it's there, but it hasn't become obvious yet. Then it's a lot more fun when you do become sexual. But I have never seen sexual attraction remain in the background for very long. Either I don't hold out or he can't hold out. I could go on for a much more extended period of time, but I want to keep seeing him, so . . . A lot of times when I say yes, I realize the relationship isn't going to continue. Sometimes I don't hear from him again. Other times he may say, "It was really nice, but that doesn't mean we're going to continue a relationship." Or, "I really want to keep seeing you, but. . . ." Translated that means, "Oh, God, I'm so glad I got you in bed. Not saying that I didn't like you; I did like you, but I don't really want anything else."

For the past few years I have just been screwing around: A man says, "Let's make love" and I do it because I want the attention. I consider myself a very sexual woman. I love sex, but I don't just want sex. I want to make love. Making love is very different. It implies you have a relationship. And you have some control. So about two weeks ago I was really, really sad. I just hated myself for giving in to men as easily as I've done. I was trying to understand it and I wasn't able to. I was sitting in my room feeling lonely, and I didn't have anyone to talk to about this. I sat and wrote down the name of every man I have ever slept with. It was pretty embarrassing because it is amazing how many men I had forgotten. I don't know if embarrassed is the right word. I felt like such a hypocrite because when I have conversations about sex with people, I say things like, "Love is very important." And I believe that. But I have never had real love, so I have not stuck to my standards in the way I think I should.

I have been to bed with 24 guys. That's how old I am: 24. Twenty-four guys within the last five years. I think that's sick because not one of them meant anything to me. Or, let's put it this way: I didn't really mean anything to them. This made me feel really cheap. I have been rejected so many times. I feel that I could have gotten into serious relationships with about 85 percent of the men I've gone to bed with.

I was not just being promiscuous. They were hopefuls. But they weren't interested.

Joan cannot understand why men apparently do not need the same things she needs in order to enjoy sexual relations. She wants sexual intercourse to be part of a relationship that includes affection, caring, verbal intimacy, and sexual fidelity. Her partners, on the other hand, appear to enjoy intercourse for its own sake, without these accompaniments. They also enjoy having intercourse with a variety of partners and expend a great deal of effort to do so. These male desires are so foreign to her that they are incomprehensible. Because she feels she has been the victim of these desires, she also finds them repugnant. Are Joan's feelings unusual? Traditionally, compared to men, women have desired more cuddling, verbal intimacy, expressions of affection, and foreplay and afterplay in order to enjoy sexual relations. Do most women still feel this way? Is this sex difference still with us despite the new freedoms granted to women by contraception and economic independence?

Basic Sex Differences

The Kinsey studies were conducted between 1938 and 1950.[1] They still constitute the largest body of information ever accumulated on human sexual behavior: over 16,000 interviews were collected, and their statistical reports were based on interviews with 5,940 women and 5,300 men in the United States. Interviewees were subjected to detailed interviews that contained checks for falsification, exaggeration, and concealment. Sorting through the mass of statistical data and tremendous variation between individuals, the Kinsey team identified certain differences between female and male sexuality as basic. Women's sexual activity, they found, is often very discontinuous. Weeks, months, or even years may elapse between periods of activity, and periods of very high activity may alternate with periods of low or no activity. This is true of female masturbation, nocturnal dreams to the point of orgasm, premarital petting, premarital intercourse, extramarital coitus, and homosexual experience—in other words, virtually all sexual activities. Such a pattern of irregularity in total sexual activity is practically unknown in men's histories. If men are not having regular intercourse, they tend to substitute masturbation; if they do not masturbate, the frequency of nocturnal emissions tends to increase.

Compared to women, men are more frequently aroused sexually, and they are aroused by a greater variety of stimuli. Men are more readily aroused by the mere sight of a potential sexual partner, by pictures of nude figures and genitals, by memories, and by the anticipation of new types of experience. Because of the ease of arousal, nearly all younger males are aroused to the point of erection many times a week and many are aroused several times daily. Many men, and particularly younger men, may be uncomfortable and disturbed unless they can carry their responses through to orgasm. Women, however, are usually not seriously disturbed if they do not regularly achieve orgasm, although a few women may be as disturbed as the typical man.

Men's sexuality is more focused on genital stimulation and orgasm, while women are more readily aroused by diffuse touching and caressing, which may eventually progress to genital stimulation. Women are more easily diverted from having intercourse and distracted during intercourse—whether by a child's cry, the ring of the telephone, the memory of tasks left undone, or the presence of other individuals in the house.

Compared to women, men more readily form associations between sexual excitement and almost any stimulus object. In a sense, all men are fetishists because males can be aroused by the mere sight of a particular part of the human body or other stimulus object that is completely separate from any person and from any emotional or relational context. This male capacity explains why fetishism is almost exclusively a male practice. Although most men respond to different parts of the human anatomy as sexual stimulants, some men form sexual associations with particular pieces of clothing or other objects and cannot be aroused without these objects, and some can *only* respond to these objects and not to sex partners: this represents the most extreme male tendency to associate particular stimuli with sexual arousal. Women are far less likely to form such associations and to be aroused by the mere sight of a stimulus object.

The Kinsey team believed that men's greater capacity for sexual-psychological conditioning and greater ease of sexual arousal helped to explain why men are more likely than women to desire sexual relations with a variety of partners. Men are more readily aroused by the sight of an attractive stranger, by fantasizing about this stranger's naked body and genitals, by anticipating new types of sexual techniques, stimulation, and variations in physique and genital anatomy. None of these factors has much significance for the average woman.

The Kinsey researchers found that their extensive information on background factors like religious and moral training and other types of socialization could not account for these sex differences. Nor did these sex differences appear to stem from any differences in the physiology or sensitivity of the sex organs. They therefore speculated that these basic sex differences were the result of differences in the neurophysiology of males and females—in other words, basic differences in the brains and central nervous systems of men and women. In this interpretation the Kinsey team presaged evolutionary psychology's view of sexuality.

There is no doubt that sexual behavior has altered since the decades of the Kinsey studies, and many experts belived that these changes would radically alter women's sexual behavoir.[2] In 1974, Hunt's study of over 2,000 adults revealed that more women had premarital intercourse, engaged in extra-marital affairs, and experienced more types of sexual activity than women in the Kinsey study, but some men still engaged in these activities with significantly more partners than did any woman. These behavioral statistics might be interpreted as indicating that basic sex differences in sexuality are waning, but studies that delved into the psychology behind the behavior revealed a different story. For example, Shere Hite's 1976 sample of 3,000 women was heavily biased in favor of single, urban, feminist, economically independent, sexually liberal individuals. Despite this bias, Hite found that almost no woman wanted sex for its own sake or for the sake of variety—although some women thought their lives might be less complicated if they did enjoy casual sexual relations. Overwhelmingly, the women in Hite's study wanted sex with emotional attachment. Many of Hite's respondents complained that their male partners tended to focus on genital stimulation and orgasm to the neglect of intimacy, affection, and emotional commitment. It is significant that the *Redbook* survey in 1977 of 100,000 women who were more "middle American" than Hite's sample revealed similar findings: women preferred sex in loving, committed relationships and were more likely to orgasm in such relationships than in more casual encounters.

A generation after Kinsey, sociologists Philip Blumstein and Pepper Schwartz studied over 5,000 couples.[3] Their sample included gay men and lesbians, cohabiting heterosexuals, and married heterosexuals. They expected that the changes wrought by the pill and the women's movement would have weakened if not obliterated the male-female differences Kinsey found. They were shocked when their data revealed the same sex differences Kinsey described. Men tend to have more sexual partners than women and fewer emotional attachments. Men tend to seek a variety of sexual partners for the sake of variety, and are more oriented toward genital sex and less toward affection and cuddling. In contrast, women prefer sex within emotional, stable, monogamous relationships.

In 1994, a study of 3,400 Americans by Laumann, Michael, and Michaels illustrated that important changes in sexual behavior have occurred in the last forty years.[4] Among people who came of age in the 1950s, 45 percent of the women and 17 percent of the men were virgins when they wed. Of those who came of age in the 1980s, 5 percent of the women and 3 percent of the men were virgins when they married. In recent years, marriage has given way to cohabitation, and more younger people emphasize sexual foreplay that includes oral sex. Despite the many changes that have occurred, the male-female differences that Kinsey termed "basic" emerged as strongly as ever. Three times as many men as women reported masturbating at least once a week, and three-quarters of men reported always reaching orgasm during sex, as opposed to only one-quarter of the women. Men were more likely to have more sex partners and were more excited by visual materials, sexual fantasies, and the idea of group sex. Laumann, Michael, and Michaels concluded, as Kinsey did, that men and women experience and express their sexuality differently and that this is a source of tension in many relationships.

Additional studies in the 1980s and 1990s continued to produce findings similar to those of Kinsey: boys experience first sexual arousal earlier than girls, are aroused more frequently, and masturbate more often. Men are more likely than women to have multiple partners and to reach orgasm during intercourse. Men are more excited by visual materials and exhibit a stronger desire for a variety of sex partners and uncommitted sex.[5]

No doubt, the new freedoms conferred by more convenient and effective contraceptives, legalized abortion, and women's increasing economic independence have changed sexual behavior. But these changes have not eliminated the differences in how men and women express their sexuality. On the contrary, the available evidence suggests that the opposite is true: *Allowing women and men to explore their own sexualities and choose what they like best makes basic sex differences more, rather than less, visible.* Greater sexual freedom allows more men and women to experiment with different partners in different situations and to discover what they truly like and dislike. The desire for a variety of sex partners, on the part of men, and the link between sex and love, on the part of women, show this clearly. The greater availability of sex outside marriage now allows more men to attempt to have sex with many partners with little or no emotional involvement, and allows more women to feel disappointed when these men succeed. Joan is a case in point. She and many other women have felt that they were victims of the sexual revolution rather than its beneficiaries.

Are men and women sexually excited by the same things?

When a woman decides to be excited by a selected partner, if she decides to excite herself through fantasies or masturbation, she can be aroused as readily as a man. But the cues for her arousal are initially internal: she must put herself in the mood, or allow herself to be put in the mood. She is not likely to be sexually aroused merely by looking at parts of a stranger's body, whereas such experiences are commonplace in the life of the average man.[6]

When a woman sees an attractive stranger, she usually wants to know more about him: his character, what he does for a living, whether he is married, and how he would relate to her. If circumstances permit, she attempts to gain this information through conversation. Although she may not be aware of it, in this conversation she is evaluating the stranger's potential for investment. Is he married? Is he dressed properly? Does he have the right kind of job and education? How does he relate to women? What have his past relationships been like? Is he sensitive and respectful toward her? In her perceptive article on how women assess men's attractiveness, Priscilla Flood wrote:

> The old saw is true: women simply do not objectify the male body the way men do the female body. That doesn't mean we take any less pleasure in watching the opposite sex. We love to look at men. But a man seeing a desirable woman walking down the street can easily imagine her undressed and available to him. He needs no response from her to continue his fantasy or even get an erection. A woman's fantasy, on the other hand, revolves around who the man is, how he fits into the world, how he might relate to her; she doesn't make that automatic mental leap into bed. For a woman, the big payoff in street flirtation is simply a look, some communication between her and the man who's caught her eye.[7]

Flood notes that in their assessment of men, women emphasize the following traits more than they do actual physical traits: signs of vitality, energy, mastery, and a genuine interest in them. She observes, for example, that the message in a man's eyes is ten times more powerful than the most gorgeous body. Of course, it is an additional attraction if the man's eyes are also beautiful, but "it's the expression in and around the eyes that makes the difference." Hands are also very important. In touching, a man's hands should convey "care, consideration, sensitivity, sureness, and strength." If a man has a good body, that is a plus, but it is not the primary determinant of his attractivenss, and a naked stranger is offputting and may be perceived as a threat. Flood concludes that when a woman allies herself with a man, she wants assurances that he is able to take care of himself, and that "he is willing and able, on occasion, to take care of her," even if she plans to earn her own living all the rest of her days.

Flood's analysis highlights the link between women's sexuality and their desire for signs of investment. When women view a handsome stranger, or a photograph of one, their typical reaction is, "Yeah, he's a good-looking man. He's attractive. So what?" He might look like someone they would like to get to know, but they do not assess him purely on the basis of his physical appearance and decide they would like to have sex with him. To make this decision, women need to have more information about the man. In comparison, a man's sexual response to a physically attractive stranger, or simply to certain parts of the stranger's body, or to photographs of these parts, can be immediate, and nudity or seminudity generally enhances his arousal.

In my class on human sexuality, a student related that a woman professor had proclaimed that it was a terrible tragedy that the sexist roles in our society had made men think they had to get an erection every time they saw an attractive woman. I asked the class what they thought of this statement, and one young man replied, "There's no thinking involved. You see a really good-looking woman with a great body, and you want to have sex with her. It's instantaneous. There is no decision. Of course, you can suppress it, but the initial thought is there." This statement launched a class discussion of sexual arousal, and we reviewed the most recent studies. This research indicates that high school boys and college-age men are aroused on the average two or three times daily, the stimulus for arousal is often visual, and the average young male masturbates several times a week. The average high school girl or college woman is aroused once or twice a week, the stimulus for arousal is almost never the mere sight of a person or object, and the average young female masturbates about once a week.[8]

The men in the class agreed that some erections were spontaneous and involuntary, and could occur in extremely embarrassing situations, such as the classroom or church. Merely looking at the woman across the room or allowing one's thoughts to stray to sexual images could produce arousal, and the sexual urge could be so strong that a person would seek relief by masturbating in a bathroom stall or some other desperate location. The women in the class were incredulous and said that this must be "awful," and they wondered how boys and men could live like this. A basketball star who happened to be in the class smiled and explained that spontaneous, involuntary arousal was most common in puberty and the early teenage years, and that "with experience you learn to control it," so that by eighteen or so young men only experience erections when they allow them.

While women can certainly be *excited* by viewing a handsome stranger on the street and by the possibility of meeting him, they are not typically aroused sexually. Physical arousal is marked in women by clitoral erection and vaginal lubrication, and in men by erection of the penis. When men respond to a psychological stimulus like the sight of an attractive stranger, a mental impulse of sexual desire and anticipation precedes and initiates the physical process of arousal. This impulse translates as: "That person is sexually attractive. I would like to have sex with that person." On seeing an attractive stranger, real or photographic, men are prone to run private pornographic movies in their minds. In these fantasies men focus on different anatomical parts of partners that they find particularly attractive, like hips, breasts, thighs, and genitals, and will make love to these body parts in their minds. Although men can see a partner as a total person with a mind, personality, and achievements, their sexual desire does not depend on these qualities, and they can want to have intercourse merely because a partner has a particular anatomical feature that provokes their desire. Men are extremely susceptible to such psychological stimulation, and if they allow their fantasy to continue, they will experience erection and the urge to consummate their desire in orgasm. Women are much less readily aroused by external psychological stimuli but can be as easily aroused as men by touch—if they are with a selected partner, or by their own fantasies when they are masturbating. The cues for women's arousal thus seem to be more internal.[9]

None of this discussion implies that women are less sexual than men. Men and women are simply different. The following statement by a 36-year-old professional woman reveals a sympathetic understanding of this difference between male and female sexuality.

Claire

I think that sex is a comfort for men, something they want and need when they feel grief or loneliness. It seems to be an affirmer of life and of their own power of life. That's not something most women feel or understand emotionally. Men tend to offer sex as a comfort, and they don't understand it when the woman turns away because she is not in the mood. It's out of joint with her feelings if she is lonely or sad. Sex is a celebration for women. You enjoy it more if you're feeling good. If I get all dressed up and go out to a party or a movie or dinner, and I feel pretty and charming, then making love puts the cap on things. I feel sexy then. Everything is going well, and if the evening ends in sex, then I feel better. If I have that "I'm a little blue, convince me that I'm pretty" feeling, then I can be coaxed. But if I'm really down, I am turned off. A lot of men (at least I've heard this is a standard complaint) don't understand why women need all that foreplay and courting and afterplay. I suppose it is boring for a man. It takes a lot of time and energy and he's tired and "she's his wife for Christ's sake," and the alarm is going to shrill in his ear in six hours. Some women might use these excuses consciously. They might not like sex or their husbands. But even for a woman who does love her man, who does enjoy sex, it's not that easy to snap into the mood.

You remember all of that fifties stuff when women really did do things like brush their teeth and put on perfume and change into a clean dress before their husbands got home from work? Well, I think that was very intelligent. I'm not talking about the "total woman" sort of crap. That seems to concentrate heavily on manipulating the man. Besides, does any woman really feel good about greeting her husband on the doorstep wearing a roll of saran wrap? With the stretch marks showing through, and a little roll around the midriff? The other thing concentrates on the woman manipulating her own mood. She's not gussying up for him, she's making herself feel good. A lot of men probably wouldn't notice, really—not what she is wearing exactly. It might even be something invisible, like a lace slip. The point is they'll both notice her mood, and they'll both react to it.

The Kinsey team found that men were much more readily aroused than women by explicit depictions of nudity, genitalia, and sexual intercourse. This was true of both written materials and pictorial media like films and photographs. Women, however, were likely to find films and stories erotically stimulating when they were less explicitly sexual and when they contained fully developed characters in a story with a romantic plot. In fact, twice as many women were stimulated by such literary materials as had responded to portrayals of sexual action, and five times as many responded to such literary materials as had responded to photographs or other depictions of nude human figures. Fully 86 percent of the women who had heard or read pornographic stories had never received any erotic stimulation from them. Yet a surprising proportion of women in the sample said they occasionally enjoyed such stories because of their intrinsic humor, or because enjoying such stories represented a defiance of social convention. Similarly, women who said they enjoyed burlesque or strip shows attended them not because they found them erotically stimulating but because they were curious or because they could share the experience with their male companions.

More recent research has tended to confirm the Kinsey team's findings.[10] For example, some women are physiologically aroused by pornographic films, but they are much more likely to respond to scenes of a man and woman making love than to pictures of nude males or to closeups of male genitals. In viewing heterosexual coitus, women tend to identify with the woman in the film and fantasize that they are the targets of the male actor's desire and attentions. Men, on the other hand, make the woman in the film the object of their lust, and imagine themselves copulating with her.

These experiments contain a substantial volunteer bias because far more women than men refuse to participate in experiments involving hardcore pornography. Even those women who do respond to pornographic materials in experiments do not usually seek them out in everyday life, and there is still no pornography market for women, while the market for men is enormous. Twenty-five years ago the total retail value of all the hardcore porn in the United States was estimated to be between $5 and $10 million.[11] The aggregate male readership of the leading magazines featuring nudity is now over 200 million. The number of hard-core video rentals rose from 75 million in 1985 to 490 million in 1992, and the total climbed to 665 million in 1996. In fact, in 1996 Americans spent more than 8 billion dollars on hardcore videos, computer porn, sex magazines, cable programming, live sex acts, peep shows, and sex devices—an amount much larger than all the revenue generated by rock and country music recordings. Americans now spend more money at strip clubs than at Broadway, OffBroadway, regional and nonprofit theaters, opera, jazz, and classical musical performances combined. These materials are designed for and consumed by men, and this includes the magazines that specialize in portraying nude men, which are designed for and bought by homosexual men.

Women's magazines that feature photographs of nude males do not contradict this basic sex difference in visual arousal. *Viva*'s introduction of a nude male centerfold was a financial disaster. *Playgirl* featured nude males and was successful for a while, but almost half its readership was male. Many of these men were presumed to be homosexual because no women's magazine without nude men showed anywhere near the male readership of *Playgirl*. Furthermore, there is no evidence that the nude photos in *Playgirl* significantly boosted female sales, or that women were sexually aroused by these pictures or used them to stimulate masturbation, as many males use such pictures. Significantly, both *Viva* and *Playgirl* died for lack of interest.

The explosion of the pornography market began in the sixties with the liberalization of laws regulating such materials, and this explosion supports my contention that more sexual freedom allows basic sex differences to become more visible. Contemporary women could easily avail themselves of this market and could do so privately if they feared social disapproval. But the evidence indicates that they do not do so simply because they do not find it sexually arousing or particularly interesting. This is exactly the conclusion the Kinsey researchers reached over thirty years ago, when hardcore pornography was unavailable to most people and was sold to men under the counter in plain, brown wrappers.

The current popularity of male strip shows for women does not contradict the basic sex difference in visual arousal. Studies of these establishments have shown that they are markedly different from strip shows for men.[12] Strip shows for women attempt to create a fun, political atmosphere in which women can defy social conventions and feel liberated by their experience. The female audience is more amused than aroused by the show, and the camaraderie and interaction with their female companions is more important than the interaction with the male dancers. Dancing skill is important for the male strippers and they are allowed (and sometimes encouraged) to dance, joke, and flirt with members of the audience. The men do not expose their genitals. In some strip shows for men, female strippers make no pretense of dancing or enthusiasm, and merely walk about, some smoking cigarettes, displaying their bodies, and if local laws allow, exposing their genitals. Some men in the audience use flashlights to obtain a better view of the women's genitals, and as in adult film theaters, some of the male audience are masturbating. In more upscale strip clubs, which have proliferated in the 1990s, a variety of attractive women perform expert dance routines, but the basic pattern is the same: exposure of the breasts, buttocks, and genital areas and suggestive postures and movements. In either type of club, men in the audience are almost never allowed to touch female strippers—presumably because some of the excited men might maul the women.

A woman medical student named Pat—from whom we will hear later—described a hilarious bachelorette party that featured a male exotic dancer. By the time he arrived at the hostess's apartment with his balloons, the women were already drunk and randy. As soon as he rang the bell, they jerked him into the room and began stripping his clothes off, which, they said, "freaked him out." When they saw that he thought they were truly bent on mayhem, they reassured him that they were just goofing around. Everyone had a good laugh, and after they had given him a few drinks, he stripped down to his G-string and did his exotic dance routine. By this time everyone was ploughed and dancing wildly with each other. Some of the women flirted outrageously when they danced with him, and after several hours, the party began to break up and he left. No one left with him nor to Pat's knowledge did any of the women plan to see him again. I asked Pat whether he was physically attractive and she said, "Of course, all the guys that do that sort of thing are good looking and have great bodies." I asked Pat why, then, weren't her colleagues interested in going home with him or seeing him again. She replied, "What would be the point? He was nice and all but not the type of guy you would date. I think he was going to school part time at some community college and doing this to support himself." Pat, however, believed that the male dancer would definitely have been willing to have sex with the women present, but the women were not interested. She also thought that if the roles had been reversed, and a beautiful woman had danced naked in front of a bunch of drunk and randy men, the outcome would have been all too predictable. In fact, the woman would have had to bring along some protection in order to avoid being manhandled.

Don't both men and women enjoy variety in sex partners?

Because men are more readily aroused, the possibility of having sex with a new and different partner is intrinsically exciting and many would engage in more casual sex than they do if they were not constrained by women's desire for male investment. Although there are women who have had more sexual partners than the average man, studies invariably show that some men have had many more partners than any woman has. The Kinsey team proposed that this sex difference was due to men's capacity to be aroused by a greater variety of stimuli, and to the tendency to limit the sexual experience to one encounter and then move on in search of a new partner. Men who enjoy one-night stands are not necessarily hostile toward women or incapable of affection and intimacy; many men who enjoy casual encounters have had stable, affectionate relationships. But they can also enjoy casual encounters because they find them stimulating and because they do not necessarily need the signs of investment most women require in order to enjoy sex. The following statement exemplifies the male tendencies to seek partner variety and limit the experience to one encounter. Patrick is a 26-year-old businessman and a frequent patron of singles bars.

Patrick

I see it as a game. Women will almost never just get picked up and leave with you, so I hustle and charm the girl until I get her phone number. Then I take her out to dinner and try to score. If she doesn't come through, maybe I take her out again, maybe not. It depends on how attractive she is, what I think my chances are, a lot of things. But once I make it, I'm not interested in her any more. I don't call her again. I mean, sure, I would like to get married some day but I wouldn't be serious about any girl I found in a place like this. I figure if I can pick her up, someone else can too, and I wouldn't marry a woman like that. You'd always be thinking about how many guys she's had and whether she might do it again.

Patrick exhibited a double standard that is typical of many contemporary men: he does not think nonmarital intercourse is necessarily morally wrong for men or for women, but he does not want to marry a woman who has acted as he has and engaged in multiple casual relations. His attitude is more pragmatic than moral. If he can pick a woman up and seduce her so easily, other men can do it also and may do so in the future. This type of double-standard reflects the dynamics of male investment. Men resist investing heavily in a woman when it is not required and when other men have invested little in order to have intercourse with her. If a man finds a woman exceptionally attractive, he may be willing to invest more. He may court, cajole, and promise her the earth. But his tendency is to invest as little as she allows him to invest.[13]

Because male and female sexual desires and capacities differ in fundamental respects, most men and women find it necessary to modify their sexual behavior in order to accommodate the opposite sex's basic desires and capacities. Heterosexual relationships thus involve a bargaining process. A man's ability and willingness to show affection and engage in cuddling, foreplay, and afterplay signal to a woman that he cares about her feelings, and her as a person, and is not merely intent upon satisfying his own desire for genital stimulation and orgasm with a variety of partners. When a man follows his inclination to focus on genital stimulation and orgasm, to spread his investments among several women, and slights these signs of caring and commitment, sexual relations tend to be less satisfying for women.[14] Because of basic sex differences, sexual relations between men and women involve a compromise between their different desires and capacities.

Because male and female desires and capacities are compromised to some extent in heterosexual relations, men's and women's fantasies, ideal preferences, dissatisfactions, and emotional reactions to sexual experience show greater differences than does their overt sexual behavior. In simpler terms, what men and women would ideally prefer shows greater sex differences than what they actually end up doing with each other.[15] Blumstein and Schwartz, for example, found that men were generally less confined to the emotional side of sex than women and were more likely to seek sexual vari-

ety. Consequently, most heterosexual men were predominantly monogamous not because they preferred monogamy, but because they adjusted to
women's preference for monogamy. Because of this adjustment, heterosexual men did not go outside of established relationships as much as they otherwise might have. Instead, they adjusted to the restrictions of monogamy by
designing their sexual activities with their partners to accommodate their
ideas of sufficient and diverse sex. The following statement illustrates the
bargaining involved in heterosexual relationships, and the consequent compromises of basic sex differences. Bryan is 23 and a second-year medical
student. Some of his male and female classmates perceive him as being very
"straight"—to the point of being dull and "a nerd." He is definitely not considered a macho type or a Lothario.

Bryan

*I met Alice when we were undergraduates. I wanted to go out with her,
but I was dating another woman at the time. I eventually dumped this
other woman because she was demanding too much of my time. It was
med school or nothing for me. If anything interfered with that, I would
cut it off. That relationship was convenient, at least for a while. I liked
Alice a lot more, but she was dating a business major who had the time
and money to go out and party. I was studying until eleven or twelve
every night and everybody knew it. Women like to go out with guys
who are fun and lively and will show them a good time, or so it seems.*

*After Alice and I started dating steadily, there was a time when
I was having problems in medical school and wasn't taking care of
her needs. She was dissatisfied and began dating a mutual friend.
That's when I thought medical school wasn't worth it, and I wanted to quit and marry her. I thought I could go into something
besides medicine. Medicine alone was not enough. I was very jealous of her other relationships, but I could understand because I
was asking for support from her but giving nothing in return. I just
didn't have it to give. We'd commute to see each other on weekends
and I'd have to spend forty hours studying. I was a wreck. She was
a senior in college and didn't have the course load I had. She had
been pressing for us to get engaged before, but I hadn't been ready
for engagement. It was when she started seeing this other guy that
I decided that I really needed her and we should get engaged. Now,
she wants to get married after my third year, but I'd rather wait
until I graduate.*

*After I'm married, I don't think I would have an affair, although I
stare at other women and am tempted. A man can get an erection just
staring at a pretty woman. It's an involuntary reaction. But I wouldn't
do anything because I'd be afraid to lose Alice.*

While Bryan is a very conscientious, devoted, and faithful partner, his desires and motives reveal the basic pattern of male sexuality. He describes his previous relationship as "convenient." When his partner's demands for additional commitment made it inconvenient, he ended the relationship. Although currently monogamous, he continues to desire intercourse with other women, and the stimulus for this desire is visual—the mere sight of a pretty woman. He increases his commitment in his relationship with his fiancee only after she threatens him with total rejection by dating other men. He adjusts to monogamy not because he prefers it, but because he is afraid of losing her if she should catch him being unfaithful. Judging from his description, her strategy has been gradually to escalate her demands for commitment and to threaten him with rejection when her demands are not met. This strategy was apparently successful: he wanted to postpone their engagement, so she dated another man; she and Bryan consequently became engaged. She wanted to get married after his third year, he wanted to wait until after his fourth year. They married during his third year.

If Bryan were free to indulge his desires without cost, he would want to have intercourse with every woman he found physically attractive, and he finds a great many women other than his wife physically attractive. His lack of freedom and opportunity to consummate his desire for multiple partners suppresses this male tendency and thus its behavioral manifestation. On the surface, he may appear to be more monogamously inclined than his wife. But it is her demands for sex with commitment and fidelity, and her threats of rejection and loss, that cause him to contain his desires and adjust to monogamy.

A study of sexual foreplay and afterplay also illustrates the bargaining process that occurs in heterosexual relationships. Women were much more likely than men to say they would like to spend more time in foreplay and afterplay. This sex difference in desires resulted in a bargaining process and compromise. Women were more likely to get their way in regard to foreplay than afterplay because they had more control over the amount of foreplay: they could always refuse to have intercourse if their demands for foreplay were not met. Women, however, did not have any obvious way of controlling the amount of afterplay. As the authors of the study noted: "At least with respect to that particular sexual encounter, she no longer has anything with which to bargain."[16]

Do men and women maintain relationships just for sex?

Vince is a second-year medical student, and his experience which follows vividly illustrates a basic difference between the sexes—men can maintain relationships purely because they offer regular sexual relations with a reasonably attractive partner.

Vince

Looks are very important but I have to be able to communicate with a person too. My first girlfriend was a high-school dropout. It was my first sexual experience so I was mesmerized. It was like a new toy. After a year the novelty of sex with her wore off and I couldn't stand her. We had nothing in common intellectually. I would try to carry on conversations with her and I would get so frustrated just by the vocabulary she didn't have. I'd talk about anything, whether it was medical or just anything, but it didn't work. It was driving me crazy. It went on for another year and a half with her just so I could go on having sex. I felt I needed it. It was like a comfortable shoe. After that I just couldn't take it anymore so I broke it off. I thought I'd rather not have anyone than go through that, so I didn't date anyone until I met my present girlfriend.

Vince is no playboy. He has only had sex with two women and he married the second one. He could not maintain a relationship indefinitely with a woman he considered ignorant, but her physical attractiveness and his sexual needs were sufficient to cause him to continue it for two and a half years. Women seldom if ever maintain relationships solely because they offer regular sexual relations with a physically acceptable partner. When women have regular sexual relations with someone, they tend to become involved even if they had not intended to do so. In the next chapter we will explore this issue further, but here I present an overview.[17] For most women, having casual sexual relationships represents a stage rather than a preferred lifetime strategy. Some women realize that they will probably not marry anyone they meet in their current environment—for example, while they in college or graduate school, or dislocated in a training program—and their own career plans, or the uncertainty of such plans, may cause them to try to keep from getting involved. On the other hand, they do not want their sexual relationships to be meaningless—that is, to be devoid of commitment, and in fact their emotions make such a course difficult. So they walk a tightrope in which they try to maintain the level of commitment and attachment that is convenient at this moment in their lives, and at the same time ensure that their partner is equally committed, or more committed, to the relationship. If the partner is overly committed, this too can be a problem, because it would restrict career ambitions and potential opportunities to find someone better. To control these relationships, women limit sexual access and keep other partners interested in case a current relationship fails. Both of these tactics allow women to limit the amount of their sexual involvement so that it does not interfere with career plans, or in case they anticipate moving into another arena with possibly better prospects. Some women are completely conscious of these tactics. Sophia has worked two summers as an intern in journalism and recently accepted a job with a major periodical in New York City. She is 22 years old.

Sophia

Your first reaction when you sleep with a guy is to feel affectionate and nurturant toward him, an emotional bond—despite who he is, even if he's inappropriate or not especially likable. If you sleep with a guy on a regular basis, you're definitely going to have these feelings, and if you like the guy, it's even more true. Women who are dedicated to their careers may consciously pick inappropriate men, just so they won't be able to get too involved. But they still have these feelings. So you get into relationships knowing they won't work out because you won't let them. Either you go after someone who's unobtainable and he won't commit, so you reject him. Or, you pick someone you won't commit to and you reject him. You're only delaying the inevitable. A woman can coast in a relationship if a man is committed and giving her lots of attention, and if he's borderline and nothing better comes along, she can always marry the old standby, but she doesn't respect him.

Jennifer has had a total of ten sex partners but only a single one-night stand, because she usually makes a man court her for several weeks or even months before she sleeps with him. For over two years she maintained a bank of male suitors to ensure that she was in control.

Jennifer

I saw Jon and Dick simultaneously: Jon when I was at school and Dick when I was at home, because he lived a lot closer. Jon is wonderful and has a good heart. He's a psych major and very insightful and supportive. He really helped me grow as a person, but I sometimes wondered if he'd ever make it. He's not ambitious. He wouldn't even do his papers or study unless I pushed him. Dick is a lot more impressive. He made it into a top medical school and is doing well. I saw Dick as an opportunity and a safety relationship. I wasn't ever really in love with him. I felt a little guilty about deceiving both of these guys but not that much because Dick wouldn't commit. Then Jon and I started having problems, I think partly because I was having trouble juggling both of these relationships. Then out of the clear blue, Jon said he wanted to see other people. I wouldn't allow it. I would feel used if he slept with me and then went out with someone else—even though I was secretly seeing Dick occasionally. I felt I could love him while still seeing someone else but I didn't think he could. So I stopped seeing Jon altogether. I think he scarred me for life. I told him, "You killed a positive person. Now I go into every relationship thinking it can't work and hoping it doesn't. If it weren't for you, I

*would believe any guy who said, 'I love you'. Now I don't believe any
of them." Maybe I should be grateful! To this day I've never let myself
love someone like I loved Jon. After I broke up with Jon, I met Kevin.
I went out with him two months before I slept with him. If you're
sleeping with a guy, it's really difficult to keep your emotions under
control. That's why I took so long before I slept with him. Now I'm
afraid to put all my cookies in one basket. I'm always looking around,
keeping someone in waiting, as a backup. I'm really getting tired of
this balancing act and all these games, though, with Kevin and Dick.
Sometimes I think I might blow off law school and start working to
have money so I could get married earlier. To me it's essential to be able
to support myself in case my husband left me. I think about having a
family so much. I feel in control with Kevin, but if I let go of Dick, it
will be impossible not to fall in love with Kevin. I'd be completely
dependent on him and I'm not ready for that. So, I have these little
ways of keeping control, like I keep reminding myself of Kevin's flaws:
he's not that ambitious and probably won't be very successful, or I
automatically think about Jon and how he hurt me. I consciously do
this to keep myself from getting completely into him.*

Jennifer attempts to control the balance between her own and her partner's investments by limiting sexual access, keeping a kind of person-bank,
and holding her own emotions in check.[18] But the more techniques she uses
to control her emotions—such as reminding herself of Kevin's flaws—the
more ambivalence and anxiety she seems to have. Her conflict is not a moral
one. In fact she is self-righteous about her deceptions and infidelity, even
though she does not allow her partners the same freedom. The strength of
her emotions allows her to rationalize her actions completely.

Do older, more experienced individuals outgrow these basic sex differences?

Large-scale investigations like the Kinsey studies in the late 1940s and
Blumstein and Schwartz's *American Couples* in the 1980s have consistently
indicated that men are more likely than women to pursue casual encounters
and relationships and this difference continues into middle age. Women continue to prefer sex with emotional bonding and commitment throughout
their thirties, forties, and fifties, and women with high-powered careers have
the same need for intimacy and affection in sexual relationships that other
women have.[19] Lillian is a good example. When we spoke to Lillian, she
was 27 and a second-year resident in obstetrics and gynecology. Although
medical residents do not have the income, status, and privileges of board-cer-
tified specialists, they are physicians, are addressed as "Doctor," and perform
the procedures of their specialty under supervision. When she was inter-

viewed, Lillian had assisted in many major operations and performed many procedures herself. She was already a physician and it was only a matter of time until she was certified to practice her specialty. She saw nothing wrong with nonmarital sex and maintained a relationship with a married physician for almost two years.

Lillian

It was really good at first. I learned a lot from him and we had a good time together. I wasn't ready for serious commitments at the time because I knew I would be leaving in a couple of years anyway, so at first, I didn't feel compromised at all, and it was quite comfortable. But I began to resent a lot of things about it, like I couldn't spend my birthday or holidays with him because he had to be with his family. I could never call him at home, and he could never stay overnight. He would come over, or we would have dinner somewhere, and then we would make love, and then he would leave. That began to bother me. I began to feel used—like I was just some port in a storm or a place where he could deposit his sperm. I didn't think the way I felt was logical, but I couldn't help it. I just didn't feel right about it and it began to affect my work. I felt off center and depressed. I finally had to cut it off, so I told him I wanted out.

I went out with other guys but there wasn't anybody I was really interested in. I would just go to bed with them if I liked—if I found them attractive. Why not? But that didn't work for very long. I was unhappy with myself, but I didn't know how to articulate it. I couldn't explain it, but one time I just talked to myself and I said, "I don't want to be doing this." This just sort of happened. I started going out with guys on a friendly basis and I wouldn't go to bed with them unless I liked them and I thought there was some potential there. It just seemed to work out better. There would be whole periods when I wouldn't be sleeping with anyone, but I could get my work done and I felt better about myself. The other thing was too emotionally draining and destructive.

Lillian did not regard her actions as morally wrong, and at first she was satisfied in her relationship with the married physician. She did not understand the negative feelings that developed, nor did she rationally accept them, but they were sufficiently powerful to cause her to end the relationship and force her to change her sexual behavior. I interviewed many women in their thirties and forties who reported incidents where they had deliberately decided to have casual sexual encounters. Their descriptions of these encounters revealed a basic pattern. They either already knew the man, or they sought information about his background, occupation, marital status, and character. They required verbal intimacy before they agreed to have sex and were critical of the man's sensitivity toward their feelings and desires, and of his ability and willingness to invest time and energy in them. In other words, they sought and evaluated signs of caring and commitment despite their decisions to have casual encounters. The following interview illustrates all of these characteristics.

Brook is 48 and maintains a successful law practice. She was vague about how many men she had slept with, although she acknowledged that the number was over 25. She has been divorced for over ten years and has experienced difficulty in finding a suitable man in her age range and occupational bracket with whom she could establish a stable relationship. She describes her experiment with a one-night stand.

Brook

I was waiting for a friend in the bar of this restaurant. I was running late, and she had left a little early, so we missed each other. I figured I would wait a little longer, and as I was sitting and having a drink, this man came over and asked if he could sit down. I said, "Sure." I was getting ready to leave soon anyway, but if he hadn't been attractive, I probably would have left immediately. He was from out of town, but he knew some people where I worked so we chatted for a little while and he said some interesting things. I certainly wasn't thinking of getting anything on with him. We went inside and danced to the band. He was actually a pretty good dancer. He was very nice, and tall and thin. He was not putting the make on me at all.

About three-quarters of the way through the evening, I knew my friend was not going to show up. I was intrigued with the idea of taking off and having sex with somebody I'd never met before. I usually make it a point to look someone over more carefully than that for safety reasons. I suggest we have breakfast or lunch, so I can see them in broad daylight. But I was curious about how I would feel doing this and how I would carry it off. He asked me if I would go to his motel room and I said, "Sure." We got to the room and took our clothes off and had sex. He was absolutely competent. He was fairly good at oral sex so I came two or three times. Another interesting thing was that he called me by name, first and last, several times while we had sex. I thought it was a nice touch that he remembered my first name, let alone my last.

So after we had sex two or three times, I said, "I've got to go home." He turned over abruptly with his back to me and said, "What do you mean you're leaving? I thought you would stay and have breakfast with me." I said that I would come back for breakfast in the morning if he really felt bad. He said he felt used, and I felt very bad, even though it was like a role reversal of a one-night stand. I understood his need. I guess his ego was hurt when I said I had to go. Anyway, he got up and put on his clothes and walked me to the car. If he had called and asked me to lunch, I probably would've gone, but he was not the kind of person I wanted to spend much time with. He just wasn't that scintillating, and there were large discrepancies in our ages and our educations. The one-night stand wasn't that great, exciting, or interesting. It was okay. I wouldn't be inspired to do it again. It just wasn't satisfying to me.

Do gay men and lesbians show the same differences in their sexual behavior as heterosexuals do?

The most compelling evidence for the existence of basic sex differences comes from studies of homosexuals. Basic sex differences are even more visible among homosexual men and women than among heterosexuals. Gay men tend to have low-investment sexual relations with multiple partners and their sexual activities focus on genital stimulation. Compared to women and heterosexual men, gay men tend to have large numbers of partners. Bell and Weinberg found that 75 percent of the white males in their sample had had over 100 partners. Twenty-eight percent had had over 1,000. Many of these contacts are with anonymous strangers, occur in public baths or restrooms, and often last only a few minutes. Although some gay men desire durable emotional attachments, they are able to enjoy sexual relations without them. In order to have more lasting relationships, gay men usually agree that sex outside the relationship is acceptable as long as it is not serious. Gay men use the word "cruise" to describe the search for casual sexual encounters, which they sometimes seek. While the AIDS epidemic has diminished gay men's numbers of sex partners, their experience with casual partners still far exceeds that of lesbians and heterosexual men and women.[20]

In contrast, lesbians are much more monogamous than gay men. Seventy-four percent of the lesbians surveyed had had fewer than fifteen partners; 58 percent had had fewer than ten. And lesbians almost never cruise. They tend to become friends before they become lovers.

For lesbians, genital sex is less important than it is for gay or heterosexual men, but affection and caresses are more important. The Kinsey team found that lesbians frequently criticized homosexual men because they were interested in nothing but genitals; gay men, in turn, criticized lesbians because "they do nothing" in a homosexual relationship. The authors point out that these are exactly the complaints they heard from heterosexual men and women about each other:

> It is the constant complaint of married females that their husbands are interested in "nothing but the intercourse," and by that they mean

that he is primarily concerned with genital stimulation and an immediate genital union. On the other hand, it is the constant complaint of the married male that his wife "will do nothing to him," which means, in most instances, that she does not tactilely stimulate his genitalia.

The Kinsey researchers had histories of exclusively homosexual women who had lived openly with women for ten or fifteen years before they attempted any sort of genital stimulation. Thirty years later, Blumstein and Schwartz found that many lesbian couples complained about the low frequency of genital sex because neither partner wanted to be the primary initiator: "each woman's reaction to the aggressive role—distaste—results in an inactivity that makes sex less frequent than lesbians like."

The sex-role approach has difficulty explaining these findings. Homosexual men and women have rejected so many aspects of traditional sex roles—including the very basic aspect of sex, marriage, and children with an opposite-sexed partner—that it is hard to see why they would not also modify or eliminate basic sex differences in sexuality. But rather than being diminished in homosexuals, basic sex differences in sexuality are *more* evident than among heterosexual men and women.[21] This finding supports the propositions of evolutionary psychology. Homosexual men exhibit male tendencies in an extreme form because they are not constrained by women's needs for commitment. They can express their capacity for visual arousal, their desire for casual sex with multiple partners, and their desire for genital stimulation virtually without limitation because they are dealing with other men who also have these desires and capacities. In contrast, lesbians focus more on diffuse touching, verbal intimacy, and signs of affection because that is what women want and what comes most naturally to them.

Changes in sex roles do not appreciably affect these basic sex differences in sexuality. Some lesbians affect masculine behavior and dress, and some gay men are effeminate and cross-dress. To some extent, dress and mannerisms are aspects of sex roles, and social training and sexual scripts do in part determine sex roles. But whether heterosexuals or homosexuals adopt aspects of the opposite sex's role or not, they tend to show basic sex differences in their sexuality.[22] Blumstein and Schwartz studied over 5,000 couples, including married couples, cohabiting heterosexual couples, gay men, and lesbians. They summarize their findings on sexual behavior as follows:

> But the extraordinary diversity in our couples' lives should not invalidate the inescapable message in the data—the continuity of male behavior and the continuity of female behavior. Husbands and male cohabitors are more like gay men than they are like wives or female cohabitors. Lesbians are more like heterosexual women than either is like gay or heterosexual men.

Why is there a sexual double standard?
In our interviews and conversations, women often complained about the sexual double standard in our society: If a man has sex with multiple partners, he's a stud; if a woman does the same thing, she's a slut. I reply that today women do not have to conform to a sexual double standard. If they want to have uncommitted sex, they can do so and many *are* doing so—as we will see in the next chapter. They retort that if they had casual sex with a lot of partners, they would get a bad reputation. I ask, So what? If a woman wants to have casual sex and is not worried about love and commitment, why would she care if men knew that? In fact, if she had such a reputation, men from far and near would be pursuing her to have sex. Why would this be bad? There may be several reasons.

Some contemporary men still harbor a traditional double standard and view women who have casual relations as degraded. But not all men feel this way. This was true in Joan's experience. Many of the men she slept with would call her again when they wanted sex. They did not necessarily see her as degraded by her complicity, and they themselves did not feel degraded by the experience because casual sex was what they wanted from her. She, however, experienced casual sex as degrading. All of this does not mean that men are inevitably callous and indifferent to women's desires for attachment and intimacy. It simply means that men are more capable than women are of enjoying sex without these accompaniments, and at times may even prefer to do so.

This principle is most evident when we examine the behavior of attractive gay men. Gaetan Dugas is referred to as Patient Zero because he is credited with being the primary agent in the initial spread of HIV across the United States.[23] He told health officials that he had approximately 250 different sex partners a year, so that in the ten years since he had come out, he had had about 2500 partners. Yet, men were not turned off by his sexual feats. It was a standing joke that Gaetan would walk into a gay bar, scan the crowd, and announce, "I am the prettiest." His friends and numerous admirers had to agree. He returned from outings with pockets full of matchbooks and napkins covered with addresses and phone numbers. Gaetan was the man everyone wanted. Why wasn't Gaetan worried about his reputation? Because having a reputation of having thousands of lovers (before AIDS was discovered) was proof that he was attractive and had what other men wanted. If a person wants casual sex, then a reputation for hundreds of admirers and partners can act as an advertisement, enticement, and challenge.

But it is clear that women do not want casual sex—or at least not for very long. As we will see in the next chapter, even when women totally reject a sexual double standard and voluntarily engage in casual relations, their emotions eventually sound an alarm, alert them that their interests are being violated, and guide them toward relationships that offer higher levels of investment: relationships with more affection, commitment, and long-term potential. The sexual double standard does not produce male-female differences in sexuality. It results from them.

How does evolutionary psychology explain sex differences?

Evolutionary psychology explains basic sex differences in terms of the different risks and opportunities women and men have faced in mating throughout human history.[24] Women face much greater risks in mating because they could become pregnant, and the number of children a woman can produce in a lifetime is severely limited. These two factors have resulted in a cautious, selective sexual strategy. Because one man could easily father a woman's maximal limit of children, women developed the tendency to select for the best mate possible: the one who makes the greatest investment in her and her children. Investment can take a variety of forms: attention, affection, time, energy, money, and material resources. Regardless of the various forms investment takes, all serve to communicate that a partner cares about the woman, her feelings, and her welfare, and is willing to devote time, energy, and resources to make her happy.

Women are extremely sensitive to the quality of their partner's investment. In many animal species the male brings a gift to the female, or offers access to a territory for feeding, mating, and rearing young. If these gifts are inadequate, the female rejects the male's sexual advances. In human mating, women look for two signs of male investment: the presence of adequate material resources and evidence of emotional involvement. The intense emphasis that American women put on signs of male affection and expression of emotions is part of the evaluative process of choosing partners who would be willing to invest in them. Women want men to show that they care about them, and are willing to invest their time and resources to make them happy. When contemporary women say that men are unwilling to make commitments, what they mean is that some men want to have sexual relations without making these male *investments,* or they want to spread their investments among several women. Sexual relations without these signs of investment are less satisfying to women. When these signs are inadequate, the woman is likely to feel that her partner is getting what he wants, and she is not. She feels as the women quoted earlier did: *used.* Although men may also desire to share these signs of investment with some of their partners, they are able to enjoy sex without these signs.

Women are sexually aroused less frequently and by a narrower range of stimuli, and women's sexual desire is intimately tied to signs of investment because these tendencies were biologically adaptive for females. Women are not sexually aroused by the mere sight of strangers or nudity because such tendencies would promote indiscriminate matings and be maladaptive for them. Women who have showed these tendencies and engaged in indiscriminate sexual relations without requiring male investment have been at a distinct disadvantage throughout human history. They and their offspring were less likely to survive and their genes were consequently selected against.

Men, on the other hand, have historically had a great deal to gain by being easily aroused and attempting to mate with a variety of partners. If a man acquired two wives, for example, he could double his fertility and the representation of his genes in later generations. A woman with two husbands, however, does not necessarily increase her fertility. Of course, men profit by investing in their offspring because they increase their children's chances of survival by doing so. But a man's biology does not require him to invest. It is this difference in minimum parental investment that has caused, over aeons, men and women to evolve different sexual psychologies.

Men do typically invest substantially in their mates and offspring. But men's ability to be easily and frequently aroused by a great variety of stimuli and by the mere thought of a new partner urges them to try also to have sex with women in whom they will invest little or nothing at all. This tendency also appears in other species where males are mated to one female at a time and invest heavily in her and her offspring. Evolutionary psychology thus not only offers a cogent explanation of human sex differences in sexuality, but also those in hundreds of other animal species. These differences are indeed *basic*. They are still very much with us and they do not seem to be going away.

2

Emotional Alarms

The Link Between Sex and Love

Is love so small a pain, do you think, for a woman?

—Euripides, *Medea*

Love and Commitment

HAVE MEN AND WOMEN BECOME more alike in their sexual behavior and attitudes? It is true that more women are engaging in premarital and extramarital sex than ever before, and often without a great deal of courtship and commitment before they decide to become intimate with a man. But have differences between the sexes really disappeared? Have some women been able to separate sexual pleasure from a need for affection, future commitment, and emotional bonding? What percentage of young women engage in sexual intercourse with no expectation, or hope, of emotional involvement? What are the motivations and emotional reactions of these women? How do they compare to men in this regard? I was interested in these questions and wanted to know if the hard-won gains women have made in the professions and workplace have helped them acquire a different view of sexuality.

Among the people I interviewed was Ingrid, a 24-year-old, second-year medical student.[1] Her classmates generally considered her to be one of the most attractive women in the class, and in her own words, Ingrid was attracted to men who are "fun, good-looking, and successful." She feels the medical student she dated for a year possessed these qualities. Now she thinks such men do not want to make commitments: "They just want to have fun and concentrate on their work." Several months into the relationship her partner began to feel confined, and complained that he wanted more time alone and to be with his friends. The relationship began to deteriorate. They fought and she announced that if he could not devote more time and energy to her,

37

she wasn't sure she wanted to continue the relationship. He answered, "Maybe we should take a break." Ingrid thought they would make up soon, but a few days later he said it was over. He said that he wanted to maintain a "special friendship" with her in which they would see each other occasionally and sleep together. Ingrid wanted more than that. Several weeks later, however, she felt lonely and decided to call him. She thought that she needed some closeness and sex, and felt that if he could handle sex on a more casual basis, she could accept it too. Ingrid went over to his apartment and slept with him.

Ingrid

He said he still misses our friendship but I think he misses the sexual relationship the most. I knew within twenty-four hours after I saw him that he's not in love with me. He didn't call the next day and I finally called him that night. He was studying and after we talked a bit, he said, "Well, I've got to get back to studying!" I felt brushed off and . . . I shouldn't use that word. Why should I feel that way if he doesn't? [JMT: What word?] Used. I feel used even though I don't think I should. It's irrational. If we had just gone out to dinner and talked, I would have felt he was interested in me. Or if he had called the next day, I wouldn't have felt bad. But I called him and went over and slept with him and he got what he wanted and I didn't. He says he wants a friendship but I think he just wants to keep things friendly so it won't be uncomfortable in classes and to sleep with me occasionally. That really bothers me. That's not even enough for a friendship. I thought I could handle it the way he does, but I couldn't and I feel pretty bad now about going over there.

Ingrid felt used because her partner refused to offer her adequate signs of love and commitment. She was surprised and perplexed by this feeling, however, because rationally she did not see anything wrong with what she did, and she honestly thought she was capable of continuing to have sex without these signs, as her partner was. Obviously she had accepted the morality of premarital sex for over one year with this man, so that was not the issue. Rather, it was the fact that she had become seriously involved with this man, had grown to love him and to entertain thoughts of a future together, and he was unwilling to talk about the future, or to invest the time, energy, and affection necessary to make her feel secure. When she tried to have sex on his terms, powerful negative emotions intervened. Her feelings of vulnerability, bonding, and closeness changed to anger, humiliation, and depression. These feelings acted like an alarm that alerted Ingrid that her interests were being violated. Ingrid reports that she is not about to repeat the experience.

In the surveys and personal interviews we conducted, one fact consistently emerged: even the most sexually experienced women perceived control of their own emotional involvement and their partners' level of involvement as a problem. The negative emotions women experienced in response to inadequate commitment were not necessarily linked to conservative sexual attitudes and, hence, were not part of a traditional double standard of sexual morality. Engaging in various forms of sexual relations with little or no emotional involvement or commitment did not necessarily produce feelings of degradation or exploitation in these women. Instead, what produced these feelings was a *lack of control* over the partner's involvement and commitment. This discrepancy between the desired level of emotional involvement and the man's actual involvement produced emotional distress. As long as the woman felt the level of the man's involvement was appropriate, feelings of being used, degraded, and disoriented did not emerge.

Sexual Strategies and Emotions

Evolutionary psychologists explain Ingrid's and Lillian's feelings in terms of parental investment and sexual strategies. As we saw in the last chapter, parental investment can take the form of time, energy, risk, nurturance, and resources. Although a man's parental investment in terms of time, energy, and resources *can* exceed the mother's, his minimal investment set by biology is the energy required for the act of intercourse and the production of sperm. Women are thus potentially subject to the same lack of male investment as the females of other mammalian species, such as dogs or cats.

Sexual strategies are not necessarily conscious. Instead, they operate as desires, attractions, and gut-level emotions. Evolutionary psychologists argue that certain emotional reactions were designed by evolution to perform specific, protective functions. These emotions alert individuals, direct their attention to certain types of actions, and evaluate those actions: Is this making me feel good or bad? Should I keep doing this or try something else? Emotions are thus mental evaluations of experience. When people's interests are being violated, their emotions act as alarms that motivate them to remedy the situation.[2]

By their very nature, male and female strategies often conflict and interfere with each other. Men and women evolved emotional mechanisms that alert them to *strategic interference* and allow them to alter their own behavior and influence the behavior of the opposite sex to eliminate or reduce the interference.

Casual sexual relations are relations that involve little investment of time, energy, and resources. Women's sexual desire and their desire to continue sexual relationships are closely tied to signs of sufficient investment. If a woman tries to continue a sexual relationship that involves inadequate investment from her partner, she experiences negative emotions that alert her to strategic interference, dampen her sexual desire, and urge her to stop having sex until adequate signs of investment are forthcoming. In our contemporary environment these signs can consist of a phone call, an invitation to dinner, a birthday card, or affectionate words and hugs. Whatever the form, these signs serve to reassure a woman that her partner cares about her and is willing to expend time, energy, and resources to show it. When women consciously try to suppress their needs for investment, as Ingrid did, they often find their negative emotions prevent them from doing so. Christine's experience provides another example of the strong emotions at play.

Christine, a 23-year-old, second-year medical student, estimates that she has had intercourse with twenty-five men (far more partners than the average man in the medical student sample). She is sociable, assertive, competes athletically with men and is better than many. She characterizes herself as "a strong person." Nevertheless, in her desires and emotional reactions to sexual experience she shows the basic female pattern. She wants sex with investment—with intimacy, cuddling, and the possibility of emotional commitment and marriage. A recent experience made her desire for investment dramatically clear to her. She believed that she could control this desire and enjoy a transitory sexual relationship for what it had to offer. But powerful emotions intervened and forced her to cut off the relationship.

Christine

I met this fourth-year medical student in the gym. He was very intelligent and nice and had just obtained a surgical residency in a great hospital. I was impressed! He began to help me study for exams. He was so knowledgeable and helpful I began to find him extremely attractive. I can see now that I was testing the waters during these study sessions— trying to decide how he felt about me and whether there was any possibility of a relationship. He finally asked me out to dinner and I slept with him that night. In bed he was very good about being affectionate and cuddling. What impressed me the most was that even the next day he was very close and affectionate. I've been with men who weren't that way and I felt I could develop a real bond with this man. The only catch was that he was leaving in four months for his residency.

At first I thought his leaving was an asset. I told myself rationally that this was okay. I wanted a romantic and affectionate relationship with a man like this but without long-term commitments. I've got another two years of medical school and then my residency, so I thought this kind of relationship would be perfect for me—you know, no complications. But it became painfully apparent his leaving was not an asset. The very next day after we slept together I wanted evidence that he was genuinely interested in me and was willing to pursue me. I wanted him to call me and show he cared. I felt like a split personality. My rational side kept saying, "You can make it work. Enjoy it for what it is. Don't worry whether he calls or not. You can do it." I've always run my life that way.

I rationally set my priorities, consider my options, make my decision, and then go for it. That's the way I've run my career. I decide what I want to do and I think, "I should, I can, and I will." This has always worked for me in the rest of my life but in this situation the gut feeling was saying, "It's unrealistic. It won't work. It's too painful. You can't do it." I was like a split-brain experiment with no corpus callosum to join the two sides. The conflict in my mind was that intense.

I slept with him again. It was the same intensity. I tried to feel him out to see if it could go anywhere. I knew it was unrealistic, but I still had a fantasy about how it could work out. I think he knew I wanted more of a commitment and he couldn't deliver. I was explicit about my feelings even when I tried to control them. When I wanted him to call, I told him. No subtleties. So it was clear I wanted a serious relationship and he backed off. There was a point in time when I would see him in the gym, but it was obvious that I had decided to cool it. I never slept with him again after that. It was too painful. In the end the side that said it's unrealistic won out, but it was a painful defeat.

Women's greater tendency to link sexual relations to signs of investment becomes more obvious when we compare men's reactions to sexual experience. Obviously, the partners of Ingrid and Christine were willing to continue sexual relationships without obligations and commitment. It was the women who needed these signs in order to continue. The following interview with a male medical student illustrates this sex difference. Men can fall deeply in love and press for commitment, but they can also maintain relationships merely because they offer sexual relations with fun, attractive partners.

Gene is 23 years old. He came from a fairly conservative background and was a virgin before he met the woman he describes here. What he learns from his experience is the opposite of what Christine and Ingrid learned from theirs: he *can* enjoy a sexual relationship without thinking about obligations and commitments, and prefers to do so until he is ready to get married.

Gene

When we started dating, I was sort of uneasy because she had been quite sexually active with a previous guy. I told her I was pretty inexperienced, so she couldn't expect miracles. It didn't seem to matter to her though. She felt we were in love and that is what counted. I decided there was nothing really wrong with sex outside of marriage and I might as well enjoy myself like everyone else. It was fun experimenting and we got to know each other really well.

Although economically her family, like his, was upper-middle class, the two families had different ethnic and religious backgrounds. Over the months he began to notice differences that bothered him: her family drank too much; her mother constantly invoked the saints; his girlfriend dealt with conflict and emotions differently than he did; she would talk to him as a mother would to a child. He became increasingly aware of these differences, but he decided to stick it out and see if things would get better. His dissatisfaction was exacerbated by the fact that her previous boyfriend had been involved in some illicit activities and she had to testify at his trial. Gene postponed telling her how he felt because she told him she couldn't get through the trial if she didn't feel good about their relationship. After the trial he told her that he was uncomfortable with the thought of getting married, and that they should cancel the engagement party and assume there were no commitments:

That lasted for about a week, and during that time I still felt that she assumed that we would be together years from now from the way she was talking—even though I had warned her that I wasn't comfortable with that idea. I felt like I was lying to her every time she expressed those feelings and I didn't say, "You're wrong; we probably won't be together in two years, or there is a good chance we won't be." She kept saying, "I really love you, and you love me." I felt it was still bad because she knew what she wanted but she couldn't see what I was feeling and she wouldn't let me be ambivalent. So again that week I said, "Look, things aren't going well." She stuck out her hand and said, "Do you want the rings back?" And I took them back and that was it.

We still see each other without any assumptions about what is going to happen. We both understand that there are no commitments. I am seeing other people and so is she. I think our relationship will go on until I meet someone else. I probably wouldn't be comfortable with meeting a girl and just going to bed with her, so right now it is very comfortable seeing Betty occasionally. Sex is part of the way we enjoy each other and she is very comfortable with that too. I think Betty still hopes, though, that we will get together, but deep down she believes we won't. Her feelings are still stronger for me than mine are for her, and it's obvious to me that if she started seeing somebody regularly, she wouldn't want to see me, although she doesn't admit to that now.

Right now, I don't think there is any possibility that I will ever marry her. That makes me sad because in so many ways we got along so well, especially the sexual involvement. So many people have so much trouble along those lines, but we had no trouble at all. It is so disheartening that I might not find someone like that again. Yet there are other things that are important. I also realize that I learned a lot about life, how to relate to a woman sexually, and I am a lot more comfort-

able now along those lines. Before, any girl I went out with for a long period of time I was sizing up for marriage. Now I want to go out and have a great time and not think about a woman's marriage potential. I think I'd better play it cool for a while as far as getting really involved with anyone because I just got out of a lot of trouble. My next couple of years will involve a lot of long hours working and an awful lot of moving and I don't want to get married.

Gene's sexual history was quite conservative. He was a virgin until he was 21 and over half of his female classmates had had more sexual partners than he. He states that even now he probably would not feel comfortable just meeting a girl and going to bed with her. On the other hand, he feels comfortable maintaining a sexual relationship with a woman he has no desire to marry but who wants to marry him. In assessing the relationship, he emphasizes the sexual aspects and how much he gained in sexual experience and confidence. In fact, the sexual aspects appear to be what he misses most and what he most regrets losing.

Charles is a second-year medical student but is professionally advanced for his age. He has already assisted on medical research teams, and has his name on several published articles. Charles moved in with his girlfriend with the understanding that it involved no commitment:

Charles

When we moved in together, I thought I might eventually marry Debbie. But even then I was being realistic about it. When we bought the furniture, she bought the sofa and I bought the table—we divided up the purchases. This got her a little worried, but I knew how fragile most of these relationships are. I'd seen my sister and a helluva' lot of other people split up even when they had been deeply in love at one point, so I just thought this was the logical way to do it. Well, she got upset and demanded to know what was going on, like, "Why the hell did we buy the separate furniture if you see us living together for the rest of our lives?" She says she wants to have kids! She's not that confused about it now. That's what we had our first arguments about. When the cosmic choice first started to arise, she asked what I saw for her in my future. In other words, will you marry me? And I couldn't say I saw her in my future, because I don't see anyone in my future right now. I see medical school and that's about it.

These problems began building shortly after we moved in together. I began to have second thoughts about the relationship and she became upset and we had all these stupid screaming sessions because of that. It came to a head when I hinted that I might want to date other people. I never suggested that directly, of course, because I knew that the heat

*would have blown the roof off the apartment building. Instead, I said
I thought we should mellow out a little bit; we were getting too serious.
Of course that meant breaking the foundations of the relationship.
She realized that. That's why we're fighting.*

*I guess I should point out that there are some other complications in
our relationship. Debbie has a medical condition and it's chronic and
it's becoming worse. She had to take a semester off from school and it's
not getting any better. I talked to my dad about it and he said, "Well,
Debbie is a really sweet girl but there are a lot of sweet girls out there."
He's a very sympathetic man, but he pointed out to me that I was not
obligated to her. I've only known her for a short time, so I don't owe
her a lifetime of taking care of her and her disabilities. Now that I
think back on it, I can see this problem was simmering beneath the surface all the time. At first, she was talking more about going to law
school and her career than about kids and marriage. But when I started to become iffy about the situation, she began to push for marriage.
It's a terrible thing, but it's true that her disability will severely limit her
options for marriage or a career. I'm sure she realizes this, so when I
became more ambivalent, it was really threatening, and she began to
push for a final commitment now: marriage and kids. I can see how
this has aggravated all of our problems.*

*I started becoming indifferent to Debbie soon after I moved in, but
probably more seriously as we went along because these things were
being aggravated by the situation she's in. But I think I was always
kind of indifferent due to some recent experiences. Last summer I started going out with Kathy, who works in the research lab where I was a
student assistant. She actually seduced me. When I first met her, I saw
she was married and thought that was it. But she started telling me
how unhappy her marriage was and finally suggested we have a drink.
So, after that, we made love five or six times and then I stopped working there and returned to school, so it kind of fizzled out. But, really, I
saw Kathy as a lovely, young, healthy, attractive girl and that was a
very positive thing. I could see my status was rising rapidly. I'm still
only a student but I've already got my name on some articles and people know who I am. Every year my status seems to go up, and it's like,
"Whoa, I'm really somebody now!" People are starting to realize that
and I'm starting to be able to take advantage of it. It's really becoming
a very powerful tool.*

*That's one of the reasons I don't want to get married now. It's too
early. I'm being realistic about it. I want to get married to have a family. I don't want to have kids now because I need to get settled in my
profession first. If I got married now, it would probably get totally
screwed up—no matter who I married. Getting married with this kind*

*of indefinite idea of having kids sometime in the future is a problem
because you've got to have something to hold you together for those
years. I think a lot of those marriages fizzle out in four or five years
because there's no real investment there. So I expect I'm going to be
facing a lot of stress in the next few years. It's something that I would
like to have someone support me with, but at the same time, I can't
have the same sort of hassles I'm dealing with now. I wouldn't be able
to deal with it. So I am not ready for any commitments right now, and
frankly, I want to look around.*

Both Charles and Gene found it impossible to maintain open-ended sexual relationships because their partners demanded signs of investment,
forced confrontations, and severed relations when the men admitted they
were unwilling to commit themselves. One of the causes of Charles' ambivalence is his desire to play the field and have sex with other women. When
their relationships failed, both men concluded that serious emotional
involvements were a source of trouble and should be avoided in the future.
Until they are settled in their professions and are ready to marry, they want
to have more casual relations. That is, they want sexual relationships, but
with little investment.

Unlike the preceding male medical students who came from fairly conservative, upper-middle-class, Protestant families, Aaron is Jewish and is
actively involved in radical politics. He considers himself a feminist and uses
terms like "macho" and "sexist" as pejoratives when referring to traditional sex roles. Nevertheless, he exhibits a distinctly male pattern of sexuality in
describing his relationship with an undergraduate he met at a political rally:

Aaron

*I met my present girlfriend four months ago at a political rally. She's an
undergraduate. We see each other a few times a week. She comes over
about 10:30 and we hang out for an hour and then go to bed. She com-
plains that I'm not giving her enough except in bed. She wants more
time, more from me. I tell her I'm busy with my work and political activities, and I am. Ideally, I would like to have a deeper relationship with
someone, create something that's working, that's stable, because this
relationship is not going anywhere. If she weren't hassling me, I could
coast and just enjoy it. It's better than nothing, especially sexually, having someone to be there, to hold. Having sex regularly is definitely important, letting out all that frustration. Having sex builds you up and you
need that outlet. Friendships are important too, but there's something
special about a sexual relationship: women will nurture you.*

*This relationship fills a need even when I know I won't marry her.
I'm not even thinking about marriage now and I don't want to marry*

before I finish my residency. Sometimes I feel a little guilty, like I'm using her, that it's convenient. But when I try to pin her down and ask her what she really wants, she's elusive. I think she wants to keep a certain amount of psychological distance in order not to be hurt. So I don't feel guilty because she's protecting herself and she's young and doesn't really know what she wants. She has lots of time to settle down.

[JMT: Has it occurred to you that she might want you to take the initiative and say "I love you," and make more of a commitment?]

Oh, no way! I'm not into that! I can feel she may cut it off because she is so dissatisfied and that frightens me because I need a relationship like this. When you're in a relationship like this and it's cut off, it's devastating. I've had that happen. Even when you're not in love and not especially committed, it's still a big loss. So I don't want to cut it off. I would like to coast for a while. She's fairly physically attractive. That's definitely a major part of it. I would like to meet some other women, and I do occasionally sleep with a woman I knew from before, but the ones I'm really attracted to are all attached.

Aaron is frightened that his girlfriend may cut the relationship off even though he does not love her and wants no obligations. This echoes a study by C. T. Hill and colleagues.[3] Men who are not particularly involved emotionally are still reluctant to end relationships. In contrast, women who feel less involved than their partners do are more likely to end relationships. Aaron pinpoints the reason for his reluctance: having sex with an attractive partner builds him up and makes him feel good. Sex on these terms, however, makes his partner feel bad and she will probably cut him off if her demands for increased investment are not met.

These interviews provide us a window into two very different sexual strategies. The men feel harassed by their partners' demands for investment and avoid confronting the issue if the women permit it. From a male perspective, the men's complaints sound quite reasonable. They want nice, easy relationships that include good sex and companionship and a minimum of trouble, so what is all the fuss about? Why couldn't these women just let it happen? But when we listen to Ingrid and Christine, we see the same situations from their perspective. For them, a good relationship is one in which they feel secure and certain that the man loves them, and they cannot feel this way unless he offers the right signs of investment. Gene, Charles, and Aaron did not exhibit a stereotypical macho desire for sexual conquests. They did not prowl singles bars trying to score. Yet their sexual experiences convinced them that they could and *should* seek and enjoy more transitory relationships in the future, because such a course would be less damaging to their mental balance and career aspirations than would more involved relationships. Their experiences, the lessons they drew from these experiences, and their resulting strategies stand in marked contrast to those of the women, whose experiences led them to precisely the opposite conclusion: transitory relationships were damaging to their mental balance, their marital goals, and their careers.

Do some women just want sex?

Perhaps our medical students weren't representative. Perhaps in a younger group of women, who were not yet concerned about finding a suitable marriage partner and balancing the demands of career and marriage, there were women who were truly indifferent to investment. The large-scale study by Laumann and his colleagues showed that younger, college-educated people were more liberal than other groups in their sexual attitudes and behavior.[4] We therefore used several different methods to try to find women who were experienced in casual sex and who were truly indifferent to signs of emotional commitment and investment. First, we asked students in a large, undergraduate anthropology class whether they would be willing to be interviewed about their dating habits, sexual experiences, and marital goals. (To establish a comfort level for the interviewees, we arranged for women to be interviewed by a woman, and men, by a man.) Students who volunteered were subsequently telephoned and informed that we only wanted to interview people who were "quite sexually active." If respondents asked what "quite sexually active" meant, they were told we were interested in people who had had sex with several partners. Participants were also requested to ask any friends or roommates who fit that criterion whether they would be willing to be interviewed. We eventually interviewed 35 women and 26 men. Research assistants made appointments for volunteers by telephone and interviewed them in their own or the interviewer's apartment. Each interview lasted from one to four hours.[5]

Women showed varying degrees of sensitivity and awareness concerning their reactions to casual sexual relations. We classified these different reactions as belonging to one of three stages.

Stage 1: Coming Out. In Stage 1 a woman begins to test her sexual attractiveness and experiment with her sexual power, its effects, and her own ability to do without investment. Women in Stage 1 are typically high school or college students, or the proverbial "gay divorcee" experimenting with the field after an unhappy marriage. These women have not yet experienced a sharp discrepancy between investment desired and investment received.

In some cases the women we identified in this stage explicitly viewed their sexual activities as an opportunity to test their attractiveness, and as competition between friends to see who could get the most attractive men. This type of competition usually occurred in some kind of public arena, like bars or parties, where the available men could be sized up and compared, and the players, tactics, and results of the competition could be observed. As one woman remarked, "It's the ultimate ego boost to have a bunch of guys come up to you and want to be with you, even if it is just for one night."

Concern about investment emerged in subtle ways among women in Stage 1, as the following interview will make clear. When we interviewed her, Jessica was 21 years old and had had five one-night stands and within the past year six different sex partners. She strongly agreed that "sex with-out love is okay," and fantasized at least once every two weeks about some-one other than her current partner. When asked whether she thought she should be emotionally involved with someone before having sex with him, Jessica answered "No." But she does worry about losing control of her emotions in relationships.

Jessica

When I first go to bed with a guy, I wonder whether sex was all he was after and how he'll treat me in the morning. If I like the guy, I worry about whether he cares about me; otherwise, I don't care what he thinks. I'm not especially bothered by a one-night stand. I think of it as opening up; if it's only for one night, that's okay. . . . I have to have control of myself. I can't get so wrapped up in him [her boyfriend] that I forget about myself. I have to maintain my own personality and ideas. I don't want to lose what is important to me. Whenever I think a guy is taking me for granted, I let him know how I feel. If he doesn't straighten up and start being more considerate of my feelings, I break up with him.

Jessica characterized herself as strongly feminist, and reported that she did not "need men in any way." She said having a career was very important to her and she did not want to marry until she was about 30 years old. In all of these attitudes and statements Jessica gave the impression that she found casual sexual relations totally acceptable. But elsewhere in the interview Jessica said she did not trust men and did not engage in casual sex very often because she does not want to get hurt. She also said she was "frustrated" that she could not "even find a formal date." On the university campus a formal date usually means a formal, public affair, such as a sorority formal, gradu-ation dinner, or parents' weekend. Such events usually require dressing up (in other words, wearing a higher-status costume) and occur in settings that bestow some prestige on the couple—going to a formal dance or to a fancy restaurant, for example. Clearly, a date of this type signifies that a man is willing to invest more than just an hour or two in bed. Although it bothers Jessica that the men she is interested in are not willing to make this kind of public display of investment, she is still ignoring the discrepancy between her feelings and her permissive attitudes.

Stage 2: Awareness and Denial. Women in Stage 2 are more experi-enced in casual sexual relations. Most of these women express permissive attitudes, yet they are becoming increasingly aware that the failure to acquire the desired level of investment generates unpleasant feelings—which they still try to ignore or supress. At Stage 2, women's worries about investment result in tactics to control (or at least give the subject the feeling of controlling) the balance between investment desired, investment given, and sexual access. Women are not necessarily conscious of these tactics. One of these tactics is to deny, to themselves and others, that they cared about investment. Alissa is 20 years old and has had six one-night stands, and within the past year two different sex partners. She strongly agrees that "sex without love is okay." When asked whether she thought she should be emotionally involved with someone before having sex with him, she said:

Alissa

No, sex is not that big of a deal. When you first have sex, it is a big deal, but once you've lost your virginity, it gradually becomes less important to be in love with the guy. The more you have sex, the less of a big deal it becomes . . . I get attached to guys I have sex with very easily because I'm very emotional. I think this is natural for all girls. If the guy is really a jerk, though, and I have nothing in common with him, then it's a lot easier not to get emotionally involved than if I like the guy. Once I sleep with a guy, I feel that there is a bond between the two of us because we've shared our bodies and left ourselves vulnerable to each other. I think of the guy as being mine in a way, even though I know we don't have a relationship.

After initial sexual encounters Alissa does worry about whether the man will call or just wanted sex, and she does have thoughts about marriage and commitment, sometimes even before she has sex with someone. She reports that she was raised to have sex only when she was in love with someone and married to them. She thinks that this is partly why she always gets attached to a man after she has had sex with him: "It's like I can justify my actions by thinking, even if I wasn't involved with the guy before I had sex with him, it's okay because I am now. . . . [In this way] I don't have to feel that I've completely gone against the morals I was raised with." Despite her liberal attitudes and statements, Alissa definitely controls sexual access with her current boyfriend and exchanges it for investment. She does not have sex with her partner when she is mad at him because it would be "belittling my feelings" and would "give him control over me because I'm letting him do whatever he wants."

Another woman said that she did not need emotional attachment to fully enjoy sex with men. She admitted, however, that she worried during and after intercourse whether men would want to see her again or were just after sex. When asked why she worried, she answered, "Because guys are cocksuckers and they can't be trusted." The female interviewer did not ask, "Trust men to do what?" The interviewee could certainly trust men to have sex, so if she was perfectly comfortable having sex without emotional involvement, why did she feel betrayed and angry? This woman seemed unaware of the contradiction between her liberal attitudes and her emotions.

Another woman we interviewed seemed to be in a transitional stage—moving from Stage 2 to Stage 3 (in which casual relations are avoided), but she was still rationalizing her behavior and denying the reality of her emotions. She expressed extremely permissive attitudes, saying that sex was "no big deal" and was the same whether it was in a one-night stand or with a person she loved, but she admitted she worried about the guy's intentions after intercourse, particularly if she liked him, because she had found "from experience that a lot of times I thought I was starting a relationship, the guy was only after sex." Now she has these worries "every time I have sex with a guy." She said that there is a link between two people after vaginal intercourse that does not exist after just petting; but "this is just a physical link and not necessarily emotional." If she really liked the guy, she might "interpret this link to be emotional as well, because we've shared an intimate moment." When asked how often this link occurs, she replied "most of the time."

Another tactic women used to control their feelings about investment was to distinguish between partners from whom they desired investment and those from whom they did not. Casual sex with men they did not really care about was more acceptable because the women had made the decision (or felt they had) that it was "just for sex". From men, however, who were suitable for long-term relationships, these women required substantial courtship and investment. One woman, for example, had very permissive attitudes and no regrets about the two one-night stands she had had, but she made her boyfriend wait two months before having intercourse with him. Another woman with very permissive attitudes said she distinguished between men who were suitable for serious relationships and partners who were "just for sex". She admitted, however, that even when she went for a one-night stand or purely sexual relationships, she tended to get emotionally attached. She explained, "I try not to let this get in the way of a sexual relationship, and try to hold my feelings back to the best of my ability." This statement echoed a sentiment that emerged consistently in our research: Sexual emotions can be involuntary, disturbing, and compelling—The women's desire for intimacy and signs of caring and their feelings of vulnerability intruded and affected their behavior despite their attempts to suppress these feelings.

Stage 3: Rejection of Casual Sex. At Stage 3 an interesting thing happens. After extensive experience with casual sexual relations, some women make a clear decision to avoid them in the future. Three kinds of events lead to this decision. The first event is the woman's realization that she can not always control the balance between investment desired and investment given, and that losing control of this balance produces negative emotions.

Amanda exemplifies this pattern. When we spoke to her, Amanda was 20, had had sixteen one-night stands, and within the past year three different sex partners. When asked whether she thought she should be emotionally involved with someone before having sex with him, she answered "No." Her emotions, however, eventually overwhelmed her abstract attitudes and led her to reject casual sex.

Amanda

If I had sex with a guy and I didn't like him, then I just wouldn't go out with him again. I would date other people. If I like the guy, then I do wonder whether sex was all he was after and how he will treat me in the morning, and I do think about marriage, what my family would think of him, what he would be like as a husband. I was very promiscuous when I was younger, in high school, but within the last six months I have become very picky about who I sleep with. It was time to settle down and start getting serious about finding a husband. [She hopes to be married by age 26.] Everyone should have their fun for a while and go crazy once they're away from their parents, but after a while, it isn't fun anymore and you want to start getting serious with someone. [Interviewer asks: Why?] I didn't like waking up with strange guys in strange places; it bothered me sometimes. It made me feel sort of used.

In describing what led to their decision to avoid casual sexual relations, women in Stage 3 talk of experiences that were unnerving—for example, being intoxicated and "waking up with strange guys in strange places"; not remembering having sex but figuring "it must have happened because I woke up naked"; always worrying whether a man would call or not; sleeping with men they didn't really know at all; subsequently running into men they had slept with who acted as if they didn't even know them. Apart from being "scary," as many of the women reported, these experiences made the women feel "slutty" and "used."

A second factor that caused women to avoid casual relations was that some women began to realize that intercourse itself produced feelings of bonding and vulnerability, and these feelings were difficult to suppress. Nicole is 21 years old and a senior in college. She has experienced four one-night stands, and within the past year six different sex partners. When asked whether she thought she should be emotionally involved with someone before having sex with him, she said:

Nicole

I would like to think this way, but in all honesty I really do not. Sex does make me feel differently about a guy, though, because we've shared something special; there's a link between us because we were intimate. This doesn't mean that we have to become great friends or anything, or it's got to lead to a serious relationship. When I have sex with a guy, I do wonder whether sex was all he was after and how he will treat me in the morning. I'm a very emotional person, so I tend to get too emotionally involved. I've had some one-night stands that have broken my heart. In the past, I was very open with my sexuality. I had no qualms about sleeping with any guy. But now I'm in a serious relationship, so I don't fool around.

Another reason women give for avoiding casual sex and "settling down" was the discovery that, with the right partner, monogamy felt right and was preferable to casual relations. Chantal's experience makes this clear. When we spoke to her, she had had eight one-night stands, and within the past year four different sex partners.

Chantal

If I was only having sex because I was physically attracted to a guy and only wanted a one-night stand, then it was easy not to get emotionally involved. Sex was just a competition between friends to see who could get the most of it. During the game, I would think of sex like a guy does; it's all about getting laid with no strings attached. But when I was after emotional involvement, I thought of sex like a woman usually does with all of the emotions involved. I would get very emotionally involved when I had sex with him. I would worry the next day about what he thought of me, whether he would call me, and I would think about marriage, what kind of husband he would make, and stuff like that. If I really liked a guy, I would hold out on him so that he wouldn't think I was easy. In the past I didn't think I needed to be emotionally involved with someone before having sex with him. But now I think I should be. I used to think I could just sleep around with whoever I wanted, but now I find this demeaning. [Interviewer: Why?] Sex is like giving a part of yourself to a guy, and if you do this without any emotional involvement, then you are showing a lack of respect for yourself. Now if I try to do that, I begin to feel used. My attitude changed when I grew up and found a serious boyfriend. I'm not sleeping around now and I have a lot more respect for myself. I like feeling this way.

Chantal categorized men as those with whom she wanted a relationship, and those with whom she was willing to have a single encounter because they were objects of competition with her friends. She even tried acting like a man with her casual partners. Her attempt to think and act like a man, however, was not completely successful because, despite her attitudes and conscious desire to be indifferent to investment, her behavior eventually made her feel degraded. These feelings caused her to become monogamous.

Women who engaged in casual relations usually had other motives than simply having intercourse. One motive was testing one's attractiveness in competition with other women. The men who were objects of this competition were considered very attractive in their circles, so merely inducing them to have sex was considered a challenge and worthwhile. We will discuss the effect status has on men's attractiveness in later chapters.

Another motive for casual relations was revenge. For example, one woman said that a man owed her attention and respect if she had sex with him, and she insisted on a period of courtship and wooing before she went to bed with someone. She told the interviewer, however, that she did not regret her four one-night stands because they were to "get back at" men who had betrayed her. In one instance she had a one-night stand with her ex-boyfriend's best friend. Several women reported that occasionally they would have sex with someone they liked but did not consider for a serious relationship to reassure themselves that they were attractive, to experience some affection and closeness, or as a consolation for some unpleasant experience. In fact, the motives of revenge and consolation were so familiar to some women that they referred to such experiences as "revenge" or "consolation fucks." But these women did not continue to have *regular* sexual relations with men they did not care for. When asked why, the usual answer was, "What would be the point?"

After completing the personal interviews, we wanted to test the validity of our findings by choosing a different kind of sample. Out of a large survey of college students, we selected the 50 men and women with the most casual partners and permissive attitudes.[6] Although these women were much more sexually liberal than the average woman in college, the men in the sample were even more so, so male-female differences were as strong on most questions as they were for the average man and woman. But even with these women, there were feelings of being more vulnerable than men after intercourse, and these women were more likely to worry whether their partners were just after sex. Women were more interested in the long-term possibilities of relationships, and they found it more difficult to keep from getting emotionally involved with their sex partners. Women were also more likely than men to refuse to have sex when they were upset with their partners.

Among these 50 sexually liberal college students, men and women were equally likely to have tried to have sex without emotional involvement. But women were much less likely *to continue* to have sexual relations with someone when they did not want emotional involvement. This point emerged in our personal interviews, and other researchers have also described this pattern.[7] Women do not continue to have sex with partners they do not like or who do not measure up because they see no point in sexual relations that do not "lead anywhere"—that is, toward a higher-investment relationship. Or they do continue sexual relations and have emotional reactions that cause them to seek investment and to end the relationship if investment is deficient.

Do sexually experienced men care about investment?

Men's motives for casual sexual relations and their emotional reactions were very different from women's. Merely having sex with someone, even with partners they did not like, was pleasurable—or at least pleasurable enough to continue doing it. Matt is 21 years old and had had sixteen one-night stands since becoming sexually active and ten sex partners within the past year. With fifteen of his partners, he knew before he had sex with them that he did not want to get emotionally involved. When asked why he went ahead and had sex in those circumstances, he replied:

Matt

To get laid. I did this about twice a week. I'd see them at a bar and take them home. This was enough because I was not attracted to them. I wasn't willing to take these girls out on a real date. I'd see them in a bar and start talking a little and chat more and more as the evening progressed, and then we'd go to my place. I got sick of these girls after a while. I was kinda' seeing this girl for a while who was too nice, like she was too materialistic and tried too hard to make the relationship work. She was looking for a husband. She would never stand up to me. It was really a turn off. [The interviewer asks, Did you still have sex with her?] Oh, I still screwed her for a long time, even though I didn't like her.

Mark was 21 years old when we spoke to him. He agreed that he should be emotionally involved with a person before having sex, and he did not think that sex without love was okay. He stated that he thought about marriage and the long-term possibilities of a relationship when he had sex with someone. He told the interviewer that he respected women and, "Before we become lovers, we must be friends. We are equals." In many of his statements, Mark appeared to reject typical macho attitudes and to show the kind of sensitivity that many women prefer. Nevertheless, Mark had had six one-night stands, and within the past year three sex partners. With six partners he knew before he had sex with them that he did not want to get emotionally involved. When we asked why he did this, he replied:

Mark

They were available. If a girl wants to put out, I won't turn her down. As soon as you get your fraternity pin a whole group of women becomes available to you that otherwise wouldn't give you the time of day. Now I get approached a lot at parties and in bars. I dunno' why, maybe it's my haircut. I don't think I'm "alternative"; I make my own style. I think girls see me as the house rebel. That's my rep, you know, like a James Dean, that's why they come on to me. I usually prefer to date girls that are younger than me because they're easier to screw.

Some of the men felt guilt about their activities and this reduced their number of partners from what it would otherwise have been. This guilt was inspired by their partners' reactions to casual relations rather than by their own reactions: really hurting a woman by "just screwing and dumping her" made some of the men "feel like shit." Rob is a senior and in a fraternity. He explained his feelings as follows:

Rob

I had sex with girls I didn't like because it was convenient. They were really into me, and it made me feel really guilty, which is why it was hard to stay detached emotionally. We'd have sex a couple of times a week. I would have preferred less, but they were wanting it more, thinking it was what I wanted. The whole thing didn't feel right. If a woman wanted just sex, it would be cool, but they always get involved. That's why I usually only sleep with girls that I really like. I really hate hurting girls. It makes me feel guilty.

The men with the greatest number of sex partners were all star athletes, leaders in their fraternities, or otherwise had high profiles. The stars of the large spectator sports, basketball and football, all had had over 100 sex partners. The stars of sports like rugby and lacrosse had all engaged in over 40 one-night stands. Many of the one-time encounters involved fellatio rather than vaginal penetration. Most of these men said that they planned to "settle down" some day and get married, but none claimed that he would remain totally faithful. About a third of these men had girlfriends now and discreetly cheated on them. The easy access to sex "with no strings attached" overwhelmed their loyalty and prudence. Several star athletes reported that they were "afraid" of women because women often wanted more than they claimed—"they want to control your time, your social life, and your sex life." The higher a man's status and popularity, the more women became available to him, and the more he tended to take advantage of this opportunity by having casual sex with a variety of partners. This means that, as a man's number of sex partners increases, an ever greater percentage of his partners is deliberately casual, whereas this is much less true of women.

We also found that women who had extensive experience with casual sex were just as likely as monogamous women to worry about whether their partners cared about them and just as likely to think about love, commitment, and marriage. Men were a different story. The more experience with casual relations men had, the less likely they were to worry whether their partners cared about them, and the less they thought about love, commitment, and marriage. In fact, In our research a common male reaction to demands for investment, once their partners committed to a relationship, was a feeling of being trapped or suffocated, of needing more space. Harvard psychologist Carol Gilligan was shocked by the violence and suspicion she found in men's reactions to materials that suggested intimacy and emotional attachment.[8] In intimate situations, men see the danger of entrapment or betrayal, being caught in a smothering relationship or humiliated by rejection and deceit. Women, on the other hand, are drawn to such materials, and project their own desires for investment and attachment into them.

So, when men decide to be monogamous, it is not normally because casual sex causes them to have involuntary feelings of being used and degraded—or because they find casual sex intrinsically unappealing. Instead, it is usually because of the difficulty of having casual sexual relationships with women: their partner's negative reactions, the threat of divorce, social ostracism, allegations of harassment or date rape, or they find a woman so desirable they accede to her demands for fidelity. As Blumstein and Schwartz concluded, most hetrosexual men adjust to monogamy not because it is their deepest desire, but because it is their partner's desire.

Evolutionary psychologists argue that the fundamental sexual desires that motivate action, and the emotional reactions that evaluate these actions differ in men and women. These desires and emotions exist in a feedback system so that even if men and women were socialized identically, they would nevertheless be motivated to engage in different types of activities, and their emotional reactions to the same activities—casual sex, for example—would differ predictably. The Kinsey team found that men's memories, fantasies, and emotions motivated them to engage in low-investment relations with a variety of partners. When men engage in casual relations, the mental feedback they receive in terms of feelings and memories is often very positive, and they motivate men to repeat the experience. For women, these feelings and memories are more often negative, and they direct women away from such experience. Worry about whether partners will call in the morning, really care about them, or are just after sex alerts women to strategic interference and guards them against sexual exploitation. Thoughts about marriage, honeymoons, and romance direct women toward relationships that can offer high-quality investment.[9] These thoughts and feelings limit women's experiments with casual relations and guide them toward higher-investment relationships—relationships that involve greater amounts of time, affection, and marital potential.

Christine's experience is a case in point. She reports that she learned a lot from her experience with the fourth-year medical student and that she is now trying a different strategy with a lawyer she met; namely, she is forcing him to court and woo her before she has sex with him. She found that it was nice to be able to plan a date five days in advance for a change: "Medical students usually give you an hour!" She went out with the lawyer five times and finally slept with him but refused to have intercourse because, "It was too soon."

In fact, I don't know what made me say "no." It's very unusual for me. I guess I didn't consciously plan it this way. I'm trying to protect myself by taking things slowly. I've learned that if you're interested in a man, it doesn't pay to sleep with him the first night. They don't respect you then. Sex is something you have and they want. The more difficult it is to achieve something, the more a person wants it. If a woman gives it away at the first shot, she's given up the game point. It's hard to go back and say "no" after that. You've given up your leverage and you probably won't get what you want, which is commitment. If I just wanted an orgasm, I could do that more easily myself, so obviously I want more than just sex.

I know I'm taking a big chance by not having sex with him because I might not hear from him again, but I have a feeling I'm trying to gain respect and keep the upper hand—call the shots this time. My affair with the medical student had a big influence. It was a very disheartening experience. I've gone to a couple of parties recently and both times a medical student came on to me. I'd been to bed with one of them before. I was tempted in both cases and in the past I would have probably gone for it, but I resisted these times because I knew it would not lead anywhere and I'd probably feel shitty about it. When I woke up those two mornings after the parties and hadn't gone to bed with those guys, I felt really good about myself.

Christine's decision not to have sex was pragmatic rather than moral. She did not come to believe that sex without love and commitment was immoral. Instead, she concluded that love, intimacy, and commitment were what she really wanted, and casual relations would not help her reach this goal. She also learned that not heeding her emotional alarms could make her feel very bad.

Emotional Alarms: Culture or Biology?

The American women I have quoted in this chapter may very well harbor an unconscious sexual double standard as a result of their upbringing. If, however, these women's negative emotional reactions were a product of traditional sex-role socialization, we must ask why these women are able to reject so many other aspects of traditional sex roles but were not able to control their feelings of vulnerability and dissatisfaction in these particular situations.

Why does this very specific link remain between failure to obtain desired male investment and feelings of sexual vulnerability and remorse? Most of these women are assertive, ambitious, and successful in their careers. Two of the women medical students competed in what were traditionally male sports and stated that they were always "tomboys," were good in math and science, and had always identified more with their fathers than with their mothers. They reported that they had never accepted a traditional female role and did not plan to do so in the future. Most of the women quoted rejected traditional sexual morality and traditional sex differences. They found sex outside of marriage totally acceptable—in one case even an affair with a married man. Because they did not accept traditional sex differences in sexuality, they were surprised and shocked by their intense emotional reactions to their experiences. They honestly believed that they could enjoy sexual relations that involved little investment from their partners. They did not expect these emotions, could not understand them, and were surprised and disturbed by their inability to control them. These feelings were not part of their sex-role ideology and that is why the women were caught off guard.

Some women engage in sexual relations that they know will not lead to further commitments and they experience no regrets. This is likely to occur when the women themselves are not ready for commitments because of their own career plans, or because they have recently gotten out of unhappy relationships. In such cases the partners are usually either well known to the women, or they try to glean as much intimacy and information as possible before going to bed. Such women, however, do not normally continue to have sex on a regular basis in relationships that involve little or no investment. They either decide a man would make a good partner and ask for more investment, or they decide he does not measure up and cease having regular sex with him. Coasting in relationships merely because sex is good is not what most women feel comfortable doing.

Some of the women quoted in this chapter had experimented in the past with more open-ended sexual relations and had experienced no conflict. But in those cases the women felt that they had made the decision not to continue a relationship and that they therefore had the upper hand. What appears crucial, then, for the emergence of such intense feelings of vulnerability and remorse in sexually liberal women is a discrepancy between the woman's desire for a specific partner's investment, and the partner's actual investment. If their partners had simply turned out to be nerds, the women would have gotten rid of them. But in some cases they found these men extremely attractive and were in love or falling in love with them. It was the discrepancy between what these women wanted from their partners and what they were actually getting that activated their intense feelings of vulnerability, remorse, and of being used. Some authors claim that these reactions are the result of socialization and are all part of a traditional sex role or script. In

Chapters 10 and 11 we will see that the cross-cultural evidence does not support this claim. Furthermore, what emerges in these women's emotional reactions is not a traditional double standard of sexual morality—at least not any that has been documented. Engaging in various forms of sex with no emotional involvement or monogamous commitment did not *necessarily* produce feelings of guilt, regret, degradation, or exploitation in these women. Rather, what produced these feelings was a lack of control over the level of the partner's investment.

The sexual emotions we have examined do not seem to be simply the product of a sexual double standard that is engrained in children from birth. These emotions emerge despite egalitarian socialization. A study of West German school children, for example, showed that, at age eleven, boys and girls did not differ significantly in their sexual attitudes.[10] As the children moved into puberty, however, their sexual attitudes and behavior began to show basic sex differences. By age sixteen, one-third of the boys but only 5 percent of the girls wanted to spread their sexual attentions among a variety of partners. The girls overwhelmingly wanted to confine their sex life to partners they loved. The authors concluded that the sexual *morality* of German adolescents is, in fact, egalitarian because the same degree of permissiveness has been granted to both sexes. Indeed, the teenage girls tended to have initial intercourse before the boys did. A liberal, egalitarian sexual morality has been actively advocated in postwar Germany, and German girls explicitly repudiate a sexual double standard in both attitudes and behavior. They do not think premarital intercourse is wrong, and before puberty their attitudes were virtually identical to the boys' attitudes. It was in puberty that attitudes and behavior began to diverge. But the girls did not begin to feel that sex without love was morally wrong. They began to think that it was *undesirable*. They simply did not want it for themselves. In a later chapter we will see that the sexual emotions we have examined appear even in the most sexually liberal societies.

Even when women voluntarily engaged in casual sex and expressed extremely permissive attitudes, their emotions urged them to test and evaluate investment, detect shirking and false advertising, and remedy deficiencies in investment. These emotions caused many of the women to avoid casual sexual encounters despite their permissive attitudes and conscious resolve to engage in such relations. Women's emotional reactions thus acted as alarms that channeled and guided them toward higher-investment relationships—relationships that involved greater amounts of time, affection, and potential for long-term commitment.

Judith Bardwick presaged these findings in her book *The Psychology of Women*.[11] She argued that as the sexuality of heterosexual women matures, it typically develops from an essentially egocentric, masturbatory activity to an active-receptive activity in which, "*Coitus is perceived as the physical and psychological fusion with the loved man.* . . . The primary source of physical sensation remains the clitoris; the site of physical-psychological fusion is the vagina." (italics in original). Although sexual training and socialization affect the development of sexual behavior and attitudes, Bardwick's thesis implies that as women gain sexual experience, they will typically develop the tendency to associate sex with love, with or without specific cultural sanctions promoting that link. In the next chapter we look at the effects rising status has on men's and women's sexual attractiveness and behavior.

What Do Women Want?

Women's Perceptions of Sexual Attractiveness

> The man I marry doesn't have to be the chief of surgery, but he's got to
> be a professional—at least at my level and preferably higher. As long as
> I can look up to him and he is highly respected in his field, I could make
> more money than he did. That's not so important, but it might not work
> for him if I did make more. He's got to achieve and be up there or I
> wouldn't respect him. Women who marry men beneath them are going
> to be dissatisfied. It just won't work.
>
> —A woman in her second year of medical school

IN CHAPTER 2 WE EXAMINED women's desire for emotional investment. Here
we will focus on women's desire for material investment. The two types of
investment are distinct but related. The signs of emotional investment indicate to a woman a man's *willingness* to invest. When a man looks affectionately into his partner's eyes and says "I love you," he shows, if he is not
faking, a genuine concern for her and her welfare. These signs are extremely important to women, as we have seen. But a genuine concern and willingness to invest are relatively meaningless if the man has nothing but time
and energy to offer. He must also have the *ability* to invest sufficiently. Men
who are sensitive, caring, and affectionate but who, in the eyes of their
female partners, cannot provide an adequate material investment are likely
to be discarded. The signs of emotional investment are important to women,
but not sufficient.

In this chapter we explore how status, ambition, wealth, and success—the
signs that a partner is *able* to invest—interact with physical traits to determine sexual attractiveness. My analysis draws on six social-psychological
experiments, survey data from over 1400 individuals, and in-depth interviews.

Do women judge sexual attractiveness the way men do? If not, how do
they differ? What are the components of men's sexual attractiveness to
women and how are these components weighed? Do women agree on who is
sexually attractive? Men emphasize physical attributes when they assess sexual attractiveness, and many women believe that physical features are primary

when they evaluate sexual attractiveness. But even when women are specifically asked to rate men's *physical* attractiveness, they are influenced by many factors besides physical features: how he is dressed, his status within their social circle, and whether he is the kind of person with whom they could have a relationship. Women are not always conscious of the influence of these traits. Pat, a 22-year-old, second-year medical student, speaks to this issue:

Pat

I think it is pretty automatic. You don't have to consciously tick off each item when you see a man: he's dressed okay, good income, speaks intelligently, that sort of thing. All of this stuff just goes into the computer and is processed automatically. Then you get a readout: this guy is attractive or he isn't. But if you analyze it later, you realize you noticed whether he was wearing a tailor-made suit or polyester, or a Rolex or Timex watch. Women notice these things whether they're aware of it at the time or not. You also notice how other people react to a man. If other women find him charming and sexy, it can predispose you to look for these qualities too. But I think the most important thing is whether he's good at what he does. It can be medicine, or skiing, or selling insurance, but if he's really good and other people know it, it makes him more confident in the way he acts with you, and you sense it and are influenced by it. But he's got to do something the woman respects. If a woman is not into the type of thing the guy excels in, then she's not impressed. I'm in medicine so I'm turned on by men who are at the top of their specialties because I know what it took to get there. I admire them. I wouldn't be impressed with a bodybuilder type, but I might be with a professional ball player—if he wasn't gross and could talk intelligently—because I love to play baseball and respect people who do it well. Respect is a big part of turning on to a man. It has to be there or it doesn't get off the ground.

Pat's statement raises three important points. Status cues and the opinions of other women greatly affect women's judgments of men's attractiveness. A man's excellence and success are major criteria by which women judge men's attractiveness, but a woman has to respect and identify with the activities at which a man excels or she is not impressed. The process by which a woman evaluates these cues is relatively automatic. It occurs whether she is aware of it or not. We will examine each of these points in detail.

Status Cues

Research has consistently shown that women's assessments of sexual attractiveness are more influenced by signs of status than men's are.[1] These studies led me to wonder if we can take a man who has been judged attractive by large number of women and render him unattractive merely by altering his costume and apparent status. Conversely, can we elevate a homely man's attractiveness by giving him the trappings of high status? Will these alterations have the same effects on women's attractiveness to men?

The costume experiment

College students saw pictures of people of the opposite sex and of various levels of physical attractiveness in different costumes.[2] They then reported how willing they would be to enter different types of relationships with people like the one in the picture—from coffee and conversation through dating, sexual relations, and marriage.

> The high-status costume consisted of a white dress shirt with a designer paisley tie, a navy blazer thrown over the left shoulder, and a Rolex wrist watch. Female models wore a white silk blouse, a navy blazer thrown over the left shoulder, and a woman's Rolex. To depict medium status, models wore an off-white shirt and khaki slacks. For low social status the models wore the uniform of a well-known hamburger chain: a baseball cap and a polo shirt with the company logo showing. Male and female models were matched for physical attractiveness.

Men said they were very willing to have coffee and conversation with the prettiest model, and they were completely indifferent to how she was dressed. Women, however, *were* affected by how the men were dressed: they were more willing to have coffee and conversation with men who wore the blazer and Rolex. In rating models' acceptability as dates, the greatest difference between men and women was in the effects of the high-status costume. For women, the high-status costume made the homely model acceptable as a date, but he was not acceptable when he wore the fast-food uniform. Men were not willing to date the homelier model in either costume. In fact, for women, the blazer and Rolex made the homely model more acceptable than the best-looking model in the fast-food uniform *for all types of relationships*. This was not true for men. We also asked men and women in the study to rate the models' attractiveness on a scale of one to five. Costumes did not affect men's ratings, but they did affect women's ratings.

Peer opinion

Pat mentioned that women were influenced by other women's opinions when they were assessing men's attractiveness. In a series of studies William Graziano showed that women's ratings of men's attractiveness and desirability as dates were strongly affected by what other women said about the

s ratings of women's attractiveness were unaffected by what
about the women. Negative assessments by peers had
on women than positive assessments did. The authors
dings in terms of evolutionary psychology: Women risk a
they decide to mate, and social information about a suitor
would be vital in deciding whether he was worthy and reliable. Given the
risks of male abuse, shirking, and abandonment, a woman risks more by
ignoring negative information about prospective partners than by ignoring
positive information. Men often show similar circumspection in picking a
lifetime mate in whom they will invest exclusively, but in simply judging
women's desirability as dates or sex partners, the woman's physical attributes may be the man's primary consideration.

Social status, competitive arenas, and attractiveness

Social status is a relative characteristic; it is determined by a person's rank
and standing within a particular hierarchy. If a woman strongly identifies
with a particular hierarchy and considers success within it important, a
man's status within this hierarchy is a primary determinant of his attractiveness to her. When he is younger, a male's age affects his sexual attractiveness because it affects his status relative to other males. In high school, for
example, the freshman male is at the bottom of the pecking order because the
most attractive girls in his class are usually dating juniors and seniors. In fact,
the most attractive women in high school often date college men, and in college they may date graduate students or men already out of school. When the
high school senior graduates, he is again demoted back to being a freshman,
and the pool of women available to him again takes a nose dive.[4]

A woman's perception of a man's status and attractiveness is also influenced by her own status within the hierarchy. If she works in the business or
professional world, where income and occupational rank determine status,
she usually prefers men who exceed her in these characteristics. Some authors
have predicted that as women gain access to better paying, more prestigious
jobs, they will begin to de-emphasize economic criteria and more strongly
emphasize physical characteristics in their selection of partners. This does not
seem to be happening. Studies of marriage patterns indicate the opposite is
true: women with more education, occupational status, and earning power
tend to raise their socioeconomic standards for partners accordingly.[5]

In our interviews with medical students, 85 percent of the men mentioned
physical attractiveness as the trait most important to them in choosing a
partner for serious relationships. Only 10 percent of the women gave this
response. Eighty percent of the women but only 30 percent of the men mentioned *respect* for partners' abilities and achievements. Thirty percent of the
men stated that physical attractiveness was overwhelmingly important for
more casual relations, but if marriage were a possibility, they would also

consider other qualities important—for example, family background, intelligence, personal compatibility. No woman made this distinction because no woman in the sample stated that she wanted to have casual sexual relations.

No woman preferred a spouse with income or occupational status inferior to hers, but about half the men expressed this preference. There was some overlap between men and women in the middle category, "prefer spouse's income/occupational status to be equal to mine." No man, however, preferred a spouse with income and occupational prestige superior to his, whereas about a third of the women did. Most of the women, in fact, preferred men who were above them professionally and financially as long as the men did not try to use their superior status and income to force the women to compromise their own career goals. Many of the women found men's willingness to date and marry "down" in terms of income and occupational prestige incomprehensible and frustrating.

When asked what they most desired in a man, over half the women medical students stated they wanted a man who was a challenge, one they could admire and respect. One third said that they wanted a man who made them feel "protected." When I asked what they needed protection from, they were vague and said it was not a rational desire. They knew they would have sufficient money and resources themselves, and they did not actually expect a man would ever have to protect them from physical danger. Nevertheless, they said that having a man they truly respected would make them feel more secure. In answer to the same questions, no man offered responses remotely similar to these. Karla was a second-year medical student when we talked to her.

Karla

I'm looking for a man as successful or more successful than I am. I don't think anyone wants to admit it, but when you're on the verge of a successful career, you want a man who's a success himself. It seems elitist, but it's true. I can't see myself having a husband who's a gas station attendant—or even someone with less education and professional prestige than I have. But it's harder for women to find the men they want as they get older. You may have to drop your criteria, but you still look for someone who will be a good provider for your future offspring. It's the feeling of protection you get from someone who has more power. Women are attracted to that even if they have plenty of money to support themselves.

Zelda is 25 and a fourth-year medical student. She is explicit in stating her requirements for a mate.

Zelda

It would bother me if I married somebody like an accountant who made $40,000, and I made $150,000 as a physician. Salary has a lot to *do with power and prestige in this society. Maybe I'm not confident enough to make that kind of adjustment, but that's the way I feel. I dated someone who had an M.A. in engineering. His dad was a doctor and so was his brother. I was in for an M.D. He'd have to get a Ph.D. just to have the title of "Doctor." We both felt that way. We considered getting married. I was in medical school at the time. But we knew he'd never make as much as I did. The problem of introducing my husband as not being a doctor is a minor one. But there is something about the power and prestige involved. When you're at a certain level and used to a certain kind of lifestyle, these things do make a difference. I would like to marry a super successful businessman or a super successful lawyer who was making the same or double my salary. I'd prefer it if he made more. I'm pushy and ambitious and I want someone who's pushy and ambitious himself.*

Evolutionary psychologists argue that women are attracted to signs of status and success because mates who had these qualities were able to invest more in them and their offspring.[6] Men who appear weak and ineffectual compared to other men are generally less able to provide and protect, and hence, have less to offer. On the other hand, the most powerful man in the world is a bad bet for a woman if he is unwilling to invest in her and her children. This explains women's dual requirements, which sometimes seem contradictory to men. Most women are attracted to men who can be tough and competitive in the outside world because the world is a tough and competitive place and only the skillful succeed. At the same time, the man must demonstrate his willingness to invest in her by being considerate, affectionate, and nurturant. Debbie talks about these dual requirements. She was very successful in medical school and eventually entered one of the most prestigious and lucrative medical specialties.

Debbie

My boyfriend is a medical student but he failed the first year and is having to repeat it. I couldn't believe he could fail anything. I never have. He's not as bright as I am or as capable. I get honors in some of my classes, but he's having a hard time even repeating his first year. I vowed I would see him through it when he failed and I try to help him when we study together, but I'd rather study by myself. I feel sometimes like he drains me and that I'm supporting him. He's talking about marriage but I have no intention of marrying him—absolutely not! I don't want to have to take care of him through marriage. I want someone I can respect. I hate to say that because it sounds so mean, but "respect" is a good word. I want a man that I can have confidence in, and I don't with him. . . . Money is definitely important. When my boyfriend takes me out in his sports car to a nice restaurant, it makes me feel good. But when I'm trying to nurse him through his exams, it turns me off. I want a strong man with one weak spot—me and our family, and we're so dear to him he'll do anything for us. But with everyone outside the family he'll be able to walk over them if he has to.

Law students

We surveyed 160 law students in order to check our results on the medical-student study.[7] We used the pictures from the costume experiment but added written descriptions of occupation and income.

When models wore the blazer and Rolex, they were described as training to be doctors with an expected starting salary of $80,000. When they wore the plain white shirt, they were described as training to be teachers with a starting salary of $22,000. When they wore the hamburger-chain uniform, they were described as training to be waiters with a starting salary of $15,000.

Coffee and conversation. Women law students were just as willing to have coffee and chat with the best-looking model as they were with the homelier one—as long as they were described as training to be a doctor and wearing the blazer and Rolex. Men, however, were more willing to have coffee and conversation with the prettiest model than with the less attractive model— whether in the high-status or low-status costume.

Date. Women law students were just as willing to date the good-looking model as the homelier one, as long as they wore the blazer and Rolex and were described as training to be physicians. Men were ambivalent about dating the homelier model even when she was paired with high status, but they were extremely eager to date the prettiest model when she was paired with high status. Men were equally willing to date the doctor and the teacher. Women were more willing to date the doctor than the teacher.

Together, our interviews and experiments indicated that men and women make different *tradeoffs* between status and physical attractiveness when they choose partners, and they have different thresholds of initial acceptance. When they are deciding whether to initiate interaction or go out on a date, men and women assign different levels of importance to partners' social status and physical attractiveness. Men often refuse to date women whose physical features do not meet their standards, regardless of how ambitious and successful the women are in their careers. For their part, women are rarely willing to date or have sexual relations with men who have lower socioeconomic status than they do, despite the men's looks and physiques.

Status Hierarchies

In the United States there are myriad activities and interests and, hence, myriad hierarchies: from bodybuilding and bowling to artistic and aesthetic appreciation. Individuals move through different status hierarchies as they grow into adulthood. In high school a girl who is conventional may want to date the captain of the football team or the student body president. A girl who identifies with a rebellious group finds these same boys too straight and square. She is more likely to be drawn to boys who are prominent rebels— who play in punk bands, have outrageous hairdos, and offer the best drugs. Either way, the male is judged primarily by his achievements, reputation, and position in a particular group.

A man's status, and therefore his attractiveness, is always relative to that of other men in his arena. A man's attractiveness therefore changes dramatically as he moves between different circles because it varies with the different definitions of success in different circles and with his achievements relative to those of the men and women in the circle. For example, a graduate teaching assistant in college may appear extremely attractive to undergraduate females because they compare his knowledge and academic achievements to their own and to those of undergraduate males. But if the same man moves into an arena where he is competing with mature men with established professions, women are likely to see him as a boy—cute perhaps, but not to be taken seriously. Ted is 35, divorced, and a successful management consultant. He describes how his attractiveness has varied with his status in different environments.

Ted

As chance would have it, I was in a plane that was almost completely vacant. I was 24 years old but I'm tall and I happened to be dressed up, so I looked older. This nice-looking stewardess came up and said, "Oh, why are you sitting here all by yourself? Why don't you come back and sit with us after the seat belt sign goes off?" I smiled and said, "Sure, why not?" Then she said, "What do you do?" and I said, "I'm a graduate student in finance." Her whole tone changed and she said, "That's nice. I think you boys should get all the education you can." After that, I didn't even bother to go back to sit with them. In those days we referred to it as wearing the brown helmet—you know, really getting shat on. It was a total dismissal.

The other side of the story is, I'm 35, wearing a $2,000 suit, sitting in first class, and a stewardess asked me what I did, and I said I'm a management consultant. She said, "Oh, that sounds interesting. What are you working on?" and I said, "A big study for AT&T. You probably read about it in today's paper. I'm quoted on the front page." She said, "I'll come right back and talk with you after I finish with the *other customers." Nowadays this kind of thing happens all the time, as soon as I was divorced and took the wedding ring off. Before I took the ring off, they were friendly, but they didn't kneel on the edge of the seat, fetch drinks, and slip their phone numbers in my coat pocket, which some of them do now. This became much more prevalent after I took the ring off. One time I had one kneeling on the edge of the seat and in five minutes she asked whether I was married. I said "No." She said, "Divorced?" "Yes." "So am I," she said, "Do you have herpes?" "No." "Neither do I." That's getting pretty direct.*

Ted's interview illustrates an important dynamic in the relationship between status and attractiveness. In the modern world there are many different circles and subcultures, and each has its own status hierarchy. A man who is attractive in one circle may be completely unattractive in another. Furthermore, individuals move through different status hierarchies as they grow into adulthood—as Ted's continuing analysis indicates:

These kinds of experiences, of getting dumped on by attractive women when you're a student and have no status, and getting overtly hustled when you're older and a success, really teach you something. In a sense, women have trained me to be what I am: achievement oriented and interested in making a good living. When I was in high school, I saw that if you wanted to date girls, you had to play football. So I was on the team. I didn't like football. It's a very painful sport. There are a lot of men walking around with injured backs and knees from playing high school football. But the girls liked it, or at least some of them liked to date the athletes, so I played. By the time I was a junior in college, I knew I wasn't going to be playing pro football, so my fiancee encouraged me to go to grad school, and to change my major from history to finance. That gave me the potential to make a lot of money in the business world. Going to grad school and being a teaching assistant increased my status with women, but I still was not on the level of a successful man. Later, when I worked in Washington, it was amazing. If you had a White House Pass [which he did], you practically had groupies. So, to a great extent, a man's attractiveness is determined by his level of success. If anything, we were better looking when we were younger, and we were certainly in better shape. But with women, the difference between having made it or not is like night and day.

Men who move rapidly up the socioeconomic scale experience an enormous increase in the number of attractive women available to them. Tod is a second-year medical student who has figured this out.

Tod

I knew doctors were status symbols but I didn't know that sexually they were doing better. But by the first year in med school, I would see all kinds of women—chirps, nurses, med students—going for the older guys: the fourth years and the residents. That's when I figured it out: the more your status goes up, the more attractive you are to women. The more you become aware of this, the more obvious it is. You see examples everywhere. I've discussed it with some of the other guys in the class. All of them know it.

In high school girls may turn on to guys' looks and bodies but that's because it's important for sports. Later, it's all what kind of job you have and how much money you make. That is why the first two years of med school aren't so great for most guys. There are only a handful of women in the class who are attractive enough to date and they're taken. The nurses don't take you seriously yet, so you've got to try and hustle nursing students and undergrads and it's hard to make contacts. Also they know how many years you've got ahead of you, so a lot of them don't want to start anything. By your third year things get a lot better because you're on the wards and meeting a lot more people and you're closer to being finished. But in your residency it's incredible. If you have the time to devote to it, you can have your pick.

Status barriers

In the delightful film *Breaking Away*, the male protagonist is a townie and high school student in a university town. He conceals both of these facts in order to date a female student at Indiana University. There is extreme prejudice among the students against townies, who are called "cutters," a pejorative term referring to quarry-stone cutting which used to be a major industry in Bloomington. When his girlfriend discovers his ruse, she tells him she is disappointed that he felt he had to deceive her in order to win her attention because he is a really worthy person who shouldn't have to cheat. On the other hand, given the events portrayed, it seems doubtful that he would have had a ghost of a chance of dating this woman if she had known his true identity, and indeed she terminates their relationship when she discovers it.

Our interviews revealed that the status distinctions depicted in the film are very real. Female students in our study were adverse to dating down, or to dating someone with an education inferior to theirs. Women university students did not frequent bars where men from the local community college hung out, nor did they date these men. For example, one undergraduate woman reported that she had encountered a really good-looking guy in the park and was initially attracted to him until she noticed the gold chain around his neck and the type of shirt he wore, which marked him as a "townie." When he asked for her phone number, she gave him a fictitious one. She reported that if he had been a university student and dressed like one, she would have definitely gone out with him.

The Preppy-Crunchy-Townie experiment

Because most studies of sexual attractiveness have been based on samples of college students, we wanted to identify social types and status cues that were meaningful to college students. Participants saw photographs of models of the opposite sex who were dressed in the costumes of a preppy, a crunchy-environmentalist type, and a townie. They then read the descriptions and reported how willing they would be to date, have sex with, or marry the people in the photographs.[8]

Preppies, Crunchies, and Townies

A survey showed that the following social types exist in most American high schools and colleges and can be recognized by their costumes: head-bangers, druggies, punks, preppies, deadheads, crunchies, guidos. Student panels then created the following portraits and costumes of two social types prevalent on college campuses (the preppy and the crunchy-environmentalist), and one type of townie who did not attend college. The Preppy costumes consisted of a v-neck sweater over an Oxford pin-striped shirt and khaki pants. The Crunchy types wore faded, torn jeans, a headband, a tie-dyed t-shirt, and a single strand of beads. Male Townies wore a silk shirt with the top three buttons open, a gold medallion, and black slacks. Female Townies wore a black body suit, a black leather mini-skirt, and ratted, sprayed hair. The descriptions were identical for male and female models except gender appropriate nouns and pronouns were substituted.

The Preppy

This is Geoffrey, a dedicated, ambitious young man. He describes himself as very motivated and says, "There is no better feeling than that of success. I have to be the best. It's not unrealistic. Like my father says, you can get whatever you want as long as you work hard enough." When asked to describe a typical morning, Geoffrey replied, "I get up and read the Times to see how my stocks are doing. After a croissant and O.J., I go on a long jog through the park, listening to my favorite classic rock like the Stones and the Beatles on my walkman." We then asked him what he is looking for in the future: "What do I want? I want it all. It begins with a first-rate grad school. I want an elegant home in a good neighborhood, a gorgeous wife, and two intelligent, beautiful children. I will be the best at my job; I want to go right to the top. Cars, vacations, golf at the country club. It's about being at the top, and that's exactly where I will be."

The Crunchy

This is Rob, a really laid back kind of guy. He enjoys the outdoors, hiking, and skiing and does them all at Colorado State University. "I love the environment at school. Everyone is very casual about life; no one ever stresses about work. I try to give myself as much free time as possible." We asked Rob what he does to keep himself busy: "I try to get to as many Grateful Dead shows as I can and I always keep my eyes open for a miracle ticket. But you aren't always fortunate enough to be there, so my buddies and I are very active in the local Greenpeace organization. We road trip to a lot of rallies and protests to help protect the environment." Rob describes himself as kind of locked in the sixties and adds, "My VW bug says it all with my stickers—Save the Whales, No Nukes, Keep the Rainforests Alive, Make Love Not War. I'm not telling anyone else who to be; I'm just saying who I am."

The Townie

This is Tony. When asked to describe his typical Friday night, he answered, "I jump in my Trans-Am and go pick up my boys. We cruise the strip for about an hour or so scoping the scene for chicks. Then we hit the clubs and jam with the crew on the dance floor." Tony describes his favorite music to dance to by quickly naming the hottest top 40 artists like C & C Music Factory, LL Cool J, and Rob Base. He was then asked to give us an idea of his priorities in life: "What's, uh, important to me? That's easy. My family is number one. Ain't no better feelin' than a bunch of us together for my mom's Sunday dinner. We look out for each other. Nobody insults the family. I would have to say that my car and lookin' good come next. You gotta look good, ya' know what I'm sayin'?"

When the possibility of sexual relations was involved, the Townie costume and description had dramatically different effects on men and women. Even with the best-looking model, women said they were unwilling to have sexual relations when he was dressed and described as a Townie. Men, however, found the prettiest models acceptable for sexual relations regardless of their costumes or descriptions.

The lifestyle descriptions caused men and women to react similarly to the Preppy and Townie in judging their acceptability for dating and marriage.

Men and women were equally willing to date or marry the Preppy and equally unwilling to date or marry the Townie.

In our interviews we had found that some women dated and slept with certain men because the men had status in local circles, but the women would not marry such men because of their lack of ambition or lifestyle. Women reacted to the Crunchy in this way. On the average they were more willing to have sex with the Crunchy than to marry him—presumably because most women expect a conventional, financially secure lifestyle after marriage—one that wouldn't include headbands and Grateful Dead tours.

Attractiveness, educational achievement, and social class

The Preppy-Crunchy-Townie study was rich in details that reflect different lifestyles and social classes. The problem with more realistic experiments, however, is that one never knows which element produces an effect. Was it the Townie's taste in music, his costume, lack of education, or Sunday dinner with mom that turned people off? In the next study we wanted to answer this question: Would men and women react the same as they did in the Preppy study if the same models and costumes were used, but the accompanying descriptions only depicted levels of education and career ambition?

Our interviews indicated that college students, and especially women, were unwilling to date Townies who attended the local community college or who had terminated their education altogether. We therefore described all the models in the Townie outfits and half the models in the Crunchy outfits as having low education and ambition, and all the Preppies and the other half of the Crunchies as having high achievment and ambition.

> **High:** This young man is attending a top-notch university now and is doing very well in his studies. He has already been accepted by a first-rate graduate-professional school, which he will attend after graduation.
>
> **Low:** This young man attended a community college but does not plan to continue his schooling. He now works at various temporary jobs and says he is not interested in a high-powered career.

Models' looks and status affected both men and women, but these effects varied depending on the type of relationship involved and the model's status. Men found the prettiest models desirable for dating and sexual relations regardless of their costumes and educational achievement. This was not true of women subjects. Women were negative about any type of relationship with the low-achieving men. In fact, even a date with the best-looking models was considered unacceptable if they were described as having little ambition.

This experiment used the same pictures as the Preppy experiment but the descriptions were different. Apparently, it was the descriptions of lifestyle rather than models' looks, costumes, or educational achievement that turned the men off from dating the women depicted as Townies. These two experiments suggest that for middle-class men, high physical attractiveness can render women desirable for dating, sexual relationships, and even marriage regardless of their occupation, income, and education—provided that they do not exhibit the obvious trappings of a lower-class status and lifestyle. For women, men's income, education, and occupation are often decisive in determining their acceptability. Our surveys of medical and law students support this view. In Chapters 6 and 9 we look at additional evidence on this topic.

Rating Attractiveness

I once showed a woman pictures of ten men. Some of these men were professional models and all of the men had received high attractiveness ratings from a panel of forty women. She said she did not find any of the men attractive because they weren't her type; they looked too "straight." Maybe if they had their heads shaved and wore combat boots and leather, she would find them more attractive. This woman was herself dressed in black, and she said she liked the band Nine Inch Nails: that was the look that turned her on. She then held up one of the pictures and tried to visualize the subject with the proper haircut and regalia, so that she could decide whether he could be attractive or not. This type of response was typical in my interviews with women.

Some research has shown that men and women agree in rating the attractiveness of other individuals, and among themselves, women show about the same amount of agreement as men do. Unfortunately, most of these studies omitted the types of cues that are more important to women than to men, and they did not exhibit models' entire bodies. We wanted to see whether men and women would show the same degree of consensus when status cues were present and models' physiques were displayed. We therefore dressed one model in the townie outfit and seven models in the preppy costumes. The other six pictures were of professional models in bathing suits. All the photographs showed models' bodies from head to knee.[9]

Women and men generally agreed on the average ranking of each model, but men showed less variability than women did in their rankings. In the second study, participants saw photographs of models in bathing suits and reported whether they would be willing to date, have sex, or marry the persons in the pictures. All of the models were professionals and were very physically attractive. The models were described as having either high or low income and ambition. We expected men to rate the women models primarily on the basis of physical attributes, whereas women raters would be more influenced by the descriptions of income and ambition. Women's ratings would therefore vary more than men's did. Men did show more agreement than women in judging models' desirability for all three types of relationships: dating, sexual relations, and marriage. The descriptions of income and ambition increased the variability of women's but not men's ratings of the models.

The sexual attractiveness of celebrities

In the third study, participants rated the sexual attractiveness of celebrities. Although the raters did not actually know these celebrities, the mass media contain enough images and information about celebrities' lifestyles and personalities to allow people to form impressions and preferences. We expected men to rate female celebrities' sexual attractiveness primarily on the basis of physical attributes. We thought women would be more influenced by factors like the celebrity's lifestyle, social type, and personality.

As expected, women's ratings of male celebrities varied more than men's ratings of female celebrities (see box). Women varied most in their ratings of actors who portray muscle-bound, working-class, or macho violent types. For example, women showed high variability in their ratings of Sylvester Stallone and Jean-Claude van Damme. We think this happened because these characteristics are unattractive to many middle-class women, yet women know that in real life these men are rich and famous and enjoy extremely high status. When women were extremely pretty or plain, the variability of men's ratings was particularly small (for example, men's ratings of Cindy Crawford and Bette Midler).

Average Sexual Attractiveness Ratings and Standard Deviations for 40 Celebrities

Celebrity	Male Subjects		Female Subjects	
	Mean	Standard Deviation	Mean	Standard Deviation
Luke Perry	3.05	1.06	3.64	1.08
Jon Bon Jovi	2.35	1.07	2.23	1.18
Harry Connick, Jr.	2.98	1.18	3.52	1.19
Richard Gere	3.10	1.12	3.80	1.16
Kevin Costner	3.42	1.07	3.90	1.16
Patrick Swayze	3.13	1.14	3.36	1.16
Axl Rose	1.87	1.10	1.69	1.11
Billy Joel	2.28	1.03	1.98	1.05
Jean-Claude van Damme	3.30	1.23	3.41	1.37

Name				
Tom Hanks	2.72	1.04	2.65	.95
Sean Connery	3.07	1.21	3.00	1.16
Bruce Willis	2.94	1.07	2.74	1.08
Christian Slater	2.95	1.09	3.83	1.20
Sylvester Stallone	2.94	1.18	2.40	1.26
Tom Cruise	3.75	1.16	4.18	1.13
Kieffer Sutherland	2.88	1.05	3.06	1.28
Michael Keaton	2.66	.92	2.57	1.08
Sean Penn	2.22	1.12	1.96	1.07
Harrison Ford	3.25	1.14	3.21	1.23
Billy Crystal	2.27	1.04	2.11	1.05
Cindy Crawford	4.52	.96	4.32	.92
Madonna	3.64	1.13	3.01	1.26
Jodie Foster	3.32	.99	3.42	1.03
Kim Basinger	4.29	.97	3.90	1.16
Michelle Pfeiffer	4.26	.95	3.99	1.07
Chynna Phillips	3.60	1.03	3.32	1.24
Julia Roberts	4.11	1.06	4.03	1.14
Bette Midler	1.79	.92	2.10	1.01
Cher	2.40	1.21	2.34	1.24
Elle McPherson	4.46	1.01	4.02	1.12
Demi Moore	3.75	1.04	3.91	.94
Kirstie Alley	3.56	1.08	3.32	.98
Candace Bergen	2.80	1.01	2.94	1.02
Sinead O'Connor	1.93	1.19	2.18	1.28
Lita Ford	2.74	1.22	1.95	1.02
Mariah Carey	3.77	1.15	3.09	1.20
Chris Evert-Lloyd	2.67	1.10	2.18	.99
Kathy Ireland	4.32	1.11	3.42	1.30
Jane Fonda	2.84	1.15	2.42	1.10
Sigourney Weaver	2.70	1.22	2.71	1.18

Sample of 153 female and 160 male subjects. 1 = very unattractive; 5 = very attractive.
Standard deviation is a common statistical measure of variability. See Townsend and
Wasserman (1997) for a description of results.

Are judgments of attractiveness conscious?

Are women aware of the roles that social status and conte
mining males' sexual attractiveness? When I discuss the e
freshman on men's sexual attractivness, I ask the women in my classes
if attractiveness is really based on good looks, these men instantly become
unattractive when they become freshman. The typical reactions are sheepish
or puzzled looks. The women know that the freshman boys are less attractive because the girls in their class are interested in the juniors and seniors,
but they are not exactly sure why this occurs. They acknowledge that it cannot be simply a matter of the men's age because few undergraduate women
are interested in dating adult men downtown, even though those men have
status in the "real" world in the form of occupations and earning power.
Most of the women do not see, or at least do not verbalize, that the freshmen
males' sexual attractiveness has plummeted because they have moved from
an arena in which their status was high compared to that of other males, and
they were therefore dominant, to an arena where their status is low and inferior to that of many other males.

Women varied substantially in their awareness and acceptance of their
actual criteria for selecting partners. Some women readily acknowledged
and accepted that social status and dominance were major determinants of
their evaluations. As Pat reported earlier, she is conscious of her criteria
when she reflects on them, but she is not usually aware of them when she is
reacting to men in everyday life. One of the reasons that some people do not
recognize or do not report their actual criteria for partner selection is that
these criteria are considered unacceptable by many in the current dating-
mating market. Women's emphasis on socioeconomic criteria and their aversion to dating and marrying down is seen as unliberated, mercenary, or
elitist. Ideally, contemporary women should have their own careers and not
be concerned about the economic advantages a man offers. Similarly, men
who stress physical attributes in their choice of partners, and who want to
coast in sexual relationships or otherwise minimize their investments, are
often considered emotionally immature, or sexist, or incapable of true love
and commitment. There is considerable opprobrium currently attached to
these sex differences, particularly in educated circles. Consequently, many
people are reluctant to admit that they harbor these tendencies and they
may not even be consciously aware that they do so.

Numerous women in my samples, both college-educated and not, stressed
that their partners had to be "intelligent." In her study, Heather Remoff
found that women from various economic levels said men had to be intelligent in order to be attractive.[10] Women's definitions of intelligence in a mate
varied, however, according to the women's own class background and education. For a working-class woman, a man with a high school education

ιο was good at fixing cars, was progressing toward owning his own gas station, and was well liked and respected could be considered intelligent and a good prospect for marriage. For a woman medical student this same man would not appear so intelligent, nor would he be likely to inspire the feelings of respect and admiration that are such an integral part of sexual attraction for women. What the women seemed to be talking about, then, was not, strictly speaking, *intelligence*, but rather evidence of a man's ability, success, social connections, and the respect he enjoyed within his own milieu. In their actual choice of partners, women do not tend to select for intelligence as measured by any standardized test; they tend to select for status and success within the woman's own social circles.

Some of the women medical students strongly denied that the reason they wanted to marry men at their socioeconomic level was because they were concerned about a man's occupational status or income. Rather, they claimed that they wanted to marry such men because they would have "more in common" with them. One woman said she would prefer not to date down because she would have nothing to talk about with a less-educated man, and he would not "appreciate a snowfall or Van Gogh." Another said such a man would not want to go to art galleries and museums. By and large, the men that the women in medical school were dating or wanted to date were in medicine themselves. Ironically, the type of education medical students receive tends to be focused and narrow. Consequently, most of these men did not appear to be particularly intellectual, witty, aesthetic, or articulate, and some of them would not know a Van Gogh from a Pollack. But they were going to enjoy a socioeconomic status and lifestyle similar or superior to what these women could achieve on their own and this is what made them acceptable. Many people with above average IQs are not highly educated, and many people who visit museums and galleries are not from the upper-middle class. When the actual partner selection of upper-middle-class women is examined, however, we see that their choices are predicted by the components of socioeconomic status (income, occupational prestige, and education) rather than by partners' IQ or knowledge of art, literature, and history.[11]

Some women deny their socioeconomic standards for partners because it sounds elitist and conflicts with their democratic ideals. This conflict may be particularly acute when a woman has moved up from her own class background. Maria is 36 years old, Mexican American, and divorced. She came from a working-class background but is now a college instructor. After interviewing her for several hours, I began to ask her whether she wanted to remarry, and what she would look for in a potential partner. She mentioned nothing remotely related to education, occupation, and income. I then asked her if she considered such things important in choosing a future mate. She said she did not think about these things. I asked her whether she would be willing to marry a man who had less education, income, and professional status than she had. She answered she did not know but she supposed so—if she really liked the man. I then tried a different tack and asked her about the men she had been interested in, or who had been interested in her in the last few years. She mentioned that a man in her church had been interested in her. I asked her what happened with him. She thought for a minute and a slow smile began to spread across her lips. She then explained, "When a woman friend at church told me he was interested in me, I remember looking over at him and thinking, 'He's 54 years old and he doesn't have a job.'"

Maria owns her own house, which is worth a considerable sum in her California community. I asked her whether she would be willing to have a man move in and live with her. She said "no." If she were to move in with a man, she would prefer to live in his home and she could rent out her own house. Or they could pool their money and buy a house together, but she would still keep her house. She said she had worked hard to buy that house and it was worth a lot of money now, and she was not going to take a chance on losing part of it in a breakup. Nor did she find the idea of a man living rent-free in her house appealing. These preferences eliminated all the men who did not own a home in the area or did not have the resources to go 50-50 on a new home—in other words, all the men not at Maria's economic level, but she was unaware of this.

Some of the medical students also came from working-class backgrounds. Mary is one of them. Concerning socioeconomic status and partner selection, Mary had this to say:

Mary

I don't like hearing women in medicine say they wouldn't marry men beneath them. I go into a fury when I hear that. Now if you were dating an electrician and he wasn't an intellectual equal, then of course you wouldn't marry him because you wouldn't have anything in common. But that's different from saying you wouldn't marry someone because they didn't have a certain degree or didn't make enough money. Women who say things like that are just status seekers. I heard a bunch of girls talking about that at school—what kind of men they will have to marry. It's gross. I really don't like the phrase "marrying down."

Mary comes from an immigrant, working-class background, so perhaps her aversion to the phrase "marrying down" reflects her loyalty to her family—a loyalty which is heartfelt and intense. Despite her protestations, however, and her denial that socioeconomic status affects her own selection criteria, she has consistently tried to keep her options open to date other people after she entered medical school, while hedging her bets by maintaining a relationship with her old boyfriend. Significantly, in exercising her freedom to date, Mary has only been involved with medical students. No doubt, Mary would be appalled by this analysis of her strategy because it does not coincide with her image of herself. To say that she would never marry a man who was not at her level would be to insult her entire family and background. But upon entering medical school, her standards began to change, whether she knew it or not. Visiting a local bar recently, she met a man she thought was extremely attractive until she asked what he did for a living. He replied that he was looking for work and wondered whether she might be able to help him get a job at the hospital. Upon hearing this, she discouraged any further interest on his part and did not give him her phone number. On observing this interaction, a woman friend challenged Mary's previous claims that things like occupation and income did not influence her choice of men. She replied that when she had said that, she had not known what it meant to be a physician: people addressing you as "Doctor," treating you as a superior, moving in different circles. Once she was in her third year and involved in patient care in the hospital, she began to experience what the status of "Doctor" really meant.

Another reason that many women are not aware of the influence of context and male status on their perceptions of sexual attractiveness is that their judgments seem completely natural and inevitable to them. Deirdre is a highly successful professional in her forties. She is not shy about expressing her class prejudices, but she is loath to admit that her perceptions of sexual attractiveness have changed with changing social hierarchies and definitions of male prowess:

Deirdre

I listen to my instincts on stuff like this. . . . I find intelligent, well-educated, ambitious men to be more attractive than stupid, poorly-educated, lazy men . . . it feels like I find them to be attractive because those traits are extraordinarily appealing and sexy in and of themselves. I've got this naive belief that unintelligent, poorly-educated, lazy men do not read, they do not make interesting conversation, and they are not attentive and imaginative and inspired lovers. I'm a bit ashamed to admit that my schema of low socioeconomic status men includes some belief that they're likely to be boring, on average. . . . When I was younger, I didn't care as much about this stuff. It was only as I acquired the experiences needed to discover how attractive and desirable these qualities were that I realized what was going on in life.

Deirdre's statement illustrates several of the points we have discussed. First, women's criteria for sexual attractiveness change as they move into adulthood because they move through different subcultures where different definitions of male prowess and status prevail. Now that Deirdre is in a professional environment, intelligence, extensive education, and career ambition are primary ingredients of sexiness. When she was younger, these qualities were unimportant.

Second, when the criteria and process of evaluation are unconscious, people's perceptions of sexual attractiveness feel natural: men appear to be sexy because they are sexy—because they possess attributes that are inherently sexy. When a person feels this way, any analysis of the evaluation process seems superfluous. Third, in order to believe that male sexiness is an inherent attribute, a woman has to ignore, or deny altogether, the tremendous variation in women's perceptions of male attractiveness, and the powerful influence of a man's status on his attractiveness. Some women consider corporate lawyers, football players, heavy metal musicians, or bodybuilders to be quintessentially sexy. Other women find these types unappealing and even repulsive. No doubt, many of the women who do find those types attractive would find the men Deirdre thinks are attractive (namely, academics and intellectuals) unappealing.

Women emphasize status more than men in their selection of mates, and women's criteria are more flexible and more variable than men's. As women age, for example, the age of their preferred partners increases accordingly, whereas men tend to prefer women younger than themselves and this gap expands as men get older. As women's own income and status increase, their standards for mates increase accordingly. These changes can occur rapidly because as women enter new status hierarchies—from high school to college, from college to the workplace—they form new standards by comparing the men in the new environment to each other and to their own achievements. Women's criteria are thus more flexible and variable than men's over the life course and across individuals because they depend more on the woman's current situation: her own age, income, lifestyle, what she needs in terms of emotional and material investment, and what she can acquire.

In Chapter 2 we saw that women's emotional reactions to low-investment sexual relations served a protective function in guiding them toward men who would make a higher investment in them. In this chapter we have seen that women's reactions to signs of men's ability, status, and success perform a similar function. Women's tendency to compare prospective partners with other men and with their own achievements channels them toward men who can provide an advantage—men who can assist, nurture, and support them in their search for security and happiness. In the chapters that follow we will explore in greater detail how and why men and women select and reject partners in long-term relationships.

4

Choosing Partners for Marriage

Male Status and Female Competition

> Aren't you funny? Don't you know that a man being rich is like a girl
> being pretty? You might not marry a girl just because she's pretty, but my
> goodness, doesn't it help?
>
> —Marilyn Monroe in *Gentleman Prefer Blondes*

Standards for Marriage Partners

IN CHAPTER 3 WE SAW that professional women prefer to date and marry
men whose incomes and job status were equal to theirs or higher, and the farther up the socioeconomic ladder they climb themselves, the higher their
standards are. Do women have difficulty finding such men? Do women have
to compete for high-status men? What forms does this competition take? Are
men threatened by ambitious, intelligent women? These are some of the
questions we will explore in this chapter.

Women and men differ more in what they would accept in a casual sex
partner than in their standards for marriage partners. For example, for
casual sexual relationships, females are choosy about partners' IQ and
socioeconomic status and men are relatively indifferent, but both sexes value
these traits when asked what they desire in a marriage partner.[1] It is also true
that most people still marry within their own social class, ethnicity, race,
and religion. From these facts one might conclude that men and women
have very similar criteria when they choose their marriage partners. But this
is misleading.

Do women compete for high-status men?

In the previous chapter we learned that men and women had different
thresholds of initial acceptance and made different tradeoffs between looks
and status. Men are often unwilling to date plain women regardless of the
women's status and achievements, and women are reluctant to date down

from their particular status regardless of a man's looks. These same differences appear in men's and women's standards for marriage partners.

Because men are relatively indifferent to women's socioeconomic status when choosing partners, higher-status women are forced to compete with attractive lower-status women for higher-status men. This competition forces some women to consider lowering their standards if they are to marry at all. But women continue to shun marrying "down" in terms of education, job prestige, and income.[2] Female competition for high-status men is therefore intense. High-status women such as doctors, lawyers, and business executives are at a disadvantage in this competition because they resist marrying down, and the pool of single men who meet their standards is relatively small.

Most of the women medical students interviewed were aware that they wanted to marry at their socioeconomic level or higher, and that this standard caused their pool of acceptable partners to shrink as their status rose. They therefore worried whether they would be able to find men who met their standards in time to start a family. Anna and Karla are second-year medical students.

Anna

I want to marry a man at least as successful as I am. Finding a man is the damndest thing. By the time you get done with your training you're in your thirties. You want to have kids but it's already too late. The worst thing about being a professional woman is that you want to have babies when you are financially insecure. It's a tremendous pressure. Right now I don't want to worry about being older and getting married, but it is in the back of my mind that it could be a problem. But I never want to be interpreted as being desperate. Nobody wants to date desperate people.

Karla

I'll be 25 when I graduate and 28 when I'm through with my residency. I'll be 30 by the time I get going and I'll have to ask how fertile am I and how many opportunities will I have to meet men. Thirty is a milestone. You only have five years left to have kids before you take serious genetic risks. Men have the advantage. They don't even have to think of this. A lot of these men will be in their residencies before they even think of marriage. They can afford to fool around. I can't afford to spend a year in a relationship with a man I don't intend to marry. I don't have the time. I try not to dwell on these things too much because it's depressing.

Pat is also worried about finding a man with the right qualifications. Like her colleagues, Pat recognizes that her criteria for mate selection are socioeconomic and she believes that other women share these criteria—although some are reluctant to admit it. Her own rising status has limited the pool of acceptable partners because she wants to marry a man who is at least at her occupational and income level, and she is aware of the competition she faces for these men from women with lower-status occupations.

Pat

Women in medicine have put themselves in a very select bracket. A lot of women with careers don't want to admit they're attracted to a man's status. It sounds too materialistic and mercenary to admit it, and they want to feel that they can make it on their own—they don't need a man to help them. But a man who's more advanced than you can help you get one step further up on the ladder, regardless of how good you are, and women are attracted to men like that. Second-year women don't go out with first-year guys, but second-year guys go out with first-year women, or with chirps or undergrads. The men talk about it. At a social function or an orientation, all the second-year men flock to the cute, first-year women. The second-year women don't care if they've got good-looking, first-year guys in their orientation groups. They see these guys as beneath them, as less advanced, and they're not attracted to them.

Zelda is the fourth-year medical student we met in Chapter 3. She is ambitious and successful and wants a man who has these qualities, and she prefers a man who earns more than she does. She is aware of the competition for men of this caliber and she has decided to apply for residencies only in cities that have large numbers of single professional men.

Zelda

I never thought too many women would be a problem. I always wanted to marry at my level, so I thought men would too. Then I heard one of my male colleagues say, "I'd never want to marry a female doctor." I was appalled! It never dawned on me until then. I've seen the evidence now. I've seen a few class marriages, then I've seen men marry nurses or secretaries because they are available when the men are. Men are willing to marry down and they are being pursued by these women and they love it! The women want to marry up. Here we are in med school and we're having problems finding men to have permanent relationships with, while there are the men next door with nothing more to offer and they have a selection of any female they want. A lot of women in my class are getting married to men they met this year. And there are a lot of women like me who haven't met the men they want yet, and we're really concerned.

Given the choice, most people would probably prefer spouses who are gorgeous and have impressive careers. Our sample of law students definitely showed this preference. But when men and women were forced to make tradeoffs between looks and status, dramatic differences appeared. For example, women were not interested in any kind of relationship with the waiter in the fast-food uniform even when he was very good looking. The men were merely undecided about marrying the best-looking woman in the waitress outfit, and 60 percent of the men were willing to date and have sex with her.[3]

Most of the women were willing to marry the homely model when he wore the Rolex and blazer and was described as a physician. Men were undecided to negative about marrying the homely model regardless of her status and costume. For women, the high-status costume and description overwhelmed the effects of the models' physical attractiveness: as long as the models were in the blazer and described as physicians, women law students were willing to marry them and were unaffected by the men's looks. For men, models' looks always had an effect, but the men were sometimes indifferent to status. For example, the men did not care whether the model was described as a teacher or a doctor. Women definitely preferred the doctor. Apparently, the men did distinguish between middle-class and working-class status and occupations, but as long as the woman was middle class, the men were not concerned about her income or occupation. Women, however, were concerned. Studies of the marriage market show that these women's concerns are well founded.

Marrying up

In a trailbreaking study in 1969, Glen Elder concluded that, as suitors, men determine to a great extent the value of physical attractiveness in the marriage market. American men rank physical attractiveness at or near the top of desirable characteristics, and this is especially true of upwardly mobile, ambitious men. Consequently, attractive women employ their bargaining advantage to secure the most successful men as mates. The result of this bargaining process is that the more a man's social rank exceeds his wife's premarital status, the more likely she is to be exceptionally physically attractive.[4]

In the late 1970s researchers found that if a white woman came from a middle-class family and attended college, her physical attractiveness did not appear to affect the socioeconomic status of the man she married.[5] For black women, physical attractiveness did correlate with husbands' status, and this correlation was even stronger for black women who attended college. The problem with studies like this is that they measured a woman's marriage mobility by comparing her husband's income and education with that of her father. Since most college students come from middle-class backgrounds, most women will show no upward mobility in marriage because they come from middle-class homes and they marry middle-class men. By this measure a woman whose father is a doctor shows no mobility in marriage if she marries a doctor. Viewed another way, however, a woman who majored in English literature, or some other subject with minimal earning power, enjoys a tremendous gain in income and occupational status by marrying a doctor—even though she herself may have come from an upper middle-class family. So, if we compare the relative earning power and occupational status of a woman and her husband, the effects of female beauty become more visible. In the interviews which follow we will see that men who are moving into high-status occupations are sensitive to signs of middle-class status, but they are relatively unconcerned about their partners' own income and occupational prestige. This laxity allows attractive women from middle-class backgrounds, and attractive women from working-class origins who adopt middle-class dress and mannerisms, to marry up in terms of income and occupational status.

A second problem with earlier studies is that women who did not marry were not included. This omission concealed the effects of female attractiveness on marital chances. In the 1980s Richard Udry conducted a study that corrected these flaws. Udry and Eckland used the husband's level of education as the criterion of marriage mobility and also included women who did not marry in their sample.[6] They found that physical attractiveness had different and even opposite effects on men's and women's social mobility and marital chances. The more attractive a woman was in high school, the more educated her husband was. The more attractive a man was in high school, the less educated his wife was. The least attractive women were ten times as likely never to have married as the most attractive. For men, there was no correlation between attractiveness and the percentage who had never married.

Putting down the competition

Signaling among animals has traditionally been viewed as a means of facilitating communication between cooperating members of a species—for example, bird calls serve to warn other birds that a predator is approaching. Contemporary evolutionary biologists, however, take a different view: communication among animals evolved to benefit the signaler rather than the receiver. Consequently, signals are a form of manipulation. They may sometimes be accurate, and they may sometimes benefit the receiver as well, but their primary function is to benefit the signaler. This does not necessarily mean that the signaler is aware of the manipulation. In fact, lack of awareness offers several advantages: awareness of our motives, tactics, and failures can be painful, and pain can reduce our effectiveness. Self-deception can help to deceive others, thus facilitating our tactics. This form of self-deception is a late development in evolution. It is most pronounced among humans because we possess language, but it also occurs in rudimentary forms among chimpanzees.

In all sexually reproducing species, individuals compete for mates. One of the ways that individuals compete sexually is make themselves more attractive compared to their peers, or make the competition less attractive. A common method of making someone appear less attractive is to derogate, slight, and insult them. In a series of studies, David Buss found that men and women slighted and insulted exactly those qualities that would have been critical to survival and reproductive success in evolutionary history.[7] Men derogated other men's manhood, ambition, achievements, and strength. Women criticized other women's physical appearance, and implied either that they were promiscuous or that they were sexual teases. Women also were more likely than men to insult competitors' intelligence, but the authors of the study did not predict this finding and offer no explanation for it.

One reason that college-educated women might derogate a competitor's intelligence is that their own criteria for partner's attractiveness—which emphasize education, occupation, and income and are not always conscious—seem natural and right, so male criteria that focus on youth and beauty seem incomprehensible, unnatural, and degraded. A second reason for this practice is that people usually pick competitor's traits to criticize where their competitors appear weak. For example, a woman whose strong suit is brains and professional success rather than beauty, and whose exboyfriend is going out with a model, would be foolish to put down her competitor's looks and body. This would draw attention to her competitor's superiority and her own deficiencies in that area. Instead, she would probably slight her rival's intelligence—perhaps also using her opponent's physical attributes as proof of her intellectual inferiority (with that body, of course she's a bimbo). Derogation of competitors' intelligence was a common tactic among the professional women we interviewed.

Most of the women medical students were acutely aware of the female competition for higher-status men. These women wanted to marry men in their occupational and educational levels or higher. Male medical students seemed indifferent to their partners' incomes and occupations and were more likely to date women in other fields and programs, for example, women in the College of Health Related Professions who were studying to be nurses, X-ray technicians, physical and respiratory therapists, and other health-related specialists. These women were known colloquially as "chirps" and provided a sizable pool of potential partners. A nearby university also offered a large pool of single, undergraduate females. In addition to these prospects, some male students were dating women who worked in the business world or were studying for graduate degrees in nonmedical fields. For their part, most of the women medical students could not understand why their male peers did not share their own criteria for partner selection. In fact, some women expressed considerable resentment toward women in lower-status occupations or programs, and they derogated both these competitors and the men who dated them. In the first statement, Zelda slights the physical attractiveness and the educational achievements of her competitors as well as the men who marry them. In the second quotation, Pat criticizes her male peers for their emphasis on physical attributes. Both women offer an explanation for men's preferences.

Zelda

I can't understand these guys going out with chirps. I don't mean that derogatively. But someone who doesn't feel education is as important as we do. Men look for someone to cater to them who always looks good: "Here's my wife, isn't she pretty." I would have expected the men to want good looks but the men in my class who married chirps didn't marry beautiful women. What do these women offer? They are not better looking than the med students. They just have more time to work on their looks. We don't always look good; we look tired.

I think the men prefer to marry down. If a person's job shows power and prestige, and they are the primary breadwinner, then the man is the boss of the house. An undergrad is a big confidence booster for him. He has to be confident enough to date us.

Pat

Men want women who are young, pretty, skinny, and have nice complexions. No matter if a guy says he wants an intelligent woman, you'll see him the next night with a pretty 20-year-old at the chirp dance. . . . Most men still want wives who will stay at home with the kids. There's a percentage of men who want their wives to have careers, but they can't stand the challenge to their male egos—the competition. I've noticed this with guys I've dated. Some may want an intelligent woman, but they want her to stay home with the kids.

Like Pat and Zelda, numerous women in my samples interpreted men's reluctance to date women in their occupational levels as indicating that men are threatened by women who are their equals—women who are as ambitious, intelligent, and successful as they are. According to this theory, men tend to prefer women who are inferior to them in terms of income, education, and occupational status because they want subordinate women whom they can dominate. This theory is used to explain why men date women who have lower socioeconomic status than they do. During my research a number of women, including several medical students, used derogatory terms such as airhead and bimbo to refer to the women their male peers dated.

Anna is a second-year medical student who faces competition from lower-status women. Note that she refers to such women as "girls":

Anna

I think I'll have to look outside of professionals for marriage. The pool is so limited I'll have to be practical. Ideally, it would be great to marry a rich, famous man. Men want to marry subordinate women because that's who they come in contact with. That is the role women are in. Men want attractive wives who are good hostesses, or women like their moms—who clean up after them. That's why a lot of men can't marry professional women. There will be constant friction over expectations. That's why most men prefer to date girls, not women. Some men are consciousness-raised and nontraditional but the majority of men go for the girls. A "girl" is someone who is not bright, looks like she'd be good in bed, and works on her looks. She's naive, and she thinks you're wonderful!

Judging from Anna's account, it seems clear that the women she calls "girls" are women in lower educational and occupational brackets who use their physical attractiveness in the competition for higher-status men. Anna does not know these women's IQ scores, so perhaps her characterization is unfair. But she knows that they are in fields that require less education and preparation, and offer lower income and status than medicine does. She also knows that the men she wants to marry—men at her level or higher—do not seem to mind dating and marrying these women, whereas she would never do the analogous thing and marry a male secretary or nurse.

Anna seems less aware than Pat of how her own rising status has restricted her dating and marital opportunities. If she were working as a secretary and earning $18,000, her pool of acceptable partners would be vastly enlarged. By becoming a physician, she has put herself in one of the top levels of occupational prestige and income in this society. Logically, she knows that she could enlarge her pool of acceptable partners by lowering her socioeconomic standards, but she does not want to do this. She would prefer to marry a wealthy successful man, but she realizes that such a man might not be willing to compromise his desire for a wife who manages the household and supports him in his career in order to marry a woman with a demanding career like hers. Her own socioeconomic criteria for a mate thus interact with men's criteria to reduce her chances of getting what she wants, but she does not necessarily see it this way. She only sees that men in her level are dating lower-status women and this presents a real problem for her. Facing this dilemma, she feels frustrated and resentful, and she vents her frustration by deprecating both these women and the men who date them.

Are men threatened?

Most of the male medical students did not accept the theory that they did not date their female colleagues because they are threatened by intelligent, ambitious women. In explaining their preference for dating women outside of medical school, the men overwhelmingly mentioned one factor: they did not find most of the women in medical school physically attractive. Dating undergraduates and other women outside of medical school afforded them a larger pool of more physically attractive women. The second reason men offered was their belief that small children needed high-quality care and attention and that children were better off when this care was provided by their mothers. About 60 percent of the second-year male medical students wanted their wives to stay home at least part-time while the children were small. Most of these men emphasized that they wanted to marry an intelligent woman who was college educated and had a career that could be resumed after the children were older. Unlike their female peers, however, they were relatively indifferent to the status and income afforded by their future wives' jobs.

Vince is a second-year medical student. His statement vividly illustrates these sex differences in partner selection criteria. He genuinely respects and likes some of his female classmates, but like his male peers, he does not find most of these women physically attractive enough to date. He severed a relationship with a high-school dropout who was physically attractive but who was so ignorant that he could not communicate with her, so he definitely requires a certain level of intelligence and education in a partner in order to have a serious relationship. But the woman must meet his physical standards for him to consider dating her. His girlfriend, whom he subsequently married, is apparently very physically attractive. She is a college graduate and works in the business world. Like most of his male peers, he is relatively indifferent to a woman's occupational status and income. He was and is willing to invest a great deal in order to continue a relationship with this woman. He also feels that many of his female classmates are doomed because their own level of physical attractiveness will not allow them to marry men at their level, and they do not want to marry down.

Vince

I met my girlfriend when we were undergraduates. She is gorgeous, unbelievable! I'd say she was in the top five percent in looks at that college. We went out as friends for a whole year before she trusted me enough to sleep with me. She had had a bad experience in a previous relationship and she didn't want to get hurt again, so I really had to take it slowly.

[JMT: Do you think that when women choose partners, looks are as important as when men choose partners?] I can only speak for myself. Looks are way, way up there: ninetieth percentile. You have to have that initial attraction. If you are going to be with that person and constantly around them, you want to look at something pretty. Actually I

was surprised when I came to medical school because I expected to see all dogs and our class has two really attractive women. Then there's a jump to ten okay-looking women; then there's an even bigger jump to the bottom three-quarters. I don't think a lot of these women have a prayer of finding the men they want—with the exception of the top two. Even the middle ten are going to have problems. A friend of mine and I take a couple of women medical students to lunch or go have beers after an exam. We're friends. These women are okay looking— a little overweight. But we would never go to a movie alone with one of them. Someone might think we were out on a date. We don't want these women to get that idea either. They're very nice people, but we just don't find them attractive in that way.

Sometimes I get the feeling that some of the women medical students are jealous of my girlfriend. No one's ever said anything, but I can tell the way they act. She's pretty and she's not a medical student. It's like, "Hey, why are you going out with her? Why aren't you going out with us?" I talked to my roomate about this and he agrees. With all these different pressures, some of these women are doomed. I think that's why a lot of them resent their classmates' dating chirps. They put down the chirps and call them airheads or whatever, and they put down the men for dating them. A lot of the chirps are very pretty and they know their field. They're not necessarily stupid just because they didn't go into medicine. I would date a chirp. I don't think that's dating down.

Vince is no playboy. He has only had sex with two women and he married the second one. He could not maintain a relationship indefinitely with a woman he considered ignorant, but her physical attractiveness and his sexual needs were sufficient to cause him to continue it for over two years. For marriage he wants both: the manners, vocabulary, and social skills afforded by a college education and middle-class background, and a high degree of physical attractiveness. Jack is a second-year medical student. He is very explicit in his opinions on these issues.

Jack

It's a problem meeting attractive women to date when you're in med school. I'm not taking anything away from the women in med school but for the most part they're not too attractive. I like some of them real well as friends, but a lot of the women in the class are fat. There may be two or three women in my class I'd be willing to date. It's not that I don't like my classmates just because they're not good looking. I like some of them a lot. It's just that looks are important. Most guys want to date pretty women whether the women are doctors, lawyers or whatever. That's the crux of it.

I've heard some of the women say the men want to date chirps and undergrads because they're threatened by an intellectual equal. That's not the case at all. You can't come out and tell them, though, that the real reason we're not dating them is that physically they're grimbos. But a lot of times that's the bottom line. It's not that men are going to feel threatened by them. That's bullshit!

I don't want to marry an airhead. There'd be nothing to talk about. I don't know if I'd be willing to marry a doctor because I believe kids need someone full time when they're small and they're better off if it's a parent. I might be willing to stay at home part of the time with the kids. I don't know. But I'd be psyched to date a really good-looking medical student. Why not?

Sex Roles and Mate Preferences

Numerous authors have argued that traditional differences in mate preferences result from sexist attitudes toward the role of women. When men fully accept women as equals, and women have equal status and power and feel like equals, these sex differences will gradually disappear. A key tenet in this perspective is that women cannot achieve true political and economic equality until they are accepted as equals in marriage, and this means that husbands and wives must have careers that are equally important and must share the division of household tasks and child care equally. We will examine the importance of sex differences in domestic roles in later chapters. Here I will focus on attitudes toward marital roles and their relationship to criteria for marriage partners.

In Chapter 2 we saw that women's sexual attitudes did not correlate with their emotional reactions. In later chapters we will see that men who espouse feminist attitudes tend to show the basic male pattern of sexuality as strongly as men with more traditional attitudes. Similarly, attitudes toward sex roles— for example, whether wives should have demanding careers, or whether they should stay home when children are small—do not correlate with people's actual partner selections. Women who espouse feminist ideology are just as likely to emphasize socioeconomic criteria in their choice of partners as women with more traditional attitudes. Men who want wives with equally ambitious careers are just as likely to emphasize partners' physical attractiveness as men who want their wives to stay home.[8] Michael is a second-year medical student. He definitely wants a woman with an equally ambitious, demanding career and he dated a woman medical student for almost two years.

Michael

I want a woman who is like me: really psyched for her career and interested in accomplishing something. For a woman to sacrifice her whole life for a man seems a great loss. I wouldn't want a woman who would want to do that. I have not thought about day care and the practical aspects of the problem so my ideas could change, but right now I want both: big careers for both of us and a good family life.

A woman's looks are definitely important to me and there aren't that many good-looking women in medical school. The three best looking girls look good compared to the rest of the women in the class, and most of the guys in the class would be willing to date them. But they wouldn't think that they're the best in the world. I think these women have it better the first two years of medical school. After that we get on the wards in the hospital and they'll have to compete with the chirps, nurses, and techs, so they won't look as good, relatively speaking. But between two equally attractive women, I think most guys would consider it an ego boost to date the med student. I know I would.

Like Michael, David is a second-year medical student and wants a wife who has an ambitious career. He does not expect his wife to bear the brunt of household chores and child care and believes that hired help and daycare will allow them both to pursue their career goals. Like the other men in the sample, however, he is not concerned about what type of career his wife will have. How much education and preparation are required and the job's prestige and earning power are not important. Like his male colleagues he emphasizes physical attributes in describing his ideal partner. His wife should be ambitious, but she should also be young, pretty, and have a good body.

David

I don't want someone with a great body who's stupid. A [woman's having a] college education is very important to me. I'd rather have a woman that runs off to college than one who runs off to aerobics. I'd sacrifice beauty for brains if I had to. Hopefully, it won't come to that. I want a woman with a reasonable body who keeps it that way. I definitely want an ambitious wife—someone with an interesting career. We can hire someone to take care of the house and use daycare if we have kids. What kind of job she has is not important to me, but she has to be ambitious.

Some of my female classmates say they don't care what a man does as long as he's ambitious. I don't buy it. How can you be an ambitious auto mechanic or plumber—unless you owned a chain of shops and then you wouldn't be just a mechanic or plumber anymore. These women want to marry someone at their occupational level and some are going to have a tough time doing it.

Brett is also a second-year medical student. He wants his wife to have a career that provides a significant income. He would only marry a woman who was willing to stay at home part-time when the children were small, but otherwise he would not exclude the possibility of marrying a woman physician. He has had two relationships with women medical students that lasted over a year. He likes smart, ambitious women and does not feel intimidated by them. He insists, however, that they must also be physically attractive.

Brett

When I was younger, I thought I would marry someone like my mother who stayed home with the kids and didn't work. But I've changed my mind since then. I think you need two incomes these days to really be comfortable, so I definitely want the woman I marry to have a career. When I was growing up, I saw kids whose mothers worked or were never home and I could see they were affected negatively, so I would prefer my wife to stay at home at least part-time when the children are small. Physicians don't have any spare time, so I probably wouldn't marry a doctor unless she were willing to take off some time while the kids were small. After the kids were older, I would expect my wife to work full-time. For thousands of years women have not been allowed to develop their talents and creativity, and I would feel bad if my wife did not have a chance to do this just because she stayed home with the kids. I definitely believe that fathers should be involved with their children too and I plan to be, but looking at it realistically, it wouldn't be on a 50-50 basis.

At this point there are two kinds of women for me: those that I just want to get their clothes off, and those I'm interested in getting to know. Physical attractiveness is important for both. The pretty women in my class you can count on three fingers. It's the rule that really attractive women generally don't make it to medical school. It's just too tough and takes too many years. I know some guys who would be intimidated by dating a woman in medical school but I don't feel that way. I want someone who has an interesting career and has opinions on matters and can express herself intelligently.

Karla is a second-year medical student. She does not want to compromise her career in order to comply with a man's desires for domestic caretaking. On the other hand, like her male peers, she does not accept the theory that men date and marry women in lower socioeconomic brackets because they are threatened by women who are equals. She understands why men would want women with less ambitious careers who would be willing to manage the household and support their husband's careers. She may not like it, because she wants a high-status man herself, and the chances of finding one who would accept her career demands are slim. Nevertheless, she recognizes men's desires in this regard as understandable.

She does not think that men prefer to date women with less ambitious careers because men want stupid women who are easily dominated. Instead, she pinpoints female competition for men as the source of her classmates' derogation of lower-status women and the men who date them. She perceives that higher-status women like herself and her classmates are threatened by these other women—particularly if the lower-status women are more physically attractive.

Karla

I don't think most men in my class want intellectual women. They wouldn't marry a retard, but they'd marry a woman with a college degree who didn't have a serious career and who was looking for a doctor. They don't want a woman who can challenge them on medical knowledge. These men aren't stupid to pick women without careers. If they want someone to do 90 percent of the housework, they won't want me for a wife. But I can't condone it when women refer to other women as "girls" or "dingalings." These women have as much right to respect as anyone else. Some of these women are very intelligent and good in their fields. Just because they're not in a profession like medicine doesn't mean they're stupid. I think some of the women in medical school are being catty when they make remarks like that. They have to compete with these other women and are jealous of them because they have time to look good. In general, I don't think the women in med school are attractive. Women who are extremely good looking find it easier to do other things than go to medical school. They get involved with men. Women who are average or on the ugly side are more apt to develop their minds. We don't spend as much time dressing and putting on makeup and trying to look attractive.

Debbie is in her second year of medical school. She does well in her classes and is judged by both her female and male peers to be one of the more physically attractive women in her class. Like most of her female colleagues, she reports that she feels pressured by the demands of her career and the biological risks of later pregnancies. Although women in medical school are typically in their early twenties, they know that they will be almost thirty by the time they finish their residencies. Then they face the years and trials of establishing a successful practice. Somewhere in these hectic years they must find a man who meets their qualifications, establish a stable relationship, marry, and begin a family. Most of the women who were not already engaged or in long-term relationships were extremely concerned about whether they would be able to accomplish all this. Debbie is optimistic because she believes that her looks give her an advantage over most of the women in medicine. She does not accept the "men are threatened by equals" theory.

Debbie

I'm assuming that I've got both brains and physical attractiveness, so I have a good chance of getting what I want. The less attractive women in medical school will have problems finding a mate because they don't want to marry down in status. There are about 40 women in the class and most of them are unattractive. A lot of them are overweight. Some of them will have to marry down if they want to marry, but I don't think it will work because they won't be satisfied doing that.

Some career women say that men are threatened by intelligent women, but I don't think that's it. It's true that some of these guys want their wives to stay home and be charming hostesses but it is not that they're threatened by intelligent women, or women with careers. It's that they want good-looking women. A lot of guys in the class are not so good looking, but they can use their status as second-year students to get women. If they can't get a woman who's both attractive and intelligent, they can go to a bar and find a dingaling undergraduate by saying they're in medical school. And there is a correlation: women who are really good looking aren't likely to be in a field like medicine. It takes too many years and is too demanding. Good-looking women have other possibilities. They can always go into another field and marry a doctor if that's what they want.

So it's not the career that turns off men, it's that a lot of women who have really serious careers like medicine are not very attractive. Women who say things like, "Men are threatened by intelligent women," are just rationalizing. It's sour grapes. The men don't want them so they say there's something wrong with the men. I'm intelligent and I don't have any trouble getting asked out. I think there's a lot of resentment among the women in the class because of the competition—both academically and for men. I had plenty of women friends in college, but now I feel alienated because I don't have any good women friends. That's one of the reasons I got into a serious relationship with my boyfriend: I had no girlfriends in the class to lean on. It's the competition.

Ingrid is also considered one of the better-looking women in the class. She describes the effects of men's and women's standards for marriage partners:

Ingrid

A woman who has a successful career and wants to marry a professional equal and have a 50-50 marriage, and she is thirty pounds overweight, has a very slim chance of getting what she wants. The women who say that men are threatened by women who are equals are rationalizing. They want successful men but they can't get them.

In this part of her interview, Pat acknowledges that most men in medical school respect their female colleagues, accept them as equals, and are willing to date some of them and be buddies with others. The problem, then, does not seem to be that men do not respect their female colleagues or are threatened by them.

Pat

The guys in our class have the utmost respect for their female peers. They think, "These women are smart and if we don't keep on our toes, they're going to step on them." They can see the evidence: some of us women are getting honors in our classes and some of the men aren't. So I do feel like I'm accepted as an equal and some of these guys treat me as a buddy. We're friends. But when you don't have a man yourself, being treated as one of the guys isn't so great. When the men really bring you into their core, you find out how physical their criteria are for judging women. Everybody has their specialty, like, "I'm a leg man," or "I'm a breast man." They tell disgusting jokes in front of you because they really are treating you like one of the guys. I know they don't mean to be insulting; for them it's second nature, and sometimes it's okay with me too. But there are times when you're interested in a guy and he elbows you and asks you to "rate that chick at the bar on a scale from one to ten." It makes you feel desexualized. You want them to notice you as a woman and they don't. Most of the time you do want to be seen as a colleague and not as a woman. But if you could be interested in a man, you want him to find you sexually attractive and it's depressing if he doesn't.

Evidently, the notion that men are threatened by women who are equals is not a convincing explanation of why men tend to date down in terms of occupation, education, and income. The following is a better explanation. First, women themselves generally prefer to date and marry men who have higher status than they do. Consequently, most men never have the chance to date up, and by dating down they get more of what they want: physically attractive women who are more willing to adjust their lives and career goals to their partners because of the socioeconomic advantages these men offer. Second, physical attractiveness is a primary criterion in men's selection of partners and many of the women in their socioeconomic level simply do not measure up to the men's physical standards. The men may enjoy friendships with these women, but they do not find them physically attractive enough to date or marry. Third, some, but not all, men want wives who can interrupt their careers when there are small children at home. This stipulation may prevent these men from marrying career women who are unwilling to do this, but it does not prevent them from dating such women, provided that these women are sufficiently physically attractive. Fourth, many upwardly mobile men are in no hurry to commit themselves to binding relationships or marriage—regardless of how career-oriented or attractive a woman is. This male reticence may be interpreted by some ambitious women as indicating that the man is threatened by their intelligence and success, but he may be equally reticent and elusive with less ambitious partners simply because he wants to look over the field and experience sexual variety before he commits himself.

Finally, men may be reluctant to date female colleagues because of the opprobrium they might elicit in attempting to have casual sexual relations. The men agreed that there were only a few women in the class physically attractive enough to date seriously and they generally agreed on who these women were. But there was a larger group of women they might want to sleep with if they thought they could do so with minimal effort and trouble. The "trouble" was that these women did not want sex on that basis and attempts in this direction could lead to hard feelings, gossip, and social ostracism. In the first two years of medical school, classmates see each other every day in most of their classes. If it were known that a man had been callous in his treatment of a female colleague, attending class could be extremely awkward, and established relationships with both male and female classmates could be disrupted. Thus, both on a personal and a group level, women's desire for investment acted as a check on male desires for partner variety and low-investment sex.

Bill is a second-year medical student. He, along with several of his classmates, remarked that neither men nor women in medical school were likely to have been the most popular, attractive, social types in high school and college. Those who got into medical school tended to be the studious types. Bill reports that in high school he was "the skinny shit with glasses" and did not have much luck with women. In college, he fared somewhat better, but medical school "has been a bonanza" for him:

Bill

Most of the guys will tell you they don't want to go out with women in their class. It's too awkward when things end and you have to see them every day. One night I was shitfaced drunk and I ended up grappling [necking and petting] with a woman in my class. I was embarrassed so I went over a few days later to see her. I wanted to slide my way out of it and keep everything cool between us. I found out she was psyched for it, [and] figured "What the hell!" so I took her out for about a month and we slept together a few times. She was more interested than I was. She had a boyfriend in another city and it was rocky, and I didn't want to deal with it. I didn't want her to break up with him to go out with me. For me there are two kinds of women: those where you're just looking for sex and the ones you are psyched for and are willing to put in the time. This woman was in the middle. Not only did I not want to marry her, I didn't want any obligations. She didn't hassle me but I knew she wanted more than I could offer so I told her from the beginning that I wasn't into anything serious. I like her; she's a nice girl and I didn't want to lead her on. I might just let it ride with someone I wasn't into or didn't have to see every day in class. You know, let the woman figure it out for herself. But I'm not a sleazy kind of guy, so I let her know right away. I finally had to be blunt about it and she knew I was blowing her off.

It was a bad scene, so I'm sort of paranoid about getting involved with women in my class. Like the other night I was at a party and I ended up with another classmate in her bedroom. I believe she had more designs than I did and she was encouraging me to stay. We were both sort of drunk. We sat on her bed and fooled around. When she told me she had a crush on me last year, I knew this wouldn't be something I could blow off tomorrow. If she hadn't been in my class, or if she had been better looking, I would have stayed in a second. I decided it was in my best interest to leave, and I did.

When I get a few drinks in me, I'm a walking erection. But I try to control myself. To seriously date someone in my class, I'd have to find her really attractive and interesting and I don't know if there's anyone in the class I'd be willing to date. As far as looks go, we're hitting the bottom in our class, but I'm interested in some of these women as friends. There are so many guys who say, "No way would I go with anybody in class." If the women were more attractive, you'd be more inclined, but you'd still be less inclined than if they were in the general population. There are plenty of guys who would be more than willing to date the two or three best-looking girls in the class, but they don't want 140 sets of eyes watching them, and if things don't work out, there's all this shit you have to deal with: friends who know both of you, gossip, different loyalties. So it's an added burden. If you go to bed with someone in your class and then blow her off, the woman feels fucked over. People gossip, word gets around, and pretty soon not only are the other women not attracted to you, they hate your guts!

Most of the medical students had observed the effects of increasing status on women's standards for partners and on men's attractiveness to women.[9] The women tended to think their pool of acceptable partners was declining as their status rose. They worried whether they would be able to find men who met their standards in time to start a family. While most of the men wanted to marry and have children, they were in less of a hurry to do so. They were beginning to notice and take advantage of the expanding opportunities their rising status offered. These sex differences in partner selection are not arbitrary and they do not seem to be waning. They have dramatic effects on people's lives. They help to determine whom we bed, whom we wed, and who will be the father or mother of our children. In the next chapter we will explore men's sexuality and criteria for partners in more depth.

5

What Do Men Want?

Men's Criteria for Choosing Partners

And it came to pass in an evening-tide that David arose from off his bed and walked upon the roof of the king's house: and from the roof he saw a woman washing herself; and the woman was very beautiful to look upon. And David sent and enquired after the woman. And one said, Is not this Bath-sheba, the daughter of Eliam, the wife of Uriah the Hittite? And David sent messengers, and took her; and she came in unto him, and he lay with her. . . .

—2 Samuel 11: 2–4

I am persuaded that there is absolutely no limit to the absurdities that can. . . come to be generally believed. . . I will undertake, within 30 years, to make the majority of the population believe that two and two are three, that water freezes when it gets hot and boils when it gets cold, or any other nonsense. . . Of course, even when these beliefs had been generated, people would not put the kettle in the refrigerator when they wanted it to boil. That cold makes water boil would be a Sunday truth, sacred and mystical, to be professed in awed tones, but not to be acted on in daily life.

—Bertrand Russell, "An Outline of Intellectual Rubbish"

Men and Mate Selection

FOR OVER TWENTY YEARS, researchers have been telling us that men emphasize physical attractiveness and women stress socioeconomic status when they choose dating and marriage partners. But numerous writers predicted that these sex differences would begin to decline as women achieved economic independence. This does not seem to be happening. Psychologist David Buss recently tested 100 college students and found that in reporting the qualities they most desired in mates, women emphasized earning capacity and education, and men emphasized physical attractiveness. Some researchers have questioned whether results that are reported by college students on abstract questionnaires are actually put into practice in partner selection. Buss also queried 92 married couples about the characteristics they preferred in mates. Women thought that good husbands should be considerate, honest, kind, understanding, fond of children, and well-liked by others, as well as having a good earning capacity, ambition, and a good family background. For men, it was most important that wives be physically attractive, good cooks, and frugal. Buss then went on to collect data on mate preferences in thirty-seven cultures. He found the same sex differences that other researchers had described. Women emphasized factors like earning power, social status, and job prestige, while men stressed partners' youth and beauty. Studies of personal ads and marriage patterns in other cultures have produced similar results.[1]

These sex differences in mate preferences are not merely hypothetical. Men's satisfaction with relationships correlates with their perception of their partners' physical attractiveness. For women, their satisfaction correlates with their male partners' ambition and success, and with the quality of emotional communication. These sex differences are at the root of the satisfaction and dissatisfaction experienced in relationships, and are frequently part of the reason for breakups. These sex differences have appeared in studies of premarital relationships, in new marriages, and even in middle-aged couples who have been married for years.[2] These differences are real and persistent—strongly affecting initial partner choice and continuing well after relationships are established.

Physical attractiveness

In choosing partners for serious relationships and marriage, most men do consider other qualities important: common backgrounds, personal compatibility, intelligence, and sociability. We will deal with this topic in more detail in subsequent chapters. But if a woman does not meet his requirements for physical attractiveness, she will not even be considered for a serious relationship. Most men show great latitude in the variety of physical types they find acceptable for sexual intercourse. But when it comes to investing in a relationship, their physical criteria usually become more stringent. Different parts of the human body act as visual stimuli for male sexual arousal. Men are turned on by what they see, and the closer a particular feature conforms to the man's ideal, the more exciting the stimulus is. The physiology of men's sexual arousal system thus seems to differ from that of women.

In fact, how satisfied a man is with a relationship is strongly affected by how physically attractive he continues to find his partner. To some extent, how physically attractive he continues to find his partner depends on the physical attractiveness of other women who might be available to him. Men's criteria for choosing partners and for maintaining relationships are thus intimately tied to their capacity for visual sexual arousal.[3] Michael, for example, is a second-year medical student who had been living with a woman medical student for about six months until he began to get restless. One of the reasons he began to want to see other women was that his partner was becoming less physically attractive in his eyes. She was gaining weight and becoming less sexually attractive. And he was becoming bored with her.

Michael

I wasn't looking for another relationship when I would look at attractive women. I just wanted something temporary with them—to sleep with them. And I began to notice imperfections in my girlfriend's body, so that it became difficult to initiate intercourse with her. She was gradually gaining weight and becoming less attractive. She had really nice curves when I met her and the curves were disappearing. She's only five feet four and by the time we broke up she had gained fifteen pounds. If she hadn't gained weight though, I probably still would have gotten bored. About a year and a half into the relationship it became obvious that I wasn't as interested in sex as I had been, and she asked what was wrong. I made various excuses: I was tired, under stress. She didn't buy any of them. She wouldn't initiate sex on her own, so it became a real problem. I would initiate it occasionally, just to keep things going for a little bit longer—just to keep her happy. When I ran out of excuses, I told her I wanted to see other women. But this did not happen abruptly.

I started by slowly telling her my goals, like I needed more time to be with my friends and to do things on my own. But every time I went out, I wanted to meet other women. When I was with her, it was okay, but when I was out with friends and saw an attractive woman, I would try to get to know her. If nothing came of it, I would go back to the security thing with my girlfriend, but give more hints about how I needed more space, more time apart. Each time I became bolder and the hints more specific. I would have slept with these other women if I could have.

Going out with friends allowed me this freedom. I did not have a good reason for wanting to go out with other women. I just wanted to do it. She was ready for a life-long commitment, so that made everything tougher. I felt she was too dependent on me. My previous girlfriend did have lots of friends and was very popular. She had a life of her own and that was good. I wanted this woman to be that way: to have her career and friends and be more independent so I could be more independent.

Michael reported that his partner's physical attractiveness declined because she was gaining weight, but that he probably would have gotten bored anyway. His analysis is probably accurate. Men's greater desire for a variety of sexual partners results from the fact that merely by being different, the sexual attractiveness of a new partner is enhanced. The thought of having sex with a complete stranger is often more exciting for men than the thought of having sex with someone familiar whom they genuinely love. Even when the new person is objectively less physically attractive than the familiar partner, the new person has an advantage because she is new and the man has not had sex with her.[4] The male capacity for visual arousal thus acted in two ways to diminish Michael's interest in his partner. First, the mere sight of physically attractive women aroused his desire for them, and their newness gave them an advantage over his partner. Second, her gaining fifteen pounds made her less attractive to him.

Michael's statement also indicates that when a man says he wants a more independent woman, or needs more "space," it may be because he wants to see other women—not necessarily for a more serious relationship, but for the satisfaction of having sex with a variety of new, physically attractive partners. We saw this pattern repeatedly in the male interviews we examined earlier. When a woman makes similar statements, her reasons are often very different. Usually she does not think that her present partner measures up and she wants to keep her options open for something better. This "something better" generally involves more material or emotional investment, or both.

Like women's sexual emotions and criteria for partner selection, men's emotions and criteria operate relatively automatically and can be experienced as involuntary. Carl is 59, divorced, and teaches music in a high school. He says he comes from the "old school" in his sexual morality and training. His parents instilled in him a strict sense of moral responsibility toward other human beings. If he sleeps with a woman he feels a level of moral obligation to her, and feels that he should be kind and considerate, concerned about her welfare, and willing to invest in order to make her happy.

Carl

About ten days ago I met this gal. She's real nice. One of the most beautiful people inside that I could ever run into—just has this wonderful disposition. Wants to do things for other people. She likes me very much, but I have found a physical flaw in her that I didn't know about until she was undressed: she doesn't have a very pretty body at all. She's very pretty in the face, but her body is sort of waistless—built like a playing card with two thin legs. But the worst part is that this gal was in a terrible, horrible automobile accident. She almost had both breasts ripped off and a fence post in her stomach. She has these terrible scars. But I didn't know that. We were in the dark, so I haven't seen it. I know she won't show me. She's such a nice person and here I am thinking, "God, now I've gone to bed with her!" The first night after we slept together, I broke out in a sweat—couldn't sleep all night—thinking about my responsibility to this woman. I should make her happy. She cares for me. When people are kind to you, you don't make them unhappy because they gave something of themselves to you. And then I feel guilty that I am unhappy with her physically, when it's something that she has nothing to do with. I shouldn't blame her because she has a body that doesn't turn me on. But when she took her clothes off, it made all the difference. This happened one other time to me. This one gal took her clothes off and she just fell apart. When she took those panty hose off, flesh went everywhere. [Laughter] It turned me off. It was like grabbing a sponge. With breasts I can pretend like they're firm. I don't care. They can throw one over the side, but legs have gotta be kind of firm. Well, this gal I'm seeing now is pretty fat. When you reach around her arm like that, where the brassiere is in the back, you can grab that much. When I met her that first night we went to bed, we had talked on the phone for about a week—long conversations. We sort of got to know each other. And when I saw her in the night club that night, she's pretty in the face, so she looked good. I was going to take her to a party and wherever. Then all these things started revealing themselves. And I said, "Oh, God, are you ever goin' to get it together." [Laughter] I thought I was playin' it so cool.

The first thing she said to me after we went to bed was, "Well, are you going to call me tomorrow"? I said, "Of course, I'll call you tomorrow!" Now she calls me once or twice a day, which I like, but I keep feeling, I gotta build some space between us. I don't want to marry her and I don't want to be her full-time lover. I would like to be her friend and maybe make love to her now and then. But I want to be able to go to singles parties, date other people, and have my male friends. See, I'm feeling guilty already 'cause I really like her as a person and thought maybe we could have something good together—up until she took her clothes off. Geez, I couldn't just cut her off now. I can't do that to her.

The guys tell me I've got a huge guilt complex with women. If I go to bed with a woman, I feel obligated. I've got to take care of her. That's why I don't go out. This is the first time I've gone out in six months. I feel right now I could never make it with a whore, but if I could, I could be a hell of a lot better off, 'cause I could go away guilt-free.

Carl's experience illustrates several points made earlier. Men's sexual arousal and desire, and hence, their selection of sex partners, depend a great deal on visual stimuli. Carl likes this woman and feels tremendous responsibility toward her—even though he has only slept with her once. His sense of guilt and his genuine concern for this woman tell him he should continue a relationship with her. Her physical appearance should not make so much difference. Rationally, he believes this. But his gut reaction tells him he cannot do this: he cannot overcome his aversion to her physical appearance. The conflict between his rational statement that her appearance should not matter and his emotional reaction to her physical appearance causes him genuine distress. Carl's gut reaction is analogous to the women's reactions to sex with inadequate investment which we examined earlier. In both cases these emotions were experienced as irrational and involuntary; in both cases individuals were unable to continue sexual relations because certain qualities were lacking. Despite what they rationally thought they should do, their emotions alerted them that something was wrong and guided them toward other kinds of relationships and partners. The women assessed their partners' emotional and material investments, found them wanting, and rejected their partners. Carl and Michael visually evaluated their partners' physical appearance, found them sexually unattractive, and rejected them on this basis. The qualities that were evaluated and the processes of evaluation were expressions of different sexual strategies. These strategies are mediated by emotions that act as alarms. These alarms warn people to get back on track. They operate whether people recognize them or consciously accept them.

Few men I interviewed appeared to play the role of playboy without guilt, and were explicit in stating their standards and their desire for partner variety. The men who did so were exceptions. Most, like Carl, were distressed by the implications of their desires and criteria. They liked the women they dated and were upset when these women acted hurt, disappointed, or betrayed. Perhaps for this reason, most of the men I interviewed were reluctant to spell out their criteria and desires and to analyze them. In many cases these male criteria and desires, like those of the women, only came to light through persistent and probing questions. Part of this reticence results from the unacceptability of these criteria and desires—particularly to educated, liberal-minded men. But part of it stemmed from the fact that these criteria and desires operated only semiconsciously. In the following case, I have included my question-probes in order to illustrate this point. When the subject, Tom, was making the decisions described here, he was not fully conscious of the process nor of how his criteria influenced his decisions. Like Maria in Chapter 3, it was during the course of the interview that Tom actually consciously analyzed how he weighed the different advantages, considered the tradeoffs, and reached a decision. Tom is in his mid-forties, divorced, and is a computer expert. He earns about $90,000 a year teaching and consulting.

Tom

T: *I was trying to decide whether I should invite Alice or Lori to this tennis resort but I finally decided on Alice.*

JMT: Why?

T: Well, I thought if I invited Lori, I would have to pay for everything. She lives clear across the country, so I would have to fly her to the resort and back, and pay for everything there too. It didn't seem worth it for just a few days' vacation.

JMT: Why would you have to pay for Lori and not for Alice?

T: Alice is a mature woman with a good job. She can pay her own way. Lori's just finishing college. She still depends on her parents, so she's not going to lay out all that money just to see me for a couple of days. We don't really know each other that well. We've only gotten together a couple of times before.

JMT: You said earlier that Alice is also a computer expert and is very bright. How does she compare to Lori in this respect?

T: Alice is a lot brighter and more interesting to talk to than Lori. Lori doesn't say much.

JMT: Then why would you want to take Lori instead of Alice?

T: Well, that could be an advantage with Lori. I planned to play a lot there and to meet some people I know. With Lori I might be freer to do my own thing. You know, less obligated to be with her all the time.

JMT: What about looks? How do these women compare on looks?

T: Alice is an attractive woman, but, you know, she's getting older and it shows. She still has a pretty good body. But she hasn't kept in shape as much as she could have.

JMT: What about Lori?

T: Oh, Lori's a lot younger. That makes a difference. She's built like a fashion model. A little too skinny above the waist, but a great ass. She looks good with her clothes off.

JMT: What about facially? How do the women compare?

T: Lori looks better. She's got a really nice complexion. And she's got nicer features. Like I said, she looks like a model.

JMT: Does the physical appearance of these women influence how you feel about them—how attractive you find them?

T: Sure.

JMT: If you were going to have a relationship, which woman would you choose? How would their physical attractiveness influence your choice?

T: Look, I'm not planning to marry either one of these women. They're nice, but I probably couldn't get serious about either one. Right now I'm not even sure I want to get married again.

JMT: But which woman would you rather have a relationship with?

T: If you're talking abut sex, Lori. Definitely. She's just a lot better

looking. With Alice I can have more of a friendship, and a profession-
al relationship, and I like to sleep with her occasionally.
  JMT: Do you think either woman is or could be seriously interest-
ed in you?
  T: Alice probably could be. She wants to get married, and she will
want to marry a guy like me—you know, a professional. And she's 35
and wants to have a kid so I think she feels the pressure. Lori's just a
kid. She's got her whole life ahead of her. She's young and good-look-
ing. She's got time to look around. I figure having a relationship with
someone like me who's a lot older is kind of exciting for her. It's an
experiment. She'll settle down eventually with some guy who can
afford her wardrobe. At least she'd better marry a guy like that!
  JMT: It sounds like Alice would be more inclined to get involved.
Does this affect the way you feel about her?
  T: Yeah, probably. I don't want to get too close with Alice because
it could be really sticky getting out of it. She's really a nice woman and
I wouldn't want to hurt her, so I try to let her know that we are just
leaving everything open. You know, no commitments.

Although Alice has the qualifications to be a much better friend and intellectual companion than Lori does, Tom would rather have sex with Lori
because he finds her more physically attractive. Tom hints that part of the
reason he finds Lori more physically attractive is that she is younger than
Alice. But he seemed reluctant to spell this out and explain why this is so. His
reluctance may stem from the fact that saying such things is considered
socially unacceptable in the educated circles in which he travels. But whether
he is willing to admit these criteria or not, they appear to affect his selection
of partners. He would have invited Lori if the financial cost had been more
equal to what he would spend on Alice.

Just as women are often reluctant to admit their socioeconomic criteria in
choosing and rejecting men, many men are reluctant to admit their physical
criteria. But research continues to provide evidence that these sex differences
in selection criteria are operating and have profound effects. Women's chances
for marriage in the U.S. do decline rapidly after age 25, so obviously something about younger women makes them more attractive as mates.[5] In the
remainder of this chapter we will explore just what this "something" is.

What is beauty?

Men emphasize physical attractiveness in their choice of sex and marriage partners and they seem to know what they find attractive and what
they find unattractive. What are the components of female physical
attractiveness? After reviewing many studies, two prominent researchers
concluded, that "identification of the physical characteristics considered

attractive in Western culture, or in any other, seems a hopeless task."[6] In a more recent review of cross-cultural studies, other researchers concluded that sexual attractiveness is a Western concept and cannot be applied validly to other societies because the standards for physical attractiveness vary so greatly among different societies. These conclusions emphasize the arbitrary nature of standards of attractiveness: whatever is deemed attractive in a particular society or historical period will be learned and accepted by most of the members of that society. Authors who emphasize the arbitrary and variable nature of standards of attractiveness often use body fat as an example. In some tribes the new brides of chiefs are virtually force-fed to fatten them up for the wedding ceremony. Similarly, the amount of fat on a woman considered desirable in Rubens' time (1577-1640) or in Victorian England would be considered unfortunate today when huge numbers of women are exercising and dieting in an effort to lose weight. Examples like these are used to support the view that standards have varied enormously in different societies and eras and that therefore there are no universal standards. This type of argument assumes that each society or era possessed an ideal of female attractiveness, that most people accepted this ideal, and that deviations from this ideal were considered much less attractive by most people. These assumptions are questionable.

Sociologist Alan Mazur has shown that within any historical period in Western society, considerable variation existed in the amount of body fat considered sexually attractive in women.[7] The fleshy nudes of Titian (1477–1576) were roughly contemporary with the slender, erotic women of Lucas Cranach (1472–1553), for example. Similarly, Rubens painted his corpulent nymphs at about the same time that Velazquez (1599–1660) painted his more slender Venus. Apparently, not all artists in these periods thought that slender women were sexually unattractive, and there is no empirical evidence that the average man of that period thought so. The fact that Rubens preferred corpulent models for his paintings does not mean that most men of this period found this body type the most desirable, nor even that Rubens himself did.

Around the end of the nineteenth century in Europe and the United States, more voluptuous types were associated with the theater and burlesque (and hence, sensuality) while more slender and demure types represented social refinement and higher status. Nevertheless, the first calender nude in 1913 was of a slender and demure type which suggests that a good number of men at the time found more slender female bodies sexually attractive. Similarly, while the voluptuous Marilyn Monroe was considered a leading symbol of sexual attractiveness in her day, her more slender contemporaries like Grace Kelly, Audrey Hepburn, and Doris Day were also considered extremely attractive—although perhaps as representative of different styles.

Evidently, there is substantial variation within any period in the amount of female body fat and curves considered most attractive. It is therefore a mistake to assume that all people, or all men, of any period found one type the most attractive simply because historians and writers have picked a particular image as "representative" of that era. Despite this variation, however, all of these images of female attractiveness share certain traits. First, the women are invariably young—generally not over the age of twenty-five, and often appearing much younger. Second, even the fleshy types are not obese; their skin is smooth and firm rather than saggy or wrinkled.

Studies have indicated that the average measurements and body weight of *Playboy* models and Miss America contestants have changed in the last thirty years. Contemporary models and contestants weigh a bit less and look leaner and more physically fit than those of previous decades. These variations in body weight and measurements at first glance seem highly significant—indicating a trend toward thinness. But if we compare the amount of variation in these women to the variation in the population, the changes are trivial. In 1930 average measurements for bust, waist, and hips of Miss America contestants were 34–25–35. In 1950, they were 35¼–25-35; in 1970, they were 35¼–23½–35¼. In 1980, they were 35–23¼–34¼. These women, who supposedly represent the physical ideals of mainstream America, thus varied minimally in terms of inches and proportions over a period of fifty years.[8]

These findings suggest that standards of female attractiveness in the U.S. have changed much less over time than some have supposed. Contemporary Playmates and Miss America contestants may weigh a bit less than their forerunners, and they may look leaner because they exercise more systematically, but women who were considered extremely attractive in previous decades would be considered extremely attractive today. The consistency of the proportions of the Miss America contestants suggests that this particular symmetry has a pervasive and persistent appeal. Men apparently find the curves implied by these proportions attractive, and as we will see, there is a very good reason why they do.

In the contemporary United States, women and men may disagree on how much body fat is attractive. Psychologists April Fallon and Paul Rozin found that college women generally believe that they are heavier than men prefer, and they want to be thinner than the figures they believe are most attractive to men.[9] But men actually prefer heavier body types than what women believe they prefer—which makes women's preference for thinness two steps removed from what men actually consider the most attractive (see figure). These results suggest that women's standards are not simply a response to what men actually want. There are other influences at work. First, keeping thin and controlling weight help to give some women a feeling of control over their own lives. Second, women believe that thinness is generally considered a very positive personal feature over and above its possible effect on men. One of the reasons that thinness is generally considered a positive characteristic is that in Western societies upper-class women are thinner.[10]

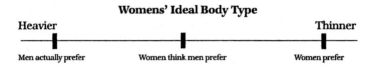

In any era, the standards of the upper classes determine what is fashionable and acceptable in dress, appearance, and aesthetics.[11] In our society, these standards are disseminated by the mass media—television, movies, fashion advertising, newspapers, and magazines—and depict what the rich and famous are doing. Whether they know it or not, the middle classes tend to emulate these standards and adopt many of them. Top fashion designers, for example, create expensive couture originals for their upper-class clientele; in time, cheaper versions of these originals will appear in department stores. The ideal of female thinness appears to have followed this same trickle-down pattern: it began in the upper classes and has now been affected by the middle classes as well.

Given the Fallon and Rozin findings, it may be likely that many women know what men prefer, but because women emphasize status more in their standards for partners than men do, they disregard to some extent what men actually prefer because they want to look like upper-class women. Presumably, they want to look like upper-class women because they want to *be* like upper-class women—to move up socioeconomically through their own achievements, marriage, or both.

Men's magazines also suggest that men and women disagree on what is most attractive. Although no systematic comparisons exist, women in fashion advertising appear to be thinner, some to the point of emaciation, than the women in magazines like *Playboy* and *Penthouse*. Women in men's magazines are trim and firm, but they have curvaceous breasts and hips. Tens of millions of men read magazines like these, and they evidently like to look at the bodies of these women. If men preferred to look at extremely thin women, men's magazines would supply these images. Evidently, some psychological research and the persistence of curvier women in men's magazines suggest that many men refuse to follow the dictates of high fashion. They continue to prefer curvaceous women to the extreme thinness that many women currently accept as an ideal.

The association between high status and thinness suggests that women who accept these standards for themselves might also prefer their men to be thin. In the Fallon and Rozin study, women did prefer thinner male figures —thinner than what men generally perceive as being most attractive to women. A man's status and success, however, so profoundly affect his attractiveness to women that these traits can overrule the effects of all but the most extreme physical defects.

George's experience provides an example. He is 42 years old and divorced and his financial interests are worth several million dollars. He enjoys the intimacy and comfort that only an established relationship can offer. Consequently, women appear to like George, not only because he is wealthy, but also because he becomes intensely emotionally involved with them. From a women's point of view, his major flaw is that he does not want to confine himself to one woman. He wants a relationship, but with more than one woman. He has been seriously involved with Valerie for eight years and with Sally for four and has no intention of marrying either one of them. He is also open to starting a new relationship whenever he comes across a woman he finds intriguing. Significantly, he focuses on their physical attributes when he explains why he is unwilling to marry these two women. Until very recently George was, by his own estimate, 30 pounds overweight, but this did not seem to affect his ability to enter and maintain the relationships he describes here, nor his ability to engage in more sporadic sexual encounters with other attractive women.

George

I have never considered myself a playboy or ladies' man, although I suppose some people would accuse me of that. I always like to get to know a woman as a person before I go to bed with her. I'm definitely not into one-night stands. Since my divorce, Valerie has been the constant thread in my life. We've been through all kinds of shit together, crapped on each other, been dishonest, and we have grown through all that and become closer. She's 37, has a lot of style and is a very good friend. She claims she left her husband for me but I don't know whether that's true.

Unfortunately, the women I've been close to after my divorce always seemed to have one or two flaws that were insurmountable for me. With Valerie, it's her calves. She has piano legs! God, she'd put a Clydesdale horse to shame! She's a beautiful woman inside and out, but this thing really bothers me. Someone else might think her legs are great, but these are the aesthetics I was raised with and that's the way I feel. The other side of that is, if this were really the right person, wouldn't I have married her a long time ago? After all, I've known her for eight years! We still spend the night together four or five nights a week.

The other woman I see regularly is Sally. She's 34. She's a very attractive lady, with an interesting background, but she was raised in a rural environment and, although her family had money, she is sort of sloppy. She's a very pretty woman, but she does little to adorn herself or fix herself up, so she usually looks a little unkempt, and her house is always a mess. I don't mind seeing that, but I wouldn't want to live with it.

At various times, I've felt pressure from both of these women to get married. Valerie has pushed for buying a house and moving in together, but I've told her that I need to get a lot of things resolved in my life before I can seriously discuss it. If I allowed her to move in, it would be a commitment toward marriage that I don't want to make. We've even looked at rings at times, but I've never actually made the step and bought one. Naturally, Sally and Valerie have no use for each other. I never discuss my other relationships with them because I don't feel it's anybody's business.

George wonders why if Valerie were the right person, he wouldn't have married her long ago. A better question might be: what would a woman have to have in order to induce George to marry her? He presently enjoys many of the advantages of marriage without its financial and legal obligations and without sacrificing his sexual freedom. He enjoys sex and companionship with both women and has the freedom to explore new opportunities when they arise. He sees no reason to marry either woman as long as he can obtain most of what he wants from them without making such an investment. As we will see in a later chapter, these women have occasionally tried to pressure George into making a monogamous commitment that could eventually lead to marriage, but he is relatively impervious to these attempts because there are many women who find him attractive and who could replace his present partners. For George, the "right person" may be a woman who can demand sexual fidelity and marriage in exchange for what he wants from her. It is likely that a good part of what she will exchange will be physical attractiveness. In the present dating-mating market, such a woman will have to be extremely physically attractive, and she will probably be much younger than George.

Since standards of health and status have apparently influenced American men's preferences for female body types, one might interpret this variation as supporting the social-role/constructionist approach. If standards of attractiveness can vary with medical knowledge and associations with status, then there should be no universal standards. But if we examine the evidence more closely, we find that the standards of female sexual attractiveness remain linked to the signs of youth, health, and fertility. The preference for large female bottoms in some cultures is not arbitrary, and neither is American men's continued preference for curvaceous busts and hips.

In puberty, the increase in female sex hormones causes fat to be stored on women's hips, breasts, and thighs. This female fat is lactation fat: reserves that help to ensure that a woman can continue to nurse her child when food is scarce. A woman will tend to lose weight in other areas of her body before she loses in these, and the fetus may even suffer from malnutrition before these fat stores in the mother are finally depleted. This explains why it is so difficult for women to lose weight in these areas. The tendency to store and maintain these reserves evolved to keep an infant alive during the first few years of life, because if the mother could not nurse, its chances of survival were slim. The fact that in modern society food is relatively plentiful and alternatives to nursing exist is irrelevant. The tendency for women to store fat in these areas evolved before the development of agriculture and the domestication of animals, and the connection between this fat and female fertility is still very much with us. Medical research shows that extremely thin women tend to be less fertile or even sterile. Wherever food is less plentiful and women continue to nurse their babies beyond the first few weeks of life, fleshier women are preferred, especially those with large breasts and buttocks.[12]

Psychologist Devendra Singh has shown that although the amount of body fat on a woman that men consider maximally attractive varies across different social classes and cultures, the ratio of the waist and hip measurements considered attractive varies very little.[13] The waist-hip ratio correlates with numerous indicators of women's health and fertility. Postmenopausal women, prepubertal girls, women with diabetes and other diseases all have waist-hip ratios that deviate from the normal range for fertile, healthy women. So curvaceous hips and breasts are not merely symbols of female fertility; they are actual indicators of fertility. When American men reject the standards of upper-class women and high fashion, and prefer women with curvaceous breasts and hips, they are preferring signs of female fertility—whether they know it or not.

So can these male preferences for youth and health in women be totally accidental? Some writers argue that these standards are purely a product of our society's emphasis on youth and health and its display of such images in the mass media. But why is youth so much more important for female attractiveness than for male attractiveness? Why do so many younger women find high-status men attractive even when these men are middle-aged, and even older, and not physically fit? Would it be possible to portray postmenopausal women, or less physically fit, less healthy women, as more sexually attractive to men than young, physically fit, fertile women merely by displaying their images in the proper contexts? Or is it simply the case that reproductive biology will continue to strongly influence the ways people choose partners—despite changing social fads and fashions?

Women conceive children and nurture them in their wombs for nine months, and a woman's health is a direct determinant of her ability to carry a child to term and deliver a healthy baby. Until bottle feeding became prevalent in the 1940s, most mothers also had to be healthy enough to lactate and nurse their children until they were weaned. Pregnancy and childbirth can entail serious medical risks. In areas where modern medical care is unavailable, many mothers and their offspring still succumb during pregnancy and childbirth. Age is also an important determinant of a woman's fertility. Women's ability to produce a healthy egg and to conceive and carry a baby to term declines rapidly in their thirties. A woman in her forties is 100 times more likely than a woman in her twenties to have eggs with abnormal chromosomes. Obstetricians therefore recommend that all women who become pregnant after the age of thirty-five undergo amniocentesis in order to diagnose potential abnormalities.

In comparison, men's fertility is much less dependent on their age and health. Men in their sixties, seventies, and even eighties can father healthy offspring if they are physically capable of having intercourse, and many are. But a man cannot produce children without a woman, so his fertility is directly dependent on his female partner's age and health—much more so than her fertility depends on his age and health. On the other hand, he can contribute greatly to his partner's health and welfare and to their children's by providing protection and resources.[14]

In the contemporary United States, the standards of female attractiveness continue to reflect the signs of youth and health. A clear smooth complexion, a full head of glossy hair, large eyes and rosy lips, firm, smooth flesh, and curvaceous bust and hips—all correspond to youth and health. As people age, their skin begins to lose elasticity, wrinkles appear, and muscle tone declines. As the face sags, eyes and lips appear smaller, cheeks and lips become less rosy, and the hair thins and is less luxuriant. When people are ill, these signs of youth and health also suffer.

Because skin loses elasticity and muscle tone declines as people age, skin and tissue tend to wrinkle and bulge. Fifteen pounds of fat therefore look very different on a 17-year-old than a 35-year-old woman. People's tendency to gain weight also increases exponentially as they get older. This means that if a woman wants to achieve the same look she had when she was younger, she must not only progressively reduce her caloric intake, but she must also exercise more to maintain muscle tone and to control sags and bulges. These facts of aging suggest that women's interest in diet and exercise are not only a response to the upper-class ideal of female thinness which dominates current fashions, but it is also an attempt to look young and physically fit. Since traits of youth and health predominate men's preferences, and women seek to enhance these traits, women are responding to these male preferences. Whether they know it or not, the enormous amount of money and energy women spend every year on diets, exercise, and beauty aids is largely an attempt to enhance these signs of youth, health, and high status.

In addition to these signs, another factor helps to determine physical attractiveness: the person's deviation from the population average for a particular feature. We tend to think of beautiful people as extraordinary, yet research shows that more conventional average-looking people are perceived as more attractive. One experiment showed that subjects had more difficulty remembering and picking out more attractive faces precisely because these faces had fewer distinctive features and were thus more "average" in appearance. Large deviations from the population mean in proportions of face, nose, lips, or ears tend to make people less attractive and more easily remembered and identified.[15] Cosmetic surgeons and beauty experts thus attempt not only to enhance or restore the signs of youth and health, but also to make a particular feature more closely approximate the population mean. Nose surgery, breast implants or reduction, hair transplants, hair styles that make the face appear fuller or thinner,—all serve these purposes. Of course, unusually beautiful people may not appear average to us, but the proportions of their features probably do approach the mean, and the deviations from the mean that set them off as extraordinary are also features of youth, fertility, and health—for example, the full lips, huge eyes, high, wide cheekbones, and curvaceous figure of Sophia Loren.

Psychologist Michael Cunningham asked male college students to rate the attractiveness of 50 women from pictures of their faces.[16] Seven of these women were black, six were Asian, and the rest were white. Twenty-seven of these women were finalists in the Miss Universe contest. The dimensions and proportions of facial features that were considered most attractive were remarkably precise and consistent. The preferred proportions of characteristics like eye width, width of face, chin length, height of visible eyeball, pupil width, and total area of nose determined what was most attractive, and these proportions were exact. Very slight deviations from this ideal caused a face to be judged as less attractive. There was a high degree of agreement on these proportions among subjects even though they did not know why they were perceiving these faces as more attractive. Cunningham argues that his findings are consistent with evolutionary psychology. Large eyes, along with a small nose and chin, are typical of newborns and, hence, youth. The high wide cheekbones and narrow cheeks are signs that a woman has reached puberty. The high eyebrows, dilated pupils, and wide smile are all signals of positive emotions: interest, excitement, and sociability. Men are thus attracted to signs of youth, recent sexual maturity, and friendliness, even when they do not know what is attracting them. Cunningham believes that human beings find such characteristics attractive because these preferences are biologically adaptive.

Thus, men's preferences are not simply a response to what high-status people or most women consider fashionable and attractive. Without knowing what this preference means, and without necessarily consciously desiring children, men are choosing these signs of health and fertility.

The Doors of Selection

In choosing mates, both sexes are influenced by partners' physical and social characteristics. But men and women weigh social and physical traits differently, and the sequences in which traits are weighed also differ. In some respects the evaluation process for women is the reverse from that of men. This process can be visualized as a series of doors—or windows—nested within one another. For men, partners' physical traits act as an initial filter that determines the pool of partners with whom they desire sexual relations. Physical traits thus open a door of opportunity for these partners in which the necessity or desirability of further investment can be explored.

When women choose partners, status is a major criterion in their initial filter. Through a perceptual process that is largely unconscious, high status has the power to transform men's physical and sexual attractiveness in the eyes of women. Women do not have to think, "Oh, now he has high status and my friends think he's attractive, so I should think he's good looking." Rather, status, dominance, peer opinion, and deference from others cause high-status men to be *perceived* as sexually attractive.

But to decide to have sex, women typically need more information than status and physical appearance provide. A positive first impression, which is also influenced by partners' physical attractiveness, typically opens the door to a first date. For women, a first date is a chance to explore partners' potential for higher-investment relationships—the man's values, warmth, ambition, and interest in them. If all of these indices are acceptable, a woman might want to have sex with this man, but her ultimate motivation is to find the *right* man— the man who will invest abundantly, reliably, and devotedly in her and her offspring. Thus men first determine which women are acceptable for sexual relations and then evaluate which might merit further investment. Women determine which men appear to be acceptable socially, personally, and physically, and then decide which might be acceptable for sexual relations.

Mate preferences among gay men and lesbians

In Chapter 1 we saw that studies of homosexuals provide strong support for basic sex differences in sexuality. Studies of homosexuals also support the notion of basic sex differences in partner selection.[17] For gay men, a man's youth and beauty are the primary determinants of his attractiveness. Gay men fear aging and worry about their complexions, wrinkles, and figures. Older men often have to pay to have sex with younger, more physically attractive men because they cannot otherwise attract the men they want. As one gay, 22-year-old man who had turned tricks for money told me, "From about fourteen to eighteen I was in demand and had plenty of money. But after eighteen, it's all downhill. It gets harder and harder unless you look unusually young and have a naturally great body." In comparison, lesbians place much less emphasis on age and looks. Intellectual and spiritual qualities, personal compatibility, and ability to communicate are more important criteria when lesbians choose partners.

The same sex differences in partner selection we see in heterosexual men and women not only persist among homosexuals, they are more visible because they are not being compromised by the other sex's criteria. Homosexual men generally tend to have sex with multiple partners, and they prefer men who look young, healthy, and physically fit. If they possess these attributes themselves, they can have many partners because they can invest minimally in each one compared to what they would have to invest if they had female partners. Lesbians do not usually seek multiple sex partners, nor do they tend to have sex with another woman merely because she is young, healthy, and has a pretty body. Lesbians tend to have relationships in which they invest considerable time and energy in verbal intimacy and in sharing nonsexual activities together. In these relationships they tend to look for some of the same qualities that heterosexual woman look for in men: intimacy, affection, and consideration. If sex differences in partner selection were solely the result of socialization and mass media influences, it is difficult to see why the same sex differences we see in heterosexual partner selection are even more pronounced among homosexuals.

Evidently, the same processes of evaluation occur in homosexual partner selection as in heterosexual selection. Men and women tend to look for quite different things when they choose partners, regardless of whether they are gay or straight. Why is this so? Constructionists will argue that these differences persist because of sex-role socialization. But it is hard to believe that men and women who have rejected so many aspects of traditional sex roles and lifestyles would retain these very specific characteristics of traditional roles. If anything, gay men and lesbians show us the enduring patterns of sexual desires, emotions, and preferences that play out in our lives.

6

The Dating-Mating Market

The Man Shortage and Marriage Squeeze

> In the eras depending on inner-direction sex might be inhibited. . . . Or
> its gratification might be taken for granted among men. . . . Only in the
> upper classes, precursors of modern other-directed types, did the mak-
> ing of love take precedence over the making of goods . . . and reach the
> status of a daytime agenda. In these circles sex was almost totally sepa-
> rated from production and reproduction . . . [now] sex permeates the
> daytime as well as the playtime consciousness. It is viewed as a con-
> sumption good not only by the old leisure classes but by the modern
> leisure masses. . . . This is one of the reasons why so much exitement is
> channeled into sex by the other-directed person. He looks to it for reas-
> surance that he is alive . . . not for display but for a test of his or her abil-
> ity to attract, his or her place in the "rating-dating" scale—and beyond
> that, in order to experience life and love.
>
> —David Riesman et al., *The Lonely Crowd*

IN THEIR BOOK *Too Many Women?* Marcia Guttentag and Paul Secord use
sex ratios to explain the problems many contemporary women face in securing commitments from suitable partners.[1] Since World War II, women have
outnumbered men in the United States. In 1970 for every 100 women over
fourteen there were 92 men. The imbalance for single men and women is
even greater: 81 men per 100 women. This surplus of women allows men to
avoid making commitments to many women they date. In these conditions
women are more likely than men to experience desertion, abandonment, and
betrayal. Women therefore become wary of commitments themselves, but it
is *men's* unwillingness to make commitments that leads contemporary women
to delay marriage, stay single, or remain divorced rather than remarrying.

In addition to a general shortage of men, women born during certain periods face a *marriage squeeze*. For example, the birthrate was rising between
1946 and 1957 (the postwar baby boom). Women born between 1946 and
1948 who want to marry men two to three years older—which is the traditional pattern—face a severe squeeze because the birthrate was down between
1943 and 1945. There are simply not enough men in that age bracket for the
women who might want to marry them. Guttentag and Secord also note that

men's tendency to marry younger women contributes to the large numbers of single and divorced women over thirty who do not marry or remarry. They argue that the tendency of women to marry older men with higher status is caused by women's relative lack of power and status in this society. When women increase their own earning power and status, this tendency should be weakened. But they admit that this does not appear to be happening: current marriage statistics reveal no trend toward narrowing the age gap between bride and groom despite the fact that increasing numbers of women are raising their levels of education and income. They conclude that "unknown factors" apparently still support this practice. These factors, however, are not unknown. They are the basic sex differences in partner selection we have been exploring.

The man shortage and the marriage squeeze are real factors, but they are misleading when used to explain the many single and divorced women in certain age brackets.[2] U.S. Census figures for 1989 tell us that between the ages of 25 and 29 13.2 percent more women are married than men.[3] Between the ages of 35 and 39 the figures are nearly even—only 1.7 percent more women are married than men. But by the forties, the sex difference reverses. Between the ages of 45 and 54, 6.2 percent more men are married than women. This trend increases until between the ages of 55 and 64, 14.9 percent more men are married than women. These statistics suggest that a large number of women are marrying men older than themselves. For men's first marriage the average difference in age is only two or three years. But when divorced men remarry, they often marry women considerably younger, and the older the man, the greater the difference is between his age and that of his partner.[4]

Age is a powerful impediment to marriage for women. One study estimates that women who reach 30 unmarried have only a 20 percent chance of marrying; at 35, they have about a 5 percent chance; at 40, they have a 1 percent chance.[5] Blumstein and Schwartz report similar statistics for remarriage. Women in their twenties have a 76 percent chance of remarrying; women in their thirties a 56 percent chance; in their forties a 32 percent chance; in their fifties or older, less than a 12 percent chance.

The concept of a marriage squeeze is not a good explanation for the many unmarried women between the ages of 45 to 64. We have seen that a great many younger women prefer to marry men who are considerably older than themselves, and they apparently prefer these men because they offer greater economic and social advantages than do men their age. So it is these younger women who are subtracting successful men over thirty from the marriage market, and the competition for these men can be intense. Bob is a wealthy, divorced businessman, aged 42. He describes his view of this competition.

Bob

I walked into a bar the other night and sat down with some women I know. They were all divorced and in their early forties. Some had been married two or three times. It was really interesting to get their feedback. It was funny because every one of them wanted to get married. They were saying the competition was really tough because there were so many young, good-looking girls in this town. No one really came out and said she wanted to get married—I guess because she'd appear vulnerable. They just talked about finding men who were willing to make commitments. But marriage was what they were talking about.

I can understand their situation. Several of them were not financially secure so that's a clear motivation. And they're worried about getting older. There's a lot of jealousy if a guy dates a younger gal. They think it is terrible if a forty-year-old guy dates even a thirty-year-old woman. They really don't like it. Personally, I've never been that attracted to the really young ones. They look good—until they open their mouths! I'd take a beautiful 40-year-old over a 22-year-old any day. Of course, an older woman has to work a lot harder to keep looking good. The women I date now range from 28 to 35. Women in their early thirties are probably about right for me.

Bob says he prefers not to date "really young" women, but the women he does date are seven to fourteen years younger than he is. He acknowledges that women in their early twenties are physically attractive but implies that they are too dumb for him to take seriously. He may honestly feel this way. But, as we will see later, it is also likely that physically attractive women in their early twenties would not put up with his lack of investment and commitment. Being more in demand themselves, young, physically attractive women are able to demand more in terms of investment. This points up another problem with sex-ratio and sex-role explanations of marriage patterns. These explanations tend to ignore women's own role in *choosing* to remain single. They tend to portray women as helpless pawns of sex-role ideology or demographic trends—as merely reacting to what men do rather than as seizing opportunities and furthering their own interests. Women are not merely reacting to what men do; they are also creating conditions to which men must react. On this issue, sociologist Jessie Bernard concludes that financial independence now allows women to be much choosier than they were in previous eras, and this means that a man has to do more now to keep a wife or even to get her in the first place.[6] Young working women have a lower marriage rate than women without jobs, and the better the job, the lower the rate.

Similarly, Blumstein and Schwartz found that women in their twenties with three children have a 72 percent chance of remarrying, while women in their thirties with no children have a 60 percent chance. This finding defies our common-sense assumption that women with children would have a much harder time remarrying than women without children. The authors attribute this discrepancy to three factors. First, the youth and beauty of women in their twenties may outweigh men's fear of taking on additional dependents. Second, younger children are more acceptable to prospective stepfathers than are older children. Third, women in their thirties with no children are more financially independent and therefore can afford to be choosier than younger women with three children. In this explanation the authors implicitly accept the existence of sex differences: youth and beauty are more important in men's choice of partners; financial gain is more important in women's, and the more economically secure women are, the choosier they can afford to be in selecting partners.

Contemporary women want both types of investment: significant material advantages and emotional attachment and sexual fidelity. If a woman has an adequate means of supporting herself, she does not have to settle for less. But a woman's own desire for high-status men can expose her to men's desires for relatively low-investment sex with a variety of partners. Higher-status men have more women interested in them so they are more able to satisfy these desires. Gwen's experience vividly illustrates these sex differences.

Gwen

The men in my life have been either one way or the other. My husband Peter was the hard-driving, achiever type. I helped put him through medical school and now he's a very successful surgeon making a lot of money. Well, shortly after he completed his residency, he bought a red Maserati and I discovered he was having an affair, or more accurately, he had been having a lot of affairs. He had been going out with all kinds of women. I just couldn't believe it! I felt like I had been living with a stranger when I realized how he had deceived me. He obviously wasn't happy and I couldn't live with a man like that, so we divorced. He's definitely a type. He's successful, exciting, drives a race car, but he's so wrapped up in his own pursuits he can't really love anyone. He won't open up and let them in. I found this very frustrating.

After I broke up with him, I got involved with a very different kind of man. Sal was from an Italian background and was very warm and expressive. In fact, he was the most sensitive and loving man I've ever known, and I had the best sex with him that I have ever had. That relationship lasted about two years. I finally broke it off. I couldn't really complain about the way he treated me. He was very sweet. But he just didn't seem to be going anywhere. He was from a working-class background and he lacked the ambition and drive to escape it. I mean he could have supported a family, but in what style? I guess what I want is a man who is generous and sweet and faithful but who also drives a Maserati. Where do I find one of those?

When Gwen's husband finally achieved high status and earning power, he began to indulge in sexual relations with a variety of attractive women. After their breakup, Gwen realized that the two types of investment were hard to find in one man, and she turned to a man who offered a great deal less than her ex-husband on the financial side, but a great deal more in terms of emotional investment. She discovered, however, that emotional investment was not enough. She wants a man who offers both. Her desire for a highly successful man who is also loving and faithful to her may be unrealistic. There are many women looking for such men and very few of them available. Gwen now earns over $50,000 a year as a buyer for a department store chain. She has no children and does not feel forced by economic necessity to compromise her standards. Statistically, she has a very slim chance of finding what she wants.

The New Polygyny

Several authors have proposed that, increasingly, men in the United States are engaging in casual, transitory relationships and avoiding binding commitments with women. If by "commitment" they mean marriage, the statistics contradict this view. Most men who can attract a mate marry and, if divorced, remarry relatively quickly. Higher-status men are especially in demand and do not remain on the marriage market very long. If, however, these authors equate commitment with sexual fidelity, their claims are probably more valid. Sex outside of marriage is much more available today than it was before the birth control pill, and successful men, single or married, can take advantage of this fact. Consequently, although most men, and particularly higher-status men do tend to marry, there may be a new class of divorced and single men emerging who use their *potential* for investment to coast in relationships, limit their investments, and indulge their desires for partner variety. These men typically tell their female companions that they would get married if they found the right person, but somehow the people they are with are never quite right. These men are practicing functional polygyny.

Polygamy refers to the practice of either sex having more than one mate at a time. In human societies, legitimate *polygyny* occurs when a man can legally have more than one wife. This form of marriage is accepted or preferred in over 83 percent of human societies. The other form of polygamy is *polyandry*, in which females can have more than one mate. Polyandry appears in less than 1 percent of human societies.[7] In Western nations, both forms of polygamy are illegal, but many men engage in relationships that are, in effect, polygynous. When a man divorces and remarries, for example, or has several sexual relationships but with only one partner at a time, he is practicing serial polygyny. When he has simultaneous sexual relationships with more than one woman, he is practicing effective, or *functional*, polygyny—whether he is married to one of these women or not. Gwen's ex-husband became a functional polygynist as soon as he gained sufficient status.

The mating patterns of songbirds may be able to tell us more about human patterns than comparisons with other mammals, including comparisons with our closest cousins, the monkeys and apes, because human males are the only primates that regularly offer provisions to females and their offspring. Interestingly, many species of songbirds do the same. What conclusions can we draw from this comparison? First, in species where mates offer resources to females in order to mate with them, we would expect polygyny to be more pronounced in situations where some males have substantially better resources to offer than others. This principle certainly holds true in human societies and is supported by observations of occasional polygyny in bird species that are predominately monogamous. In fact, in one experiment a researcher artificially improved the quality of some males' territories by increasing the available shade, and the males who held these territories were able to attract three mates—something that never occurs in this species without experimental intervention.[8]

A second point of comparison is the principle of the *polygyny threshold*, which is found in many species of birds. Female songbirds will choose to be the first mates of males who offer the best territories and resources until all the best males have been chosen. Once that happens, female songbirds will choose to be the second mate of a high quality male rather than the single mate of a lesser bird. And in fact, the offspring of the males chosen first do tend to do better than the offspring of the males chosen later, and the higher-status males are also the first males to acquire second mates. Furthermore, females who opt for secondary status do about as well reproductively as the females who choose monogamy with lower-quality males at the same time. These birds are not stupid. Somehow females know when choosing to be a second or even third mate of a higher quality male is a better deal than choosing to be the only mate of a lesser bird. Women probably do not have as precise a mechanism for exhibiting a polygyny threshold as these songbirds. But women's attraction to higher-status males and aversion to dating and marrying down are strong, and many women are currently choosing to have sexual relationships with higher-status, polygynous men rather than having monogamous relationships with lower-status men.

In the United States there are enormous differences in the amount and quality of resources different men can offer. We would therefore expect the incidence of functional polygyny to be high. We would also expect that women with economic independence and the possibility of effective contraception would be freer to express their basic desires in mate selection than those women who are forced by economic necessity and dependent children to marry or remarry. As we saw earlier, women without adequate means to support themselves are more likely to adjust their standards to what the market offers in order to marry or remarry—particularly when they have children to support. In comparison, women with higher earning power and no children are less likely to lower their socioeconomic requirements for a mate and are therefore less likely to marry or remarry. Higher status females are competing with each other as well as with lower-status females for the small pool of higher-status men. This competition and the possibility of effective contraception allow higher-status males to practice functional polygyny.

Bob is the wealthy businessman we met earlier in this chapter. His ex-wife received a million dollar settlement in their divorce. Bob's children eventually came to live with him and he raised them, so he states that he has no desire at this time to have more children or to help raise someone else's. Bob is a functional polygynist. The women he dates all work and maintain at least a middle-class lifestyle, but Bob is rich and could offer tremendous advantages to these women, particularly when they have children to raise.

Bob

There are about five different women I see regularly now. Most of them know this and occasionally they try to give me flack about it, but I just say I'm not making any commitments. I like my freedom. This one gal wanted to know how I felt about commitments, but I feel you're just together for the time that you want to be—whether that's for tonight or the moment. I told her that right then I had a commitment to finishing my salad. That was as far in the future as I could plan. Most of them don't talk about it because they know it won't do any good. I don't react well to ultimatums. I tell them I probably would get married in the right situation, but to tell you the truth, I don't know what that situation would be.

I realize now that I don't need a wife. I'm probably as self-sufficient a guy as there is. I don't need a woman to cook for me. I don't need one to keep the house; I can pay a housekeeper to come in and take care of that. I can cook better than 99 percent of the women anyway. So for me now there's really no pressure to get married. Twenty years ago it was different. You had a hard-on to get married because you had to get married to get relieved. When you got out of high school, you had basically three choices—especially growing up in a small town like I did. You went to college. You were facing the draft, so you either got drafted or joined the service to evade the draft, or you got married and started making babies. You didn't have the choice like you do now to just float around and stay single and date different women. That wasn't possible. If you were dating somebody, you had to go steady, and even then you probably weren't getting laid. There are lots of reasons for these changes, but I think one of the big things is contraceptives. They've changed our sexual habits more than anything.

Maybe it's a reflection on my maturity, but I haven't found one person I want to spend that much time with. Any one person eventually can get on your nerves. Besides, business is slow now, so I like to take off for three-day weekends, and it's hard for a lot of these gals to do that on the spur of the moment. They've got jobs or kids, or other responsibilities, so when I want to go, I keep calling until I find someone who's available. I'm not sure that having more than one gal to date does allow me more freedom because there are times that I end up going places by myself because I don't plan ahead, and you never know when one of them is going to be pissed off. I don't think that any one that I date sees me exclusively. That's something I don't ask them. I can't really expect that when I'm not that way. Sometimes it's tough, though, because I can't always find somebody to go with. Like, if I wanted to fly my plane up to the lake this morning, I don't know whether anybody could go with me. But do I need marriage just for that? I think of marriage as a contingent liability just to have a companion. It's very risky these days. Even if you have a premarital financial agreement, these things are challenged in court all the time. Do I need to lose another million dollars just to have a steady companion? No, I don't! Besides, the companionship I get this way is better quality and more fun than you find in most marriages anyway.

Some of these women get pissed off because they can't be Number One in my life. But I don't think I ever treat anyone unfairly because I don't promise them anything, I don't lie, and I don't break dates. I think a lot of their frustration comes from their insecurity because they have kids so they need a father and a provider. I don't need it. I've raised my own kids. Why should I raise anyone else's? I want my freedom. If I want to take off and go skiing or on a trip with some of my buddies, I want to be able to do that. I don't want anybody saying that I have to stay home or go play bridge tonight or whatever.

Honest and dishonest advertising

In many species males advertise their potential for investment in order to attract mates. In some cases this advertisement is honest and the female knows what she is getting. In other cases males falsely inflate their potential for investment, or they inseminate the female and then are unwilling to invest what they advertised. Male bobolinks are honest advertisers. They let a female know she is a second mate and cannot expect any help in raising their young. On the other hand, the second mate enjoys the advantages his superior territory offers. In other bird species, the male leaves his first mate unattended when she is incubating her eggs, long enough to court a second female on another territory and convince her of his good intentions. Once he has established this other nest, he abandons the second female and returns to help his first mate. In this case the polygyny threshold has not been surpassed and an informed choice made. There are still bachelors offering better bargains, but the female has been decieved.

When men practice functional polygyny, the degrees of honest and dishonest advertising are seldom so clear-cut. The man himself may not know for certain that he will never marry a particular partner, or he may know relatively soon in a relationship that such a commitment is highly unlikely but refrain from stating this explicitly. It also happens that some men experience sufficient guilt about coasting in relationships so that they do not consciously analyze their intentions—until their female partners force them to do so.

George is the divorced, wealthy businessman we met in Chapter 5. Like Bob, he is a functional polygynist, but the two men employ very different tactics. George has maintained long-term, simultaneous relationships with Valerie and Sally, and yet remains open to relationships with other women.

George

I was always close to my mother and still am. We're soul mates. And my grandma, she would do anything for me! Having these close relationships with women in my family has made me attractive to women, yet independent at the same time. Women perceive that I am sensitive and that I sincerely enjoy their company, so they usually like me. The problem is, they often get serious about me faster than I would like, and I feel like I am walking a tightrope between not wanting to hurt their feelings, and needing to be honest with myself and them.

I read Nathaniel Brandon's Psychology of Romantic Love recently, and I believe that there are different types of love: the hot, erotic rush, another one based on esteem and affection, and another on similar aesthetic appreciation. In my opinion the kind that is really enduring is the one that goes through all these stages and maintains parts of them coherently—a very comfortable, interwoven interdependence. One of the reasons I remain close to Valerie is that we've both grown together in this way. We enjoy the same art, the same tastes. We even went to the same therapist, so we share a lot psychologically.

I think Sally would also like me to marry her, but recently she's backed off. She's gone back to school and she mentions things like she couldn't get married until she finished school and her kids are gone. I laughed when I heard that 'cause I figured, "Okay, whatever you say!" Maybe this is her new line of attack, I don't know.

I would really like to marry when I find the right person. I just haven't found her yet. A few years ago I made a list of all the qualities I would look for in a wife. It ran four or five pages. I showed it to my therapist and she agreed that, while I was particular, my requirements were not impossible. I'll just have to look a bit harder

*than some people. I needed to do that to reassure myself that I was
not chasing an impossible fantasy.*

*Right now, I feel no pressure to get married. I would like to get mar-
ried someday because I think there can be a comfortable, warm bonding and sharing that is not really available without the commitment.
Now a relationship like that does not necessarily have to be reinforced
with a piece of paper. But given that we're raised in a society that says
the paper is important, it does make a difference psychologically.*

*Speaking of meeting the right person, I met a woman recently who
is quite intriguing. I like her body configuration a lot and she seems
very sharp. She's having some difficulties now getting out of her marriage, but she's going to a very good therapist and she'll grow out of it
fast. I don't know if it's just because she's a new face on the block or if
she's a person with real potential, but I'm definitely going to check out
the possibility and see.*

George has more reliable access to female companionship and sex than
does Bob, but George pays a price for this reliability. Over the years he has
had to learn to counter his companions' pressure tactics and demands for
more investment and security, and this has required a considerable investment of time and energy in itself. George is emotionally involved with his
women friends, particularly with Valerie, and this is apparently part of the
payoff for them. George must also continue to hold out some hope of marriage in order to maintain these relationships. In the interview he stated that
he would never marry either of these women, but he apparently has never
stated this explicitly to them. Instead, he procrastinates. As he mentioned in
Chapter 5, he and Valerie have even looked at rings but he has never gotten
around to buying one.

In comparison, Bob does not want to make the investments of time, energy, and emotions that George makes in order to secure reliable access to
companionship and sex, so he refuses even to discuss the possibilities of sexual fidelity, living together, or marriage. In this way Bob avoids the hassles
George has, but he pays another kind of price: he gives up certainty of availability. There is a constant turnover in the women he dates because they
tend to move on to search for more likely prospects when they discover how
intransigent his desire for freedom and avoidance of marriage are. And even
while they are dating him, his women friends are frequently unavailable to
satisfy his needs. As he said, "You never know when one of them is going to
be pissed off." To secure more availability, he would, like George, have to
offer more investment to the women he is involved with. At present, Bob is
unwilling to do this and seems reasonably content with his choices.

Wes is 38, an engineer, and has never married. He is not as wealthy as Bob
or George, but he makes a good living.

Wes

I'm not a confirmed bachelor. I never pictured myself as remaining single. As a kid I always thought I would get married and have sons in the Boy Scouts. Why it never turned out that way, I don't know. It's either the women I 've met or what I've put out there. On the other hand, I can't really see getting married without having a family. For me, marriage doesn't seem to be the big play, but if you have children, marriage gives them a home base and it is more traditionally accepted. I think marriage offers women a sense of security— that the man is not going to leave and that they have a home to come back to. Me? I'm independent. I don't need them or their money. I am perfectly able to cook for myself, and I have a home. I always have a woman—an attractive, intelligent, nice lady, so I don't want for that. There has never really been any pressure or reason to get married from my end of it. Probably I have had four or five relationships where most people would have gotten married. There was a lot of love and a lot of good things going on, but it wasn't enough for me.

I have met a lot of women that I share certain outlooks with, but there has always been some major one that hasn't worked out. Like the woman I see now has two little boys. I adore her children. If we were married, we would be a family, but it's not like they would be mine, so I can't see getting married. I don't know if I'll ever meet a woman with enough pluses, but I'm not too concerned about it. I don't need marriage to be happy, and I guess the women I've dated eventually figured that out. All of the women I have had serious relationships with broke up with me because I didn't have a strong urge to get married. They said that they had to find someone that wanted to marry them.

Wes is a serial polygynist. He gets involved with a woman and enjoys a few months or years with her until she realizes that she is wasting her time and moves on. Unlike Bob and George, Wes reports that he is sexually faithful once he is seriously involved. All three of these men maintain their own homes and avoid living with women companions because they know that such a move would restrict their freedom, be construed as a step toward marriage, and could result in financial and legal obligations even without the formal commitment of marriage. Significantly, these men tend to date divorced women in their thirties who are financially secure. These women do not want to date down and with these men they are definitely dating up financially. The shortage of single, higher-status men in these women's age brackets gives men like Wes, Bob, and George tremendous bargaining power. They can have sex and companionship with numerous women while limiting their investments and commitments because they are in demand. If they wanted to date attractive women in their twenties, they would have to offer more investment and marital potential.

Susan is a twenty-two-year-old nurse. She is blonde, blue-eyed, and has the figure of a gymnast. She knows this is an asset and exercises daily to keep in shape. Because she is young and physically attractive, she has more bargaining power in the dating-mating market than many women do. She does not have to give into men's sexual demands—or at least not so quickly—in order to be courted and romanced. Nor does she have to enter relationships with men who have no intention of marrying her, as the companions of Wes, Bob, and George do.

Susan had total emotional investment from her high school boyfriend, but her dating experience has told her she does not have to settle for him. There are available men with much more to offer. She wants to play the field before making a choice so that she can select the best mate possible. Her actions, experiences, and opportunities in the dating-mating market will look familiar.

Susan

Last January I broke up with this guy I'd gone out with for five years. Our relationship was really great. We were talking about marriage and stuff. We broke up because, well, my family has money. My father is a doctor and my mother is a sales executive for a major computer chain. Joe came from a mining town, and all of his brothers worked in factories. I think when I was with Joe, I didn't realize all that I had going for me. I was bringing all of these things into this relationship that weren't getting returned. I'm finding out that maybe I do have a lot to offer, and maybe I should find someone who has as many things to bring to me as I can bring to them.

The weird thing is that Joe is going to law school in the fall in Boston and I will be working in Boston when I graduate, so I could continue seeing him. But I keep telling everybody, "No, Joe has a lot of good things going for him personality-wise, but he has never been exposed to the things I enjoy." The way I look at things, the differences in our upbringing are so vast. That's what it comes down to. I mean, even if he were to become a lawyer and make a lot of money, he'd still be Joe from Pittsburgh, Pennsylvania, you know?

After I broke up with Joe, I just went out like crazy. It was almost like making up for lost time. I was going out with four or five different guys every week. I just needed to date, to go to movies, concerts, dinner, and everything else. I was having a great time, except when somebody would begin to get interested in having a relationship with me. I would say, "Oh, we're just friends," and laugh it off. I think I hurt some people doing that, and that wasn't good.

About May I started to reevaluate all of that. I didn't think this was very good at all and I thought I'd tailor out the pack. I'd only go out with two or three people at a time instead of ten, right? I wasn't super-involved with any of these guys, so sex was out because I wasn't interested in any of them for long-term commitments. I just wanted to do all of the things I hadn't been able to do before because I was locked into the relationship with Joe. "Let's stay home together!" was nice, but I felt I was missing something during that time, and what I was missing was all these different experiences and meeting these other people.

I haven't really picked out what I do want, because I have no idea what options are out there. Every time I meet somebody else, I think what an interesting combination this person has, and I would've never thought of that if I was making a list of what I want. So I add it to the list. I guess what I'm really looking for is a husband. I'm in the competition. It's strange, because I'm really afraid to get involved in something like I had with my old boyfriend, something that had really good things about it, but also had points where love was blind. I don't want to get involved in something that isn't going to end in marriage, and at the same time, I don't want to meet that person yet. I'm still having fun. I guess if I were married, I would still be having fun, but a different kind of fun. I guess I'm not really sure what I want, but I know that I'm looking for a husband.

Marrying Up

Hypergamy refers to the tendency of either sex to mate with individuals of superior status. When women date or marry up, it is called *hypergyny*. When men do so, it is called *hyperandry*. In societies with economic inequality, the more powerful men tend to be polygynous, and they acquire many of their sex partners from lower socioeconomic levels.

Anthropologist Mildred Dickemann has shown that polygyny and hypergyny caused higher-status women to suffer drastically reduced fertility rates in the traditional, highly-stratified societies of imperial China and India and medieval Western Europe.[9] Because there were no suitable mates for them, higher-status women were systematically removed from their breeding populations through female infanticide, religious seclusion, and vows of chastity. Compared to women in China and India, women in medieval Western Europe had more economic opportunities in crafts and trades, and they could hold land in their own names and receive part of their husband's land upon his death. Because of these greater freedoms, female suicide and infanticide were less common in Western Europe than in China and India, but vows of chastity and celibacy were more common in Europe. For example, in Europe there was no formal pattern of widow suicide, but it was not uncommon for higher-status widows to assume vows of chastity or enter a nunnery. Polygyny and hypergyny led to such a surplus of higher-status women in Florence in the fifteenth and sixteenth centuries, that as much as 13 percent of the city's higher-status women were religious celibates.

In the United States today, women's hypergynous tendencies allow higher-status men to be functionally polygynous. Should a higher-status man want more children, the high divorce rate allows him to divorce his wife and remarry a younger woman with whom he can have more children. Research indicates that this type of serial polygyny enables some successful men to enjoy higher fertility rates than women who are their peers and share their status.[10]

Surveys among young women continue to show that more than 90 percent enter adulthood with the expectation or desire to have children.[11] It is also true that of the minority who do not do so, some will change their minds when they are facing the biological clock in their thirties. Some women are choosing to have children without being married, but a woman's preference to mate with an acceptable man who will provide investment and support in the child's upbringing appears to be strong. Current statistics therefore suggest that many older single and divorced women who are financially independent will remain childless, or will fail to have more children, because of their inability to find suitable partners and because their fertile years are limited.[12]

Indeed, the reduced fertility rates of higher-status single and divorced American women are not unlike the chaste religious celibacy of a large percentage of higher-status women in medieval Europe. In medieval Europe a woman's family usually made the decision that she would not be allowed to marry and reproduce. In contemporary America, the individual woman chooses not to marry because she cannot find an acceptable partner and this reduces her fertility rate. In both cases, however, the same principle appears to precipitate these decisions: hypergynous and polygynous tendencies produce a lack of suitable partners for higher-status women, which in turn reduces their fertility rates. Ironically, current dating, marriage, and fertility patterns in the United States suggest that effective contraception and female economic independence increase the incidence of hypergyny and functional and serial polygyny, and reduce the fertility rates of higher-status women.

Ruth is a tenured professor who feels that her tendency to be hypergynous, and men's tendency to be polygynous, may have caused her to miss out on having a child.

Ruth

I'm thirty-six years old, and I've never been married. It's funny, because I didn't used to think I wanted to have children, but I cannot remember a time when I didn't want to get married. Even as a child, it was understood that I would marry a man with a fancy, professional job. My mother, who is well-known in her field, started hassling me at eighteen about not having a boyfriend. She would tell me to forget about the hip, stylish men that I was interested in and would direct me towards the schlubby Jewish guys who would be good providers.

That's where her greatest competitiveness with me came out, because my father isn't a pretty man, but he is super successful. So she got a really classy man and I thought she wanted me to have a less classy man, when actually, her intention was largely good. She didn't want me to be an asshole and chase men who wouldn't treat me right. What that did, though, was accentuate my tendency to look for super high-class men and price myself out of the market.

If I were to meet someone who wanted to marry me and he demanded that I quit my job or move to another city, he would have to set up a trust fund of $5 million for me. Okay, the guy marries me and I can count on him, sure. I am naturally trusting. When I see everyone getting divorced, then I know I can't count on it any more than anyone else can. That's why I would have to bargain hard about giving up my job, because I am a tenured professor and if I quit this job, I'll never get another one.

I'm thinking of having a child without getting married, but I'm worried about it. I still think it is better for a kid to have two parents. I don't feel that I am the most important person in the world, so the question isn't, "Will this fulfill me?"—it's, "Will this be a happy, well-adjusted child? Is this fair?" I think having one parent is a disadvantage and life is rough enough without disadvantages. On the other hand, I don't want to join the cluster of gooky, self-righteous, disgusting mothers who are both the saints and the martyrs. I am neither one. I think children are the most important thing in the world, but this cultural cliche of, "You aren't a woman until you've had a child," makes me say, "Fuck you. I am so!" This one woman I know who gushes about it the most doesn't even like her kids to touch her. I have seen her scream, "Jason, get off me!" and then she would gush, "My children, my children!" I felt like saying, "Who are you kidding?" If I ever have a child, I'll genuinely love it.

Ruth has learned that when some men say they respect her independence and career, they actually intend to minimize their investments and commitments. The younger man she goes on to describe profited in many ways from his relationship with her—including having a nice house to live in and good food for the four years he was in graduate school. He was in no hurry to marry and have children, and could look forward to many more relationships before he settled down—if he ever does. The older man Ruth describes was apparently more dishonest in his advertising. He told her he would give her a baby and then reneged on his offer.

In college I was interested in wild romance. I didn't date very much because I wouldn't do the half-baked dating scene. I wanted to fall

madly in love. Now I see I would've been better off to go out with peo-
ple, maybe screw them, and then end it. In graduate school, marriage
was definitely part of my agenda. I picked the graduate school I attend-
ed because there were loads of scientists there and I was going to marry
one of them. People were urging my mother to encourage me to go to a
better school, but she supported my decision. At that time I had no
intention of having a career. I had a boyfriend in graduate school whom
I actually lived with for awhile. He was extremely handsome but very
dumb. My mother loved him. I was so desperate to get married that I
would have even married this stupid guy if he had asked me. I wanted
him to ask me so badly, and it would've been such a disaster.

When I was 31, I met a 20-year-old man I lived with for four years.
This truly was a Pygmalion trip. He lived in my house and ate my food
while he went to school. The biggest problem was simply that he would-
n't marry me and let me have a kid. I kept saying, "I'm 35 years old. I
can't wait forever." I didn't even care if he married me; I just wanted a
kid. He made it clear he would leave me if I got pregnant. He would not
live in the house with a kid. I didn't want to fight about it. I just want-
ed him to marry me and I wasn't going to beg. I didn't want to say,
"I'm going to kick you out if you don't marry me." That was ugly.

I was really angry about this, so I guess it was my subconscious
knocking me on the head when I fell in love with someone else. We met
when he came over to my house for a party. He was 25 years older than
I am. He looked around, sizing up my house, and gave his seal of
approval. He was a very charming and successful artist. I was
enthralled. He promised me he would give me children. I was 35,
which is the gynecologist's magic number. That was the hook. I spoke
to my internist, who advised me to break up with the young guy, as nice
as he might be in five years, and go with this older man and the baby.
"Men come and go," he said, "you can always get remarried when he
kicks off, but you've got to have that baby soon." So we lived togeth-
er for a year. He drove me crazy. He was the child. And what was
worse, he was impotent most of the time we were together. He lived in
my house, off me, even though he made twice as much money.

After all this, I'm not making any plans. It doesn't do any good.
Right now I'm enjoying having my house to myself. I haven't been
alone in this house for a long time. I ceded it to these men. They would
work in the living room and have control of the entire house, and I
would be sitting in my bed with all my books spread out—just one
small corner. Right now I'm enjoying this, and I think that's good,
because the less afraid I am of being alone, the more attractive I will be.
I feel like, "If I have time for you, fine. I may not. But you better be
good to me or I won't bother with you." I know my standards for a

*mate are very high, and I price myself out of the market, but I don't
care at this point. I would rather live alone than live with somebody
who doesn't deserve me. I guess I'll be even more demanding now;
I've never asked men for any services or money. I've always supported
myself and them. I find it morally repugnant to consider that now. I
wouldn't mind having a man stay home with the child as long as he
was content and not secretly resenting it and taking it out on me in
little ways. He would have to be self-respecting, and I don't think a lot
of house-husband types are. My experience tells me that most are
weirdos, flakes, and losers.*

Many men who are functionally or serially polygynous do not want children or do not want additional children. But some higher-status polygynists encourage their partners to become pregnant, or at least do not discourage them. When women become pregnant in these situations, it is often because they believed or hoped that their partners would eventually make a commitment. This hope is fostered by varying degrees of dishonest advertising, procrastination, evasion, and reticence on the man's part. Women who are caught in such situations are often reluctant to admit that they were deluded, and if they decide to keep the child, they may pretend that they preferred to have a child out of wedlock. But in most cases, they would have preferred to marry their higher-status lovers and receive all of their material and emotional investments.

Alison is 36 and a practicing attorney. She had a five-year affair with a married physician who was twenty years her senior. He told her that his marriage was very bad, but he could not get a divorce because his children would disapprove. Alison was worried about her age and the increasing risks of childbirth, and so became pregnant when she was 35. When she informed her lover that she was pregnant, he did not call her again. Seven months into her pregnancy, she decided that he might be more open to continuing a relationship if she formally absolved him of all legal responsibility for the child. She therefore drew up a legal contract to this effect and arranged to meet him to discuss it. Her lover found Alison's offer reasonable and generous, and signed the contract. He then told her that he had left his wife and begun dating.

Alison did not hear from him again until her baby was born. About a month after delivery, she called her erstwhile lover and suggested that they get together so that he could see his child. When they met, he held the child for a few minutes and said, "Cute baby!" He then informed Alison that he was getting married to "a lovely girl" he had met recently. They were just waiting for his divorce to be final. Alison now has difficulty caring for her baby and maintaining her practice. She spends most weekends at her parents' home.

Julie has also experienced the connection between hypergyny and polygyny firsthand. She is 27, pretty, and an airline stewardess. About a year ago, she met a wealthy man from Stockholm who was on business in the States. They dated and eventually began to have a sexual affair. Two months after his return to Sweden, she discovered she was pregnant. She did not want to have an abortion. She informed her lover in Sweden of this and he acted very excited and positive. He offered to fly her to Sweden and pay for her housing, clothes, medical expenses—in effect, to support her totally. He told her, however, that although he is not married, he has been living with a woman for ten years. This woman has not wanted to have children but he desperately wanted them, so he would love to have Julie come to Sweden and have his baby.

Julie decided not to go to Sweden because she would have no supports or contacts outside of him, so she tried to persuade him to join her in America. He said that he would love to but his business interests were all in Sweden and he could not afford such a move. They continued to exchange romantic, transatlantic letters. About six months into the pregnancy, he informed her that his live-in lover was pregnant and due to deliver two months after Julie was. Julie was extremely upset by this news because all along he had said that his Swedish lover was happy for him and Julie, and had encouraged him to bring Julie to Sweden.

Julie now believes this woman was afraid of being displaced and so became pregnant when she heard that Julie was pregnant. She does not know for certain if any part of what her lover told her was true, because she never went to Sweden to check out his story. He may be married with three children or be single and have no live-in lover. This higher-status man, like Alison's lover, has succeeded in being polygynous and siring a child in whom he will invest minimally if at all.

Julie and Alison did not make informed choices to be the second mates of higher-status males. If these women had known from the start what the outcome would be, it is doubtful that they would have chosen this course. What is clear, however, is that these women did end up having the offspring of higher-status, polygynous males rather than marrying and having children with lower-status, monogamous males.

Apparent anomalies

Evolutionary psychologists argue that women's preference to marry up and men's preference to have a variety of lovers are facultative—that is, they are predispositions, and whether they emerge in behavior depends on environmental conditions. But these predispositions appear to be robust because they tend to emerge wherever opportunities allow, and even do so in the face of considerable impediments and conscious suppression by men and women. As we have seen, women can engage in low-investment sex, or mate with lower-status partners, but they will not prefer to do so. Researchers Guttentag and Secord suggest that the current lack of suitable partners might cause some women to turn to men they would not otherwise consider: someone of a different race or someone considerably older. Some women are currently doing this. But consistent with the evolutionary perspective, these women do not typically maintain regular sexual relationships with such men. They see them on an occasional basis and do not take them seriously. They do not normally fall in love with such men, nor do they marry them. These women take care to maintain an emotional as well as a physical distance from such men.

Brook is the lawyer we met in Chapter 1. She is in her mid-forties, divorced, and sporadically sees two different men. One is black and about fifteen years her junior. Although he earns a middle-class living now, he came from poverty, is uneducated, and has been in prison. She enjoys seeing him because he is fun, charming, a good dancer, and good in bed. He has a potentially more serious relationship with a black woman in another city, but he will not marry her because he does not want to assume responsibility for her children. Brook also sees another man, her childhood friend, Tom, who lives in another state. He is a judge, in his fifties, and divorced.

Brook

Tom and I have a nifty relationship because he lives in New York and I live here. He hops in his plane and we go to Martha's Vineyard. We do all sorts of fun things together, but we still maintain a separate existence. I think we would have trouble living with each other because he's a playboy, and I'm not a playgirl. We have an open-ended relationship that works out well under the circumstances. We are 700 miles apart. He has a stable life. From what I can gather, he has a stable of five or six women that he sees between the ages of 25 to 45.

This is a good arrangment for me as it is. I don't need marriage that much as long as I have this comfortable arrangement. Of course, the older I get, the less feasible it is for me to date a handsome, 30-year-old black man and a nice, stable politician. It's like I have the best of all worlds. There are a lot of women my age who don't— like this 50-year-old friend of mine who has money and travels to Europe all the time, but she can't find someone to date. It's her age.

This nifty situation is going to end; it has to. My career is interesting enough and hopefully I will continue to do well enough that I'll sink into a nice, unmarried, relatively celibate way of life in ten years. It's hard to imagine, but I think women can do that more easily than men can. I can take care of my home. I'm comfortable financially. I have my daughter to enjoy. So I don't have any problems facing this prospect.

Brook's ex-husband was a successful politician, and in the early part of their marriage, she frequently attended White House parties. At 45, she adjusts to the market and dates men with whom there is no possibility of a serious commitment. One of these men is black and not of her educational and occupational level. She reports that she would never consider marrying this man although she enjoys seeing him occasionally. Significantly, he has not offered to marry her, and is a functional polygynist. The judge is wealthy, influential, and flies his own plane. He is also polygynous and, like Bob, maintains a "stable" of women he dates. He does not seem particularly eager to get married. Brook is perceptive and frank in assessing her situation. She knows that as she gets older, the quality of men she can date will diminish to a point where she is no longer interested. She will then sink back into a comfortable life of relative celibacy. Because she is financially secure, enjoys a good relationship with her daughter, and genuinely enjoys life, she believes she can face this prospect without fear.

Brook's ex-husband was a high-powered man. Her current boyfriends are masculine, self-assured, and successful, but they do not enjoy the celebrity and status her ex-husband did, and she has made no formal commitments with the boyfriends. What kind of compromises are women willing to make between men's status, fidelity, and willingness to commit? How are these tradeoffs managed and rationalized by the women and their partners? One way is through therapeutic philosophy.

The therapeutic mentality

George went to a female psychotherapist for several years, and he cited a popular book on romantic love in describing his goals in relationships. Most women seek companionship, intimacy, and a comfortable, interwoven interdependency in their relationships. George would prefer to enjoy these benefits without the legal and financial obligations of marriage, and he wants to do this with more than one woman. George can use popular psychology and psychotherapy to rationalize and defend his polygyny because these sources tend to advocate situational morality rather than an absolute morality. In situational morality, premarital sex, extramarital affairs, divorce, and simultaneous sexual relationships are not categorically and unequivocally wrong and bad: they could be bad in some situations and acceptable in others, or they could be bad for some people and okay for others. George can therefore use these sources of authority to defend his actions. Of course, so can the women he encounters.

George

Valerie is more prone to try brinksmanship than Sally. For example, Valerie will threaten that she's going to go out and sleep with someone else, and occasionally she does it. I just tell her calmly that if that's what she feels she wants to do, then she should do it. Of course I find it threatening, but I know she does it to pressure me, and I just try to deal with it reasonably.

To me "jealousy" and "possessiveness" are really synonyms for the fear of loss. When you act jealous or possessive about someone you love, it's not because you feel you own them; it's because you fear losing a relationship where you've made an investment of your time and love and money and feelings. When you've extended your hand, your being to someone, you don't want them to say "Gee, I don't want you anymore," and just chop it off. That hurts! That's why it does get me when Valerie sees other men. I don't really mind sharing her with someone else as long as I know she'll be there for me when I need her.

Anyway, Valerie found a picture of me and Sally at the yacht races and she got really pissed because she had gone to the races with me many times. So one day she saw my car at Sally's and she came in and created a scene, did a lot of yelling and screaming, and then left. I told Valerie later that she should have expressed her anger directly to me rather than barging into Sally's home and yelling. It wasn't the appropriate thing to do, although I have to give her credit for having the balls to do it!

I did have an exclusive commitment with Valerie for a short period after she found out about another woman. That was a long time ago. Thank heavens we've gotten past that type of thing. She really pressured me so I said, "okay." That lasted about a week. I went back and said that I had agreed because I was afraid of losing everything, of being totally alone, and those were bad reasons. They came from fear. I told her that I took responsibility for coercing myself. She wasn't coercing me; it was me doing it to myself and I didn't want to do that. Well, she didn't buy it. [Laughter] She was pissed that I broke the commitment and accused me of procrastinating indefinitely—as she has many times.

George's statements are examples of therapeutic philosophy, and in dealing with Valerie's jealousy and anger, he uses therapy-speak. The moral tenets of therapeutic philosophy are so vague they can be used to rationalize almost any position or self-interest. As Robert Bellah and coauthors wrote in *Habits of the Heart*:

For therapeutically liberated individuals, obligation of any kind becomes problematic in relationships. . . . The therapeutic attitude liberates individuals by helping them get in touch with their own wants and interests, freed from the artificial constraints of social roles, the guilt-inducing demands of parents and other authorities. . . . the therapeutic attitude redefines the real self. . . . which instead consists of the experience and expression of feelings. For such expressive selves, love means the full exchange of feelings between authentic selves, not enduring commitment resting on binding obligation. . . . even [the] deepest impulses of attachment to others are without any more solid foundation than [one's] momentary desires.[13]

Psychotherapy has also helped George to maintain his polygynous arrangement in another way: it has enabled him to recognize emotions like guilt, fear, and anger that make him vulnerable to the manipulations of others. When Valerie demanded monogamy after she found out about another woman, George feared losing her, so he agreed to her demand. He then analyzed his feelings and decided he did not want to be intimidated by fear, so he withdrew his commitment, saying, "You are not coercing me. I'm coercing myself, and I don't want to do that." From her point of view, this was psychological double-talk because she *was* trying to pressure him and it was not working.

Mastering his emotions has allowed George to resist the psychological pressures from both of these women over the years. For example, after Valerie burst into Sally's home and created a scene, George calmly told her that she should have expressed her anger directly to him. Psychotherapy can teach you to identify and understand you own and others' emotions. When you can do this, you can prevent people from manipulating these emotions to make you do things you do not want to do. Obviously, this skill does not always operate in the interests of those surrounding the person in therapy. Valerie went to the same therapist as George, so presumably she is armed with the same skills and is a fair match for him.

While George's polygyny causes conflict with his partners, it also helps him to resist their attempts to pressure him. In their research, Blumstein and Schwartz concluded that women are "the keepers of monogamy" because women want sex to stay within the relationship and to function as a strong emotional as well as a physical bond.[14] Putting this less euphemistically, we can say that women prefer monogamy, in part, because it allows the possibility of obtaining all of a man's emotional and material investments and because it gives women more sexual bargaining power. As we saw in Chapters 1 and 2, women are less likely to want to have sex and enjoy it if their needs for investment are not being met, and their sexual availability and response can be powerful chips in bargaining to get what they want. This power is greatly reduced if the man has sexual access to other equally attractive women. George is threatened by Valerie's dating and sleeping with other men, but his knowledge of his emotions, and the immediate availability of love, sex, and reassurance from another woman enable him to control his fears.

Some readers might call George sexist, immature, macho, or irresponsible for stringing these women along while he continues to check out other partners. The situation is not so simple. Both of these women are attractive professionals. No one is forcing them to date George. They know about each other; he makes no promises, and yet they have continued to see him over the years. They could date other men and sometimes do, but evidently they prefer to date a wealthy man, with a faint possibility for marriage, rather than a poorer man who is a sure thing. They are making this choice.

Why are women attracted to men like George, Bob, and Wes? Is it that their status makes them dominant compared to other men? What does "dominant" mean? What happens when women date or marry men they can easily dominate? In the next chapter we will seek answers to these questions.

Romance, Male Dominance, and the Quest for Investment

The great question . . . which I have not been able to answer, despite my thirty years of research into the feminine soul, is "What does a woman want?"

—Sigmund Freud

Without an office, you have no power, and I love power because it attracts women.

—Henry Kissinger

Women's Quest for Investment

SIGMUND FREUD WAS CONFIDENT of his ability to unravel the deepest secrets of the unconscious mind and to explain the fundamental processes of psychological development and gender identity. Yet in his often-quoted statement, he admitted he was at a loss when it came to understanding what women want. Freud is not alone: a great many men are perplexed by women's behavior. They often find it contradictory, frustrating, and incomprehensible. One of the reasons for men's confusion is their failure to recognize the distinction between emotional and material investment. Most women want men who are loving and tender with them but they also want men who are winners. This desire for both types of investment often causes them to behave in ways that men find baffling. For example, women tend to want more cuddling and tender shows of affection than men do, and women's complaints about men in this respect are perennial. But at times many women also want their male partners to act passionately, lustfully, and masterfully. A woman can alternate between wanting to cuddle and nurture the man, wanting the man to cuddle and nurture her, and wanting him to act as though he were ravishing her. And all of these alternations can occur in one encounter. The same alternations can occur in verbal transactions. Sometimes a woman wants a man to be sensitive, considerate, and compliant. Other times she may want him to take a stand and argue with her. In the early stages of a relationship, some contemporary women are adamant about their independence and equality. They make it clear to men that they can be tough, ambitious, and independent. They may even insist that men not show the traditional trappings of male gallantry and courtship—no car doors should be opened for them, they can pay their own way at the restaurant or theater. But if the relationship passes beyond this initial stage, most women begin to want signs of investment. These can be material, like his ability to support a family at the level she has attained or aspires to, or emotional, like remembering her birthday with flowers or a sentimental gift. Men are often shocked by women's reactions to a forgotten or slighted birthday or anniversary. As one woman told me, it is not necessarily the value of the card or gift the man offers that is so important, but rather the evidence that he was thinking about her, he cared enough about her and her feelings to remember, and to take the time to buy flowers or perfume and scribble a sentimental message on a card. Such behavior does not come naturally to most men. They usually have to be trained to satisfy women's desires for these signs of affection and intimacy, and these lessons can be extremely frustrating for both them and their partners.

Some women seem to be attracted to men who treat them callously, but apart from exceptional cases, these women are not pathologically attracted to exploitation and abuse. Rather, they are attracted to men whose status makes them attractive to many women, and this allows the men to indulge their desires for partner variety and low-investment sex. Such men offer high risk and high potential. If a woman can secure a reliable commitment from such a man, she has garnered a top-quality man, but the risks of his philandering and eventually deserting her are high. Other women are more cautious and look for reliability of investment: the good steady provider who will be a good husband and father. But women today often leave such men, as we shall see later in this chapter, particularly if their own income and resources obviate the men's. The central goal in women's selection of mates, then, is to obtain the maximum investment possible, and this involves weighing different factors, like potential for investment versus reliability and risk. It is for this reason that many contemporary women dichotomize the world of men into wimps, geeks, and nerds on the one side, and pricks and bastards on the other. The former are men who would probably be willing to commit themselves in a relationship, but they do not measure up to the women's standards. The latter group are men who measure up, but are unwilling to confine their investments to this particular woman. A joke that I heard in San Francisco while I was conducting interviews points up this dichotomy:

Question: What is the difference between porcupines and Porsches?
Answer: With the porcupines, the pricks are on the outside.

Why would folk humor make a connection between owning an expensive sports car and being a dastardly person? Because men with expensive, imported sports cars are often attractive to a lot of women and the men take advantage of this by having casual relations with them. Gloria is a thirty-six-year-old businesswoman who did her own research on men's polygynous tendencies after she broke up with her husband. She has had difficulty getting men she finds really attractive to invest in her, so she has experimented with dating men in lower socioeconomic levels.

Gloria

I was deeply hurt and angry when I discovered that my husband had been having affairs with several different women. I challenged him but he never admitted to any of it. He wouldn't even discuss it. It was impossible to continue a marriage like that, so about six months after I moved out, I figured, "Hey, I am at rock bottom. Everything has been destroyed, so I am going to go out and find out what is in men's heads, and there is not one of them that is ever going to do this to me again." I have an investigative personality anyway, so I am always gathering more information. I talked to about forty different people about these issues. I met some very interesting people, some good people, and I learned a lot.

One thing I learned was that if you want a monogamous relationship with an aggressive, goal-oriented man, just forget it. That is simply not part of the package. These guys want their security needs fulfilled at home, and they need that image for their work environment: the perfect little family. In a lot of corporate environments this is still critical; it's a matter of evaluation when they hire someone. But while these guys need the secure, little happy home, they want to screw around too. I worked for a smaller corporation, a 40-50 million dollar business, and it went on all the time. And there is no question about it, the higher they are, the less likely they are to be monogamous. It comes with the territory. They are businessmen and it's part of their personality. They are used to wheeling and dealing and manipulating people, and if they have an itch, they scratch it. If they want to screw someone, and someone is there and she's attractive, they go for it.

I love powerful, aggressive, self-made men. They are exciting because they are winners. They are the gladiators of today. They have a kind of sexual energy that most men lack. But I know how they are. They are selfish and self-centered and they are not good lovers. Some of them are talented at the mechanics of love-making, but they are not being emotional with you, and they aren't into saying, "Hey, this is your evening and I will just totally please you." They are into getting pleased and having their needs satisfied. They are used to women waiting on them—at work and at home. I can't relax around them. I can't be vulnerable because they will use me. My relationship with them is always defensive.

I look at myself and I see that I have all the capabilities of acquiring all of the money that I want. So I think a lot about the type of man I want. Because of what I have seen and the people I have talked to, I see that the sexy, exciting, super-achiever and the loving, caring guy do not come in one package. So what do I do? I think I'm gravitating toward a more passive man who can fulfill those love needs because I don't need one that fills the financial needs. I can do that part. I'm not talking about a house-husband type, but about a man who has a job but is a lower achiever.

I am dating a couple of working-class guys now and it's different. I'm in control. I like to get into their bodies and minds. I'm more sophisticated than they are and it's a challenge to bring them out. The plumber I date would freak out if I took him to a nice restaurant. He's a good Catholic man whose wife ran around on him. He's very working class. I mean he didn't even know where the State Park was, and he grew up around here. That is what fascinates me. It's like taking a young child who has never seen anything out of his village. I know that I am playing with these men in a way, but I am trying to find out where I do not play games, where is that level that satisfies my needs. These relationships are stretching me. That's good. See, if I can push them around, then I get bored with them. I sort of push them away if they want to be in love with me, because I don't want to be in love with them. I can't satisfy their need. I could never marry any of these men.

Chelsea was 21 and a senior in college when we spoke to her. Like Gloria, she felt used and abused by the men she found most attractive, so she consciously decided to date down in terms of social class to increase her bargaining power and control the amount of emotional investment she received.

Chelsea

I came to college looking for a committed relationship, dating, monogamy, courting, the whole shooting match. But college guys are not interested—at least not the best-looking, most popular guys, which was what I was trying to date. So I ended up having a bunch of one-night stands. In four cases I went out with guys I wasn't really attracted to and soon got bored, or saw someone better. These relationships were not satisfying. I went out with about 23 guys, and had sex with sixteen or seventeen of them. "Meet, eat, movie, fuck, see ya' later, bye," was the pattern. I really got sick of this! I couldn't get the level of attention, consideration and compliance I needed—like whose schedule do you run on, yours or his? So when this woman friend I met where I was working part time asked if I wanted to go to a townie bar, I said "sure." This was the kind of place where all the guys drive pickups and their big goal in life is to bag an eight-point buck in deer season. In that town any woman with anything going for her gets some training and is gone to the middle-class world, so I was the star attraction. It was like ringing the dinner bell. Men flocked. I thought, "This is more like it!" It was a conscious decision to date down. I could call the shots and have as much adulation as I wanted, as long as I was careful in choosing. Some of these deer-hunting types are violently possessive. They think it's okay if they mess around, but they beat you up if they think you are, or if you challenge them in any way. But I knew what I wanted and picked well. The disadvantages of this arrangement are that I get bored because this guy is so manageable, and it's not real. I know that I would never marry any of these guys, but we can play house. You want to feel like you have a mate, even if you know it's only temporary.

What is romance?

The dominant theme of virtually all romantic fiction is the problem of attaining this goal: How does a woman get a highly attractive (that is, high status) man to pledge eternal love and devotion and to invest his considerable resources exclusively in her and her future offspring?[1] The story details the trials and tribulations the heroine suffers en route to this goal. In the classic gothic romance, the man is invariably a count or duke, usually a womanizer—because his high status allows him to be—and a very difficult man to tie down. In the modern romance, the man may be a successful doctor, attorney, or businessman, or he may even be struggling to make his way in the world, but he must succeed or he will not get the woman in the end. In many romances, there is a man hanging around who is sensitive, devoted, and willing to commit, but the heroine can not truly love this man, at least not sexually, because he is simply not the man in her eyes that the hero is. She may be very fond of the hanger-on, but basically she sees him as a wimp. Scarlett's relationship to Ashley in *Gone with the Wind* is the prototype of this pattern.

The market for romantic fiction is enormous, international, and almost exclusively female. Many educated, financially independent women read such literature, whether in the form of the classic pulp novel or as short stories in women's magazines like *Cosmopolitan*. Indeed, in 1990 one company alone sold over 200 million paperbacks, and this is just a fraction of the market. The comparable markets for men are adventure stories and pornography. But as we have seen, women are much more likely to be sexually intrigued and aroused by romantic literature and films than by pornographic materials. As gender expert John Money stated, romantic fiction *is* the true pornography of women.[2] Some women consider romantic fiction trite and inane. But whether they know it or not, their selection and rejection of partners, and their goals and dissatisfactions in relationships, exhibit the same basic tendencies and themes that make up the core of romantic fiction.

Do women like dominant men?

Many social scientists have predicted that these female tendencies will disappear once women attain economic independence and higher social status—that once independent women no longer have to acquire status and resources through men, these female preferences will become less prevalent, both in fact and in fiction.[3] Yet this is not happening. As we saw in Chapter 3, women with more resources tend to raise their socioeconomic standards for partners. Women's achievements in other areas also cause them to raise their standards. The more educated, articulate, and ambitious a woman is, the more she demands of a man in these respects. For example, when asked what they most desired in a man, over half the women medical students stated they wanted a man who was a challenge, one they could admire and respect. One-third said that they wanted a man who made them feel "protected." When I asked what they needed protection from, they were vague and said it was not a rational desire. They knew they would have sufficient money and resources themselves, and they did not actually expect a man would ever have to protect them from any physical danger. Nevertheless, they said that having a man they truly respected would make them feel more secure. When asked what they most desired in a woman, no man offered responses remotely similar to these answers from the women. Women's acceptance of feminist ideology did not appear to correlate negatively with such responses. In fact, some of the most outspoken advocates of feminist principles were the most explicit in describing their desires for strong, decisive, successful men. These women tended to prefer men who were above them professionally and financially as long as the men did not try to use their superior status and income to force the women to compromise their own career goals.

Carol is a second-year medical student and received a good liberal arts education at a private school before she entered medical school. She enjoys the biological sciences but she feels that a truly cultured, cultivated person must also know art, history, philosophy, and literature. She is outspoken in her feminism, but she still prefers a man who is a bit ahead of her—someone older who is worldly and wise. Such a man is a challenge to her precisely because he has greater knowledge and achievements in certain areas. This advantage makes him worthy of respect and admiration and, hence, more attractive.

Carol

A lot of male medical students say, "I'd never want to marry a med student. I want a wife to stay home and keep house while I'm in surgery sixteen hours a day." These men are intellectually lazy. They aren't willing to make fairness a lifestyle. It's too easy to do what your parents did—to have a wife whose job is to clean and watch kids. That way, when you're home, your time is your own. You don't have to worry about making dinner. I don't go out with guys who are sexist—who are not as supportive of my career as I am of theirs.

My ideal husband is one who is older and wiser in the ways of the world. He could be a little better at things than I am. I am attracted to the maturity of an older man. I want a man I can be proud of. I need someone to challenge me. Nobody wants all the power in a relationship. It's no good if you know you're better than your partner. You tend to look around for someone else when that happens. A certain amount of male aggressiveness is needed by women in order to be happy. You don't want to be pushed around, but you want a man that you can respect. I wouldn't marry someone who wasn't on my level because the man would tend to feel jealous of my successes. I wouldn't like it either. He just wouldn't grow at the same rate as I would.

In high school I had a lot of male friends but I didn't date because it was a small school and with most of the guys it would have been dating down. I spoke two foreign languages well and had traveled and lived in foreign countries. I'd seen a lot of the world. These guys drank beer and threw up. Marrying someone of my level is the only thing that would work. If you can't share experiences with someone and haven't had a good conversation in days, you don't feel like having sex. The guy I go with now is close to my ideal. He's very intelligent, warm, and unpretentious. He knows all the Greek tragedies, but he doesn't have to talk about it to prove himself. We're fairly serious but we have no plans. He's a year ahead of me in medical school, so he's on call every other night and in the hospital for days.

Zelda is the fourth-year medical student we heard from in previous chapters. She describes what she wants in a man.

Zelda

I believe in sexual equality but I still have the Scarlett O'Hara fantasy of being swept off the stairs by a Rhett Butler. I've succeeded academically and professionally so those are the standards I have for a man. I want him to succeed in these areas too. It's not that I want to be dominated or protected by a man. But I would prefer him to be physically stronger than I am, taller, and to make more money. Men who are ambitious and good at political machinations are exciting. I loved JR on Dallas. He was such a bastard!

JMT: Why do you think the phrase "melted in his arms" appears in almost every romance novel?

The term "melt" is used because that is how it feels when you're with a man who really turns you on and you're embracing. I actually feel like I'm melting into him. The women who read romance novels are not on an isolated track. We all feel the same. And you can't talk yourself into it. A man either does it for you or he doesn't. It's a chemical reaction. I see some men who would make good catches. They have the right background and profession, the whole bit, and I wonder why I can't love them, why I don't melt with them. It's a sense of mastery that's conveyed, and some men don't have it. Sexually, I don't always want a man to be considering what I want and waiting for my cues all the time. He should know what he wants to do and he should be passionate and spontaneous in doing it. I want the option of being the initiating person, but I don't want to do it all the time. There are times when a woman wants to be treated like a beast. I don't like to say these things because I'm a feminist and it sounds like I want a man to dominate me, but that isn't it.

I think all this makes it more difficult to find what I want. Being successful myself, there are fewer eligible men and even fewer that are men. It's a dilemma. I want a man who accepts me as an equal and accepts my career, but men who are more willing to do this are more wimpy—at least many are. A man has to believe in female equality to accept me as a wife, yet a lot of men who are that way will have these traits I dislike.

Anthropologist William Jankowiak interviewed fourteen professional women who were deeply committed feminists.[4] Originally, in choosing their male partners, these women had intentionally picked men who were attempting to transcend traditional notions of masculinity and femininity—men who were able to express their insecurities and vulnerabilities and willing to share household tasks. As their careers prospered and their incomes equalled or surpassed their male partners' incomes, all of these women became dissatisfied with their partners. A business executive, 31, related that initially she was attracted to androgynous men because:

You could seduce them and that was nice knowing that you had the power to decide when and where you would have sex. Though other times it became too much of of an obligation. The men's inability to assert themselves—once the novelty wore off—got on my nerves.

Another businesswoman, 37, initially shared an avid commitment to radical feminism with her male partner. She reported, however, that as she grew older and achieved success in her career, radical ideology began to bore her and so did he:

About this time I noticed David's irregular work patterns. I began to resent his lack of effort. At the same time, I felt increasingly incomplete. It was as if something was amiss with my home life. No, it was more like something was amiss with my love life. I resented David's passivity . . .

I found myself wanting him to be assertive, even dominate me [laughs] at times. I guess that's why I've decided to drop in on these weekly chats. I wanted to know what's going on with me.

A physician, 33, reported that she became a feminist early in life and became a doctor so that, unlike her mother, she would never have to "play second fiddle to a man." She found most men were too arrogant, macho, or bossy to support her in her career ambitions. Consequently, she deliberately chose lovers for their "gentleness, wit, and general appreciation" for her and her work. She reports, however:

Unfortunately, the men I always seem to become involved with possessed gentleness but not wit . . . what's more they never seem to be able to invoke in me sexual passion [her emphasis].

And a high school teacher, 31, described her relationship with her male lover in this way:

He was so nice. He was a lawyer, with a growing clientele. He loved me. He was gentle, caring, and maybe too kind. I just never felt passion for him. I felt that I could manipulate him to the point where I found him puny. I felt a bit guilty in dropping him . . . after all, I thought the qualities he possessed were the ideal. Now I'm not so sure.

Most of the women we interviewed said that they liked a challenge—a man who was "hard to get" but not impossible.[5] When guys are too easy to get, the women are likely to be bored because there is no fun in the chase. When queried about what "getting" a guy meant, women gave various examples of willingness to invest: take her to nice places, call frequently, be affectionate, willing to spend quality time not related to sex, treat her with respect, not pursue other women. Men who came on too quickly with signs that they were willing to invest were likely to be labeled nerds, wimps, geeks, or jerks. In the college subculture, a popular term for a man who is willing to court a woman and do anything she wants is *whipped*, which is an abbreviation of the phrase *pussy-whipped*. This term seems to be as popular among women as among men, at least in the university subculture.

Do women test men?

Women's standards for mates tend to increase with their own achievements and their perception of possible alternatives, and consciously or

unconsciously women test, compare, and evaluate the quality of their partners' investments. Some women test the quality of their partners' investments by provoking them into competition with other men, evoking shows
of jealousy, or in domestic arguments. Among the sample of women who had
had multiple casual partners (see Chapter 2), about half said they flirted
with other men and provoked jealousy to see how much their partners cared
about them and to increase their partners' interest and willingness to invest.
Forty percent said that they tested their boyfriends to see where he stood, or
how far they could push him before he drew the line. One woman who said
that she needed a challenge added, "If a guy is too nice and sucks up to me
too much, it gives me an inferiority complex because a guy who would do
that may not be as great as I think he is." Another woman reported that if a
guy agrees with everything she says, she tries to provoke him, "just to see if
I can get an argument out of him." She also brings up topics he knows more
about than she does, so that he has to take the lead with conversation.

Numerous women acknowledged that they sometimes provoked arguments in order to get a rise out of their partners. Sometimes they wanted to
see if their partners cared enough about them to express intense emotions.
They said that they would rather have a good fight occasionally than live
with a man who seemed emotionally indifferent and withdrawn. At other
times, the confrontation served to test the man's limits. The woman would
keep pushing her partner on an issue to see how far she could go. No woman
seemed to want a man who was totally compliant; an altercation could show
her just how much stamina and self-respect he had, where he would stand up
for himself and draw the line, and how much he cared about what she did or
felt. Most women who engage in such testing behavior are not conscious of
their purpose when they do so. Some women only see their motivations in
retrospect; some never do. But some are extremely insightful in describing
and explaining their behavior. Pat is one of these women.

Pat

*I've gone out with guys that treated me like a queen but I didn't respect
them. I once dated a super-sensitive guy and I walked all over him. I
felt like saying to him, "You're spineless! Stand up to me. Don't let me
walk all over you." I ended up having no respect for him because I
need a little challenge for a relationship to work. Once the challenge is
gone, it's boring. I like a good argument occasionally. If the person
can't give that to me, I will stomp on them. I need a lover who can say,
"Shut up, Bitch!," once in a while, and then rip my clothes off.[6] I think
most women need that too but they can't admit it. If a man is so sensitive or timid he can't stand up to you, you begin to look at him as a
child—someone you protect under your wing. For me that kind of feeling is almost incestuous. It's not good sexually. I think there's a thin line*

*between a guy being sensitive and being a wimp. I want a man who
loves me and is considerate, but if he can't stand up to me, I can't
respect him and it won't work.*

Debbie's experience supports Pat's analysis. As we saw in Chapter 3,
Debbie's boyfriend failed his first year in medical school and was having to
repeat it. For her this was the major dissatisfaction with the relationship. She
felt he was draining her, and she did not want to have to take care of him
through marriage. She decided she wanted to look around.

Debbie

*I'm living with my boyfriend now. Sexually, the relationship is great.
Before my junior year of college, I got no physical pleasure out of any
sexual activity. Only very recently I discovered what turns me on and
I'm not bashful about what I want. I hadn't orgasmed until this year
and then only through cunnilingus. My boyfriend's a dream in this
respect. He's willing to do whatever I want to satisfy me. It's outside of
bed that we have problems.*

*After he failed medical school I began to have doubts and was
against living together but he agreed to move out if we broke up, so I
agreed. I dated a lot in college but never anyone seriously. They weren't
ambitious enough. I want a man who is ambitious, handsome, bright,
all those things.*

*What I want in a husband was like this guy [the rich Frenchman she
had a one-night stand with]: sophisticated, worldly, sexy, knowledgeable. I want a man who can make life more exciting for me. I'm a
romantic! I've read some romance novels. I admit it! Maybe I'm not
being realistic, but I want all of these things and I don't want to settle
for less. When my boyfriend takes me out in his sports car to a nice
restaurant, it makes me feel good. But when I'm trying to nurse him
through his exams, it turns me off. I don't want a man who cooks and
serves dinner and takes care of the kids. We can hire a maid for that.
My boyfriend will do these things now, so I've seen it but it's not what
I want. I get bored with a man who isn't a challenge—who is too willing to please. This French guy was very gracious and charming but a
little aloof until we got drunk. He was definitely a challenge.*

*When it was summer and I was home and doing well, my boyfriend
was unnecessary, but when I'm at school and have a heartache, he's
necessary; he's comforting. He's got some money now from a trust
fund, and that's nice because it allows us to do things that a lot of medical students don't get to do. But his money is running out now, and I
can imagine being married to him and doing better professionally than
he is and he would be unnecessary. When I'm in my third year and*

working in the hospital, I'll be meeting doctors and residents and fourth-year students and I'll find a new attraction. My boyfriend's draining and I won't need him then.

Women did not call it "testing" and often had no specific term for these actions. But if they were asked if they sometimes pushed their partners to see if they could get an emotional reaction out of them, or to see how far they could go before their partners drew the line, or if they sometimes flirted with other men to see whether their partners would get jealous, most women had no problem recognizing and acknowledging these actions. Some of the women we interviewed were not aware of these actions until discussing them put them into focus. But conscious or not, the type of testing and evaluation of male prowess and dominance described in our interviews is a pervasive element in heterosexual relationships.

Not all women are as assertive and direct in expressing their requirements for male investment as Pat and Debbie. Some women hate to have arguments with their male partners, and the level of verbal banter and altercation that Pat finds gratifying and reassuring, would be intolerable to many. I believe, however, that all women test the quality of male investment although their methods are usually much more subtle and covert than Pat's. Indeed, such testing is one of the elements of women's behavior that men find most perplexing and frustrating.

Dominance, Attractiveness, and Polygyny

Psychologist Edward Sadalla and colleagues conducted a series of fascinating experiments on dominance and sexual attractiveness.[7] In the first experiment subjects saw video tapes of simulated job interviews. Half the male subjects saw an actress who acted in ways that are known to convey nonverbal dominance. She made direct eye contact, maintained an erect posture, and used confident gestures. The other half of the men saw the same actress but in that video she acted insecure and subordinate—she slumped in her chair, looked nervously around, and twitched. The procedure was identical for female subjects except that they saw a male actor being interviewed. When the actor acted dominant, women found him much more sexually attractive and desirable as a date. But men's ratings of the actress's attractiveness were unaffected by whether she acted dominant or not.

The experimenters then had additional samples of college students rate the attractiveness of descriptions of people who were either described in ways that made them appear ambitious, successful, and competitive, or unambitious, noncompetitive, and less successful. In every experiment women's ratings of men's attractiveness and desirability as dates were strongly affected by the descriptions they read, while men's ratings of women's attractiveness were unaffected. Like the women we interviewed, the women in the experiments did not like domineering or aggressive men. When the effects of these characteristics were removed, the correlation between dominance and women's ratings of men's attractiveness increased.

Some sex-role theorists claim that dominant women are not considered attractive because the traditional role for women is passive, so women who violate this role expectation are considered unattractive. If this were the real cause, the actress should have been rated as less attractive in the dominant videotape and more attractive in the passive tape. But this did not happen. In all four experiments, when women were described or portrayed as dominant, it did not make them less attractive—it simply had no effect at all. These results are consistent with our interviews that addressed the question of whether men were threatened by strong women (see Chapter 4). Men are turned off by domineering, aggressive women, just as women are turned off by these traits in men. But men are not necessarily turned off by women's confidence, competitiveness, and success. In fact, as we saw, many men want to marry women with good educations and jobs. In judging sexual attractiveness, however, men are relatively indifferent to women's dominance, prowess, and competitiveness. But when women judge men's sexual attractiveness, these traits are essential.

Evolutionary psychologists argue that men and women have evolved different reproductive strategies, and because of this, dominance has different meanings for men and women.[8] A women who mates with a dominant man gains both long and short-term advantages. In the long-term the woman may pass on to her offspring traits that confer advantages in competition for status and resources. She gains the short-term advantage of greater access to resources, which gives herself and her offspring advantages over the mates and offspring of less dominant males. Although females do compete to mate with the most desirable males, their reproductive success is less closely related to their position on a dominance hierarchy.

This link between male attractiveness and dominance is not confined to our culture. Dominance hierarchies are universal in human societies; dominance is an attribute of the male role in all cultures. Male sex hormones correlate with assertiveness and dominance and induce men to attain rank in the social hierarchy. All over the world, men display rank, achievement, and skill as part of courtship. And in a majority of primate species, females are attracted to dominant males.[9]

In our research, women considered men "challenges" when it was difficult to induce these men to be sexually monogamous and to invest heavily and exclusively in them. These men have sexual access to several women and therefore do not have to invest heavily in any one woman. Typically, men who enjoyed high status within their social circles had multiple casual partners. Men who had public profiles such as musicians and athletes, all

more than 100 different sex partners. Many of their one-time
rs were with "groupies."[10]

re interviewed were quite conscious that their attractiveness was
dependent on status. For example, three football players who were certain to
be drafted into NFL teams said that their attractivness to women all depended
on status and environment. At some frat parties, said one, the "women are
into the frat boys there and not into football players, so you have to be in the
right environment, where the women are into football players." One campus
bar in particular is known as a football hangout and these men made many
of their conquests there. These men explained that when they attend functions in other cities or states where they are not known, they are virtually
ignored by women until, for example, a star professional athlete or network
sportscaster introduces them and confirms their status. One of the players
said that he took off his helmet as often as possible during games so that he
would be recognized off the field by fans, particularly women. The male
athletes also acknowledged that they usually wore their varsity jackets to
broadcast their status when they went out partying.

Eight college men we talked to who were not varsity athletes said a primary
motivation for joining fraternities was to gain access to women. They stated
that when they joined the frat house, their access was near zero but was trans-
formed virtually overnight when they became upperclassmen and prominent
in their fraternities. They also said that they tended to "hook up" with
younger women—freshmen and sophomores—because it was easier. Thus,
when the men dated down in terms of age and status, they got more of what
they wanted: low-investment sex with physically attractive women.

And the men's interviews confirmed a point that had emerged in the
women's interviews: women who have multiple casual partners have their
specialties. Football groupies are not usually interested in members of punk
rock bands; basketball groupies were not interested in wrestlers; counterculture intellectuals typically despised athletes and fraternity men. But none
of these women referred to themselves as groupies; if they commented at all
on their preferences, the women would say they had dated or "gone out
with" some of the guys on the team. Status in a particular hierarchy, rather
than specific physical attributes, determined these men's attractiveness—for
example, some male counterculture and punk-rock celebrities do not have
the physical prowess of athletes yet they still have their groupies.

Some of the athletes said that in the past, they had led women on—
promised or implied more investment than they were willing to make. Now
they made it very clear up front that it was a simple copulation with no further contact. Many of these men had begun to restrict this approach because
of the risks of allegations of date rape, paternity, other entanglements, and dis-
ease. These men each had ten to twenty women whom they could call any
time they wanted sex and companionship, and they remained open to novel

partners who appeared safe and were particularly exciting. They thought this tactic was both safer and more convenient than the random, multiple "hookups" in which they used to engage. The men with the greatest numbers of partners did not boast and in fact were reluctant to offer details because of the opprobrium surrounding male exploitation of women, and their awareness of how such information could damage their careers and reputations.

The football stars who were African American acknowledged that most of the girls they slept with were white. They said that this makes the black women on campus angry, but the men figured those women are just jealous. One player recalled a black woman upbraiding him for "sleeping with all those white girls." He asked her if she would go to bed with him and she refused. He said, "Then shut up!" The men said that they did not discriminate, but that "decent-looking" black women were not nearly as sexually available as white women. And these men affirmed that they did not think these white women would ever have sex with African American men who did not have extremely high status. For their part, these men said they would never marry a white woman, and would probably not have a serious relationship with one. These men thus acknowledged that their status gave them sexual access to hundreds of women who otherwise would have been unavailable.

Political scientist Jeffrey Benedict classified groupies into three types.[11] The "collector" accumulates sexual acts instead of autographs. The "would-be wife" hopes that an affair will lead to a long-term emotional relationship—although she may deny this is her goal until something works out. The "sniffer" wants to bask in the reflective glow rather than have sex with the celebrity. Being a member of a celebrity's entourage can bestow prestige, draw attention, and perhaps lead to a desirable relationship with someone else.

In a study by psychologists David Buss and David Schmitt, women rated high and immediate investment as more important in short-term than in long-term relationships.[12] The authors explain that in long-term relationships investment is more certain and cumulative—for example, a long-term relationship could lead to marriage and the support of children. In short-term relationships there is no expectation of this type of payoff, so, women want male investment up front. This explains some women's willingness to be groupies, or otherwise engage in sexual relations that involve minimal investment. In such encounters, women test their sexual attractiveness in competition with other women and exchange sexual access for the attention and time of men who otherwise are unavailable to them. In these cases, inducing a man to have sex becomes a challenge and worthwhile simply because the man has so many other women available to him that simple intercourse becomes an affirmation and rewarding.

Do men test women?

About half the men we interviewed said that they tested for jealousy and how much their partners cared for them, but this was only with someone they were really interested in—in other words, someone in whom they might be willing to invest.[13] Most of the men also said they wanted their girlfriends to be challenges, and able to "stand up" to them, but what the men meant by this was a mirror image of the women's definition. A woman who did not demand investment would get neither "respect" nor investment. The men indicated that they would court and invest as little as was necessary, but would still sleep with women whom they did not respect and did not even like, provided that the women were sufficiently physically attractive. Most of the men had done this numerous times in one-night stands. Thus, a woman's being sensible, having backbone, and demanding investment were prerequisites for males' willingness to invest, but these qualities did not determine women's *sexual* attractiveness. Physical traits were the primary determinants of women's sexual attractiveness.

Testing one's limits

It is the nature of competition that people keep testing themselves until they reach their limits. When women say they like a man who is a challenge, they mean someone who is attractive and secure enough that he does not have to rush into commitments and investments with any woman who will accept him. He is attractive and he can afford to be choosy. Women are attracted to men whose investments and commitments are difficult to obtain, not only because the difficulty itself is exciting and challenging, but also because the difficulty can signal male quality and prowess: men who are in demand can more easily get what they want from women while limiting their investments. It is then the woman's task to convince such a man that she is so special that he cannot have her without making the required commitments and investments, and that she is worth it.

The tendency to test one's limits in this way means that virtually any woman, no matter how attractive, will eventually experience rejection if she stays on the dating-mating market long enough. This happened to Susan. She reported that she met a man who was "a real challenge" because her previous boyfriends had always been more interested in her than she had in them, but this guy had the potential to "turn the tables" on her. He dated her for six months and they began having intercourse. He remained charming and warm but made no moves to intensify their relationship. After they began having sex, she felt that she was beginning to fall in love with him. But when she asked for some signs that her feelings were reciprocated, he was elusive and reticent. She also began to suspect that he was seeing other women. He was unwilling to make commitments, or even to say he loved her, so she cut the relationship off. She reported that she was very hurt. It was the first time she had been dumped herself instead of "doing the dumping."

How women form their standards

In choosing partners for serious relationships, a woman will measure potential mates against her own achievements. Women want to marry men in levels that are equal to or higher than the levels they have attained themselves, as we saw in Chapter 3. Another determinant appears to be a woman's own social class. If she comes from a professional, upper-middle-class family, she generally expects to marry a man who can provide a similar or superior lifestyle—even though her own earning power may be minimal. Women from the working class might prefer to marry up if they could, but they might also be content with finding men who are successful within their own class. Some of the medical students came from working-class backgrounds. Mary is one of them.

Mary

Joe is the most understanding and supportive guy in the world. He just graduated from business school and has a real job in the city, and money, and time—all the things I haven't had because I have been in school. He was my first serious date in college and we've been together ever since. It took me a year to decide to sleep with him, and during that time I think he was the most sexually frustrated guy in the world. But he was very patient and understanding.

When I decided to go to medical school, I was in my junior year of college. When I told Joe, he said he was behind me 100 percent. If he had said he thought I was crazy, I would have agreed, so he provided the impetus for my decision. I don't like being away from him because a lot can happen in three years. I know I could go down there now and get married and live happily ever after. I could escape this torture. The grind. He said, "I would love to have you down here, but I won't let you because I know that in two years you would be bored as anything and I don't want to be blamed for keeping you from what you want to do. So don't consider it an option because you won't be happy in the long run." He is the biggest support for my staying here.

I know that I couldn't be a housewife and have some meaningless job. Now I realize that getting respect is important to me. I want to control my own destiny. If I want to work, I'll work; if I want to make a lot of money, I can. Or I can work in a clinic and make my own hours. I'll be self-sufficient. Sometimes I wish I was married, but I want to know that when I get married, it will not be a mistake. I don't think it would be a mistake marrying Joe, but people change.

Our senior year in college we decided to date other people. I guess we got afraid because we hadn't really dated anyone else seriously. I'm the one who said it, but I had gotten vibes from him that he wanted to date. It turned out that I had a great time going out and he didn't. I think men have more of an appetite for sex than women, so they have to put forth more effort to have dates and get their needs fulfilled. It was a problem for him. I didn't have to do anything to have guys chase me. We got back together then and lived together for a year. It was the best time we ever had together.

The first year of med school I didn't tell anyone I had a boyfriend. I didn't want to be labeled. I was not married. As a medical student you are deprived of so many things, you don't want to be deprived of your social life too. He wasn't here with me, so I wanted to be free to date. I soon got involved with a guy in my class. We were both involved with other people, so it never got really serious. I think I was more interested in him than he was in me. He's very Jewish and I don't think he would ever marry a Gentile. This was the only time I ever cheated on Joe, and since we've always been honest with each other, I told him. He freaked out. He started going out with someone else then, and we didn't see each other for seven months.

I enjoyed it when I was dating but you know how the grass is always greener on the other side of the fence. I found out that when you're just going out and having a good time, it's great, but when you need someone's shoulder to cry on, there's no one there. I also found out that a person is subject to lose a lot by looking farther down the pike. I don't want to risk what I've got by looking around anymore. Joe put me up on a pedestal, so I thought that I could keep looking but he could only turn to me. Then I found out that a lot of women would be happy to scoop him up. He was going out a lot. It shed a new light on it. Subconsciously everyone is looking. It's human nature.

Having the freedom now to see other people if I want to makes me feel that I don't have to. Having the ring and the commitments can make people feel trapped. Also, I think maybe his devotion to me made me feel that he wasn't that great. Maybe that made me want to look around. Yet no other man I've dated has even compared to him. So why don't I say, "Let's get married"? Why do I keep looking? I'm scared of what medicine does to people and their relationships. So many people who marry before they're finished with their residencies break up. And if you don't make commitments, you don't lose. I don't want to risk losing a good mate because there aren't that many good men out there. We are feeling the pinch now of waiting and we wouldn't make it another six years, so I will get married when I graduate. There! That's the first time I've been definitive about it. We can make it through the next three years and then we'll get married. That's pretty safe.

Mary states that one of the reasons she has postponed marrying Joe is because marriages contracted during professional training have a high failure rate. But premarital relationships like hers have a much higher probability of dissolving than do marriages, so if her sole motivation were to preserve the relationship, she would be inclined to marry. Of course, breaking up a premarital relationship may not appear to her to be as serious as breaking up a marriage, so perhaps her fear of divorce does contribute to her ambivalence. But her other statements make it clear that a major cause of her ambivalence has always been that she was not convinced that Joe was the best she could do. Although she appreciates his patience, understanding, and utter devotion to her, she recognizes that these very qualities caused her to take him for granted and to want to look around. She no longer saw him as a challenge. Although she made him wait for a year to have intercourse with her, she became sexually involved with another man soon after she entered medical school. She consciously attempted to enhance her chances of meeting someone in medical school by concealing her relationship with Joe and acting like a person who was unattached.

Mary tested her attractiveness on the market while hedging her bets by maintaining the relationship with Joe. If she failed to find someone else, there was always Joe. Although Joe had a business degree and a professional job and was basically acceptable, he was not a physician, and it could have been a long time before he acquired the income and status in his field, if he ever did, that she would acquire automatically by becoming an M.D. Mary may have underestimated Joe's attractiveness, however, or overestimated hers. While Joe and Mary were exercising their freedom to date, Mary began to notice a waning interest on Joe's part. He did not call as frequently or make the effort to get together on weekends. She suspected that he had found someone else and eventually drove to the city where he lived to find out for herself. Waiting outside of his apartment in her car, she saw Joe arrive with a very attractive woman on his arm. She walked up and confronted him, demanding to know who the woman was and what was going on. Joe's companion became upset and left. Joe explained that he had become seriously involved with this woman, was going to marry her, and since Mary and he had agreed that they could date other people, she had no right to complain. He later called her and told her that it was over. She was deeply disturbed by these events and thought that she had ruined a good relationship by insisting on looking around. For a time she had trouble getting involved with other men. The last we heard, she still had not married.

Men and women share many characteristics and traits, and women now successfully compete with men in almost every field and enterprise. But men and women continue to differ most radically precisely where evolutionary psychology predicts: in their sexual psychology. The different reproductive strategies of men and women have been a central feature of our evolution, and our sexual behavior and reproduction are mediated by our sexual psychology—the emotions, desires, fears, and aversions that motivate and channel our sexual behavior. For women, an essential component of sexual attractiveness is dominance—a sign that a potential mate has the wherewithall to outfox a foe and protect and provide for her and her children. When modern women use words like "challenge" to describe such a man, women are really playing out ancient rituals that have become unconscious—and even objectionable—to many in today's society. Some consider women's attraction to dominant men unliberated and obsolete. But dominance signals a man's ability to win the respect of his peers, meet life's challenges, and defend himself and his loved ones against their enemies. If a woman can garner such a man's investment, she enhances her own success and that of her children. For their part, men are uninterested in whether a woman is dominant or not. Dominance may make a women more interesting as a person, but it has little effect on her sexual attractiveness. In the next chapter, we will see how men's desire for a variety of sexual partners, and women's desire for dominant yet nurturant men, affects the stability of their marriages.

8

What Men and Women Want in Marriage

The concept of romantic love did not appear in Europe until the time of the thirteenth century troubadours, and these experts ruled at first that it was impossible to married people. Even as late as the eighteenth century it played a very small part in European marriage. All societies recognize that there are occasional violent emotional attachments between persons of opposite sex, but our present American culture is practically the only one which has attempted to capitalize these and make them the basis for marriage. Most groups regard them as unfortunate and point out the victims of such attachments as horrible examples.

—Ralph Linton, *The Study of Man*

The Evolution of Marriage

IN ALL SOCIETIES throughout history the fundamental basis of marriage has been a contract between two family lines that has assigned rights and duties concerning property and children. In a few preliterate societies an intense, emotional bond is expected to develop between husbands and wives, but even in these societies this bond is not the primary basis of marriage. In most traditional societies the exchange is quite clear: men and their families are expected to pay the bride's family for her procreative powers and domestic skills. The custom of dowry is relatively rare. Traditionally, in Europe a woman's dowry remained her property and provided for her in case she was widowed or otherwise left destitute. Dowries were not a payment to the groom's family for his fertility.[1]

In all societies, and until very recently in ours, a sexual division of labor existed. Women and men performed different tasks. Consequently, they were economically dependent on each other. In industrial nations this sexual division of labor has declined, and so has the sexes' interdependency.

Historian Edward Shorter describes marriages in preindustrial Western Europe as strictly economic affairs.[2] The primary purpose of the traditional family was to produce the next generation and transmit to it property, position, and knowledge. Family lineage was important. An individual's feelings, or being around the dinner table together as a family, were not important. Marriages were often without affection and were maintained by strict marital roles. Although some marriages were loving, this was not typical. If spouses fulfilled their economic roles adequately, their partners were expected to be content. One physician in eighteenth-century Germany estimated that about one marriage in a hundred was happy. When a peasant lad proposed marriage, the girl's father would inspect his family's resources, including the manure pile, as an index of the true size of his family's herd. Only when he thought the match was economically sound would he give his approval. Whether a couple found each other attractive was considered relatively unimportant. At best, the family offered the son or daughter two or three choices in a partner. Sexual freedom was similarly restricted.

Before the availability of the birth control pill, the fear of pregnancy severely inhibited sex outside marriage. Illegitimate children were a public shame and a private financial burden. Abortions were dangerous, illegal, or unavailable. Only the upper classes could afford to make a hobby of sexual affairs. In Western Europe prior to 1750, the chastity of young women was closely guarded. Courtship was strictly supervised by family and community. For example, in Northern Europe "night courting" was practiced into the eighteenth century. Groups of young men would walk through the village streets at night, stopping at various houses to talk to the eligible young girls, who would lean out of their windows. If a girl liked one of the boys, she would invite him in with her parents' permission. The young swain could go to her room, lie on top of the covers (while she was under the covers), and the couple could talk and get to know each other. If everything proceeded satisfactorily in further formal meetings, and the families and community approved, the couple could marry. Rarely, if ever, was there a chance for the couple to be alone and unsupervised. Premarital sex was kept at a minimum. Even as late as World War I, courting couples were supervised. If parents were against the match, there was usually no marriage.

Two sexual revolutions have occurred in Western history. Beginning in the eighteenth century, individuals' feelings toward each other became more important in partner choice. With the rise of industrial cities, parental supervision of youngsters became more difficult. The economic considerations of the family carried less weight, and children were more likely to reject their parents' choices. People were more mobile and could seek out the privacy necessary to explore each other's personalities—and bodies. Consequently, there was a drastic increase in premarital pregnancy between 1750 and 1850. This was the first sexual revolution.

The greater availability of effective contraceptives reduced premarital pregnancy rates between 1850 and 1940. After 1945 there was another increase in illegitimate births, but until the 1960s parts of the basic pattern remained: dating was still part of courtship; premarital and extramarital sex were socially unacceptable; and most people needed to get married and stay married. Divorce was not respectable.

When the pill was introduced in the 1960s, the second sexual revolution occurred. The enormous increase in premarital intercourse produced a commensurate increase in premarital pregnancy. It took several years for the effective use of the pill to reduce premarital pregnancy rates. In the 1970s and 1980s, the increase in premarital pregnancy shifted to teenagers.

The Industrial Revolution and technological development have obviated the sexual division of labor: today, most if not all jobs can be performed equally well by women or men. The pill, unisex jobs, and women's increasing economic independence have revolutionized relations between the sexes. And for the first time in history, marriage is not necessary for sex or economic survival.

As the sexes' economic interdependency declined in the nineteenth and twentieth centuries, the basis of marriage shifted, at least ideally, to that of romantic love: couples should stay together because they find each other attractive and love one another. A good marriage today is expected to provide exciting sex, companionship, economic security, and not hinder personal growth. These are high expectations. The present divorce rate suggests that for many people they are unrealistic.

Satisfaction in Marriage

Men and women now possess genuine alternatives to marriage, including the possibility of choosing to have a child out of wedlock. The sexes are therefore freer to express what they actually want in marriage and to leave it if their standards are not met. This greater freedom allows sex differences in marital goals to become more visible than in previous eras, when more couples stayed together out of necessity. Human beings are social animals, and both sexes need friendship, companionship, and love. Long-term relationships that are happy fulfill these needs for both partners. Men and women in such relationships are likely to report that they are each other's best friend, that they admire and esteem each other, and that they appreciate the loyalty and support they have received from their partners over the years. It is also true that most modern marriages still involve economic partnerships. This partnership may entail a traditional sexual division of labor, or a more equal division of household tasks, child care, and careers (see Chapter 9). But the ultimate goal of most of these partnerships, whatever their form, is to have children, raise them, and provide for them financially. Women and men often overlap in these goals and in their means of reaching them, and the greater the overlap, the happier the marriage. Even in happy, long-term marriages, however, men and women differ in their priorities, in the ways they love, and in the causes of their satisfactions and dissatisfactions. All of the sex differences we examined in previous chapters persist in contemporary marriages and affect their stability. Wives are more satisfied in marriages that offer high levels of emotional and material investment. Husbands are more satisfied in marriages that offer regular sex with a partner they find physically attractive.

Sexual gratification

The Kinsey researchers found that regular sexual gratification in marriage was a more central goal for men than for women. When men were dissatisfied with the sex they were receiving, they were more inclined to consider the marriage unsatisfactory and to feel justified in dissolving the relationship. Concerning marital goals, the Kinsey team wrote:

> The average female marries to establish a home, to establish a long-term affectional relationship with a single spouse, and to have children whose welfare may become the prime business of her life. Most males would admit that all of these are desirable aspects of a marriage, but it is probable that few males would marry if they did not anticipate that they would have an opportunity to have coitus regularly with their wives. This is the one aspect of marriage which few males would forego, although they might be willing to accept a marriage that did not include some of the goals which the average female considers paramount.[3]

Studies in the 1980s indicate that this sex difference is still very strong. A study of over 2,000 Canadian couples found that wives were more dissatisfied than husbands with every aspect of married life except sexual relations. Husbands were more dissatisfied with sexual relations.[4] Similarly, Blumstein and Schwartz found that in newly married couples only husbands' dissatisfaction with sexual relations correlated with breakup.[5] Heterosexual couples who were living together showed the same sex difference.

In 1984, columnist Ann Landers asked the women among her estimated 70 million readers if they would be content to be held close and treated tenderly, and forget about the sexual act? Over 100,000 female readers responded. Seventy-two percent of her respondents answered "yes," and 40 percent of those answering "yes" were under 40 years old.[6] Some of the women who answered in the affirmative explained that they enjoyed intercourse, but only when they were rested, in the mood, and intercourse was accompanied with tenderness and affection. Their male partners could more readily desire and enjoy intercourse without these conditions and this discrepancy was a common cause of marital strain.

Some popular authors have claimed that men's sex drive peaks at age eighteen whereas women's sex drive peaks in their thirties—implying that women over thirty have greater sex drives than men their age. These authors have misunderstood the Kinsey reports. Kinsey's findings on peaks reflect changes *within* each sex's lifetime rather than the relative strength of men's and women's sex drives.[7] Concerning relative drives of the sexes, the Kinsey studies established that men generally showed a greater need than women for a regular sexual outlet until their middle to late thirties, when the sexes tend to be about equal. By their fifties, women are more physiologically capable of sexual intercourse than most men their age, and by their seventies, there are many more women who are physically capable of intercourse than there are men. This does not necessarily mean, however, that women in their forties, fifties, or even sixties desire sexual intercourse more than do their male partners, or are as frustrated as men are when their sexual needs are not met. Women over 50 may be physically more capable than men their age, but they do not necessarily want sex more.

Recent improvements in the methods of measuring levels of sex hormones in the blood have revealed that sexual interest and activity correlate with testosterone levels in both men and women. Men show high levels of both sexual interest and testosterone levels from puberty to age 50, and only decline thereafter. In women a decline in testosterone levels has been observed between ages 20 and 35. Richard Udry and his colleagues analyzed data from the United States, Japan, Thailand, and Belgium.[8] The results from these four societies suggested that the decline in frequency of intercourse that occurs up to age 50 in most marriages is more a result of female age than of male age, and this decline is related to women's testosterone levels.

Jon is a 33-year-old psychologist who has been married for seven years. He describes how his satisfaction with his marriage is affected by the frequency of intercourse, by his wife's lesser interest in intercourse, and by her physical attractiveness.

Jon

My wife said, "If you're going to do this interview and you're going to complain about our sex life, just remember we had it four times this week!" She's five months pregnant, so considering that, I guess our sex life is pretty good now. There was a period after she had our first child when we didn't have sex that often. I guess I want to screw a lot more than she does. My ideal would be about once a day if I had my choice. But when I get tired, I don't care as much. We probably average two or three times a week.

Our main conflict is that she never initiates it. Once I initiate it, she usually gets into it, but often she doesn't care whether she has an orgasm or not, and I guess that's not getting into it as much as I would like. She never orgasms during intercourse. If she wants to have an orgasm, she'll tell me and I'll stimulate her manually or orally so she'll orgasm. And she will then. No question. But most of the time she doesn't tell me she wants to. She makes the decision. In other words, she's not as into it as I would like. It gets to be we don't spend a lot of time at it. It makes me feel like I'm just getting my rocks off and I don't like

that. Sex becomes routine for both parties. I'm always complaining
I'm not getting enough. I make a lot of jokes. She doesn't like me com-
plaining because it's implied criticism.

She seems to enjoy sex, though. She gets aroused and she's affec-
tionate. I tell her I love her, but I know I don't show her as much affec-
tion as she would like. On the other hand, she knows I find her
attractive. She knows she's attractive. She gets a lot of attention. When
I call her "fatty" or something, she doesn't take that too seriously. She
knows she's good looking, and I do find her attractive—even preg-
nant. So I think she understands.

Physical attractiveness

In a study of premarital couples, Bernard Murstein found that only for men
did the perceived physical attractiveness of partners correlate significantly
with their satisfaction with their relationships. Murstein then collaborated
with Patricia Christy in a study of middle-aged married couples.[9] Even in
long-term, stable marriages, husbands' marital adjustment correlated with
how attractive they thought their wives were, and the more the husbands
thought their wives exceeded themselves in physical attractiveness, the more
satisfied the husbands tended to be. Correlations between the wives' marital
satisfaction and their partners' physical attractiveness were not significant.

Blumstein and Schwartz report similar findings and conclude that the
value men place on physical attractiveness is an important part of male sexuality and that this emphasis affects their satisfaction with their partners.
Gay men also desire physical beauty in a partner. Only lesbian couples do not
let physical beauty affect their happiness with each other. When husbands
and heterosexual men who live with their partners place such great emphasis on having a good-looking partner, their relationships are less likely to
last beyond the first few years—presumably because for these men "the grass
is always greener elsewhere."[10] Men whose relationships are unstable
because they are constantly being attracted to other partners are men who
give in to these desires and have the opportunity to act on them.

Extramarital affairs

Ben is 42, divorced, and is now living with a woman to whom he is sexually faithful. Looking back, he describes how increased status and sexual
opportunities affected his previous marriage. Attaining national recognition
in his field, traveling widely, and teaching young women professionals
enhanced his attractiveness and expanded his sexual opportunities. Ben is no
Lothario. His background and moral training have made him sexually reticent. But the expansion of his opportunities unleashed his desires for sex
with a variety of young, physically attractive partners. He was not in love
with one woman; he was in love with several at the same time. Even though

he was not particularly successful in consummating his desires, he still wanted these women, and his lust for them had drastic effects on his marriage.

Ben

The two years my wife and I lived in Rhode Island were particularly bad. She could not get a job in her field, so she was pretty unhappy. Our sex life just dropped off to nothing. Part of it was that I was uninterested, but she was uninterested, too. I kind of wished I was having affairs, but I wasn't. While we lived there, I was chosen to direct a national training program for business managers. This sort of unglued me because I fell in love with about eighteen of the women in the group. I had plenty of gropes with them, but I don't think we ever fucked. That didn't make any difference, though. I was hook, line, and sinker for about three of these women. I thought of them constantly.

So I was the special fellow doing these training sessions and there was a sense of power in it. I traveled around a lot. I was the big honcho, the expert from back East. I was wined and dined wherever I was, and that made me very dissatisfied with my wife. There was all of this sexual opportunity; it was really wild. I could get whatever I wanted for the first time. It was the beginning of being able to fulfill a lifelong fantasy.

I also began to believe in my uniqueness. When I lived in New York City, I would go by a building 50 to 60 stories high and six blocks wide, and I would look in the tiny windows and feel that behind every tiny window was someone just like me. It's hard to be a big fish in New York, so I liked Rhode Island because I was the big fish. I stood out. Once you have made it, all you have to be is a nice guy. You don't have to prove you are good because everyone knows you are, and women come on to you instead of your having to convince them.

I felt really guilty about my philandering. I tend to be impotent with women the first time we try to make love anyway. I have all this guilt from my background—you know, the Jewish mother syndrome. But any woman who would bear with me after the first encounter would see a real improvement. My tendency to be impotent the first time was only accentuated by these random encounters, so sometimes I wouldn't even try to pick up women because I knew in advance it would be a bad scene. Also, I was not going to philander around where I lived. I did it elsewhere. The practical matter was that I was not much of a philanderer anywhere, but I was more interested in laying other women than my wife, and all these new opportunities made me even more dissatisfied with her.

Given men's tendency to wander, and given the availability of convenient, effective contraceptives, it is no wonder that extramarital affairs are prevalent.

And with this new freedom, women can now use their sexual favors in competition for higher-status men. Women who have ambitious careers are just as likely as women without careers to engage in this competition. As Ben discovered, married men are no longer off-limits for many women today. Ted is the management consultant we met in a previous chapter. He describes his reaction to temptations at the office.

Ted

I am a partner in a large consulting firm. There was an intern in the office whom I thought was very attractive, but I was happily married at the time and was not willing to initiate an affair. I think she overtly set one up though. She would take opportunities to lean over my desk and to make sure I would look down her blouse. She talked to me about very personal things and would bump against me suggestively. So one afternoon I put my hand on her back and turned her around and we started kissing. I got very excited and she said, "We can't do anything here." I said, "Oh, god, what can we do?" and she told me to sit down in the chair. She unzipped my pants and blew me right there. That was a surprise!

We got involved, but only in the office. She always wanted me to go to her apartment, or out to dinner, but I did not want to do that. I didn't want to get all involved with her and screw up my marriage. I'd say to her, "You shouldn't be doing this. You're not getting anything out of this." And she would say, "If you're my friend, you won't let me walk around being horny." Then she'd pull up her skirt and bend over the desk. I can't see how this was satisfying to her, but I think she was fascinated by the power she had over me. And me, hell, sometimes it was just too tempting to resist.

When he met her, Ted's lover had just graduated from a prestigious Eastern college for women and was earning her M.B.A. in a highly competitive program. Although she said that just having sex in the office was okay and that she did not want anything else, she tried to initiate more involvement by inviting him over to her apartment and out to dinner. She was progressing very rapidly in her own career, but she still was attracted to a married man who was more advanced than she, and she was willing to use her sexuality to entice him into a deeper investment. He resists making a deeper investment, but not the sex.

What people do often reveals more than what they say. When married women have affairs, they are usually seeking to improve on the emotional or material investments they already have—even when they are not clear themselves about their motives. Women whose husbands are financially successful often complain that they do not spend enough time together, their husbands do not really communicate with them or express enough affection.[11] These women miss the intense, emotional interchange and intimacy they enjoyed in the early stages of their relationships, and they seek this type of interchange and intimacy with their lovers. Women who do not feel their husbands measure up in terms of ambition and success tend to be attracted to men who could offer superior material investments. Some wives who have extramarital affairs state that their marriages are satisfactory and that they only want the excitement an affair can offer. Even in these cases, however, there is usually an element of disappointment or resentment that motivates their search for better quality investments.[12]

Jake is a 34-year-old, married professional.

Jake

Both of the affairs I've had were instigated by the women. One was this very forward secretary. She was young—nineteen or twenty. She just came up and invited me to a rock concert, so I went. She was cute. Not as good looking as my wife, but she was cute. She was single, she knew I was married, and she said she didn't want to break up my marriage. She just wanted an affair. She was very responsible about it—never called me at home. I just saw her a few times. All she wanted to do was smoke grass. I like to smoke a little bit, but it was a drag to some extent. Sex with her was not good. I think she had to get really stoned to get it on. She's a foolish girl, so I stopped seeing her.

My second affair was with a married woman who worked in the office. She came in and said something like, "I'm having trouble working on this report because I'm too concerned about your opinion of my work because I'm attracted to you." She's very responsible about it. She's got a kid, a good marriage. I've been seeing her sporadically for a few months. I don't want anything more, and if it interrupted or interfered with my marriage, I'd cut it off fast. I want to keep it, at most, limited.

I suppose the payoff for me is the excitement. Even though my wife is more beautiful than any of these women, sex in a marriage becomes routine. With this woman, it's great! We make it sometimes in the car. She's very limber. Incredible! Also outdoors. She comes in my office, and sometimes we can't really do that much because it's too risky, so she's perfectly satisfied to blow me and then leave. I can't believe it! I say to her, "That isn't fair to you. You're not getting anything out of this." She says she is. She claims her affair with me improves her marriage because when he does something she doesn't like, she feels she can put up with it, so she lets it go. It's like she's got something on him so she can tolerate things he does better. I suppose there's an element of revenge in it for her. Kinda' "tit for tat."

I feel real guilty about it and that's one reason I haven't seen her recently. It's like a betrayal of my marriage. It is a moral compromise and a lie, and it's kind of dangerous too. Also, it's already lost some of its excitement. The intensity of the first few times is gone already. I've considered cutting it off. I think I'll just keep it on hold—keep it intriguing.

For Jake the stimulus for infidelity seems to be the novelty, his partners' physical attractiveness, and their sexual performance. He feels guilty about his affair, but not enough to cut it off. Rather, his declining interest seems more due to the novelty wearing off. His married lover says that she has a good marriage and only wants an affair, but clearly part of her motivation is resentment toward her husband. Significantly, both of Jake's partners worked in his office, and were sleeping up by initiating affairs.

Researchers have consistently found that men are more likely than women to have sex outside their marriages, and adulterous men tend to have more partners than do adulterous women. Nevertheless, women's adultery is much more likely to lead to a breakup of the marriage. Blumstein and Schwartz outline two reasons for this sex difference. First, when a married woman is unfaithful, it usually means that she is dissatisfied with her marriage and is looking for alternatives. When a man has sex outside his marriage, it more often reflects a simple desire for sex with different partners. When sexual variety is his major motive, the man usually tries to avoid disrupting his marriage while he enjoys some variety on the side. Second, women tend to associate sex with emotional involvement more than men do and are therefore more likely to fall in love with their extramarital partners. Both of these female tendencies help to explain why women's adultery more often leads to divorce. Some adulterous women claim that they are satisfied with their marriages, bear no grudge against their husbands, and do not want serious involvements in their affairs. But even among such women their adultery is more likely to lead to divorce than is the adultery of men with comparable motives. Perhaps such women are rationalizing and really would like more involvement with their lovers, or they are more angry and dissatisfied with their husbands than they are willing to admit. But there is a third reason why women's adultery results in more breakups than men's adultery: men are less likely to tolerate their partners' infidelity, and when they discover it, they are more likely to act in ways that precipitate breakups.

Blumstein and Schwartz found that men were more likely than women to say that it would not bother them if their partners had sex with other people. Women tended to insist on sexual fidelity. This finding must be interpreted with caution. Although some men say they would tolerate their partners' infidelity, it is not clear they are more tolerant than women when confronted with the reality.

Jon is the psychologist we met earlier. He is educated, politically liberal, and does not think extramarital sex necessarily wrong. Before he discovered his wife's affair, he had thought that such a discovery would not bother him too much.

Jon

How did I find out my wife was having an affair? I'll tell you. It's a great story. Some guy had been calling for the last six months and saying it's a wrong number when I would answer. Same voice always, with a foreign accent. The last time he calls, I say, "This is not the right number! Who are you after?" because I'm getting a little pissed. Then the guy calls again, and he says, "Mr. Burns, I think we need to have a talk." I think, "Oh my God, who is this guy?" and he says, "I want to come by tomorrow and have a talk with you." So I tell my wife she should take the baby and get out of the house tomorrow because this guy is coming over and I don't know what he wants. She breaks down crying and confesses that she had had an affair with this guy and broke it off, and he threatened to tell me about it if she stopped seeing him. This guy is an asshole!

She started seeing him about a year after the baby was born. She met him at a bar where she was with her girlfriends. They even told me about it the night she met him. They were joking about how he kept pursuing her, so I knew his name. I even teased her about it at the time. Anyway, I finally met him because he followed us around. He would drive by the house three or four times a day. This guy is nuts, so I finally confronted him and told him to stay away. He was older, not an attractive guy, balding, uneducated. Different looking! So I asked her what she had seen in this guy. She said she thought it was funny at first, the way he kept pursuing her, but then she decided to go out with him. She said she liked the attention he paid her. I guess she didn't feel she was getting enough at home, and this guy really pursued her.

How did I feel at the time? That was the big one. I asked myself, "Seriously, am I going to break up my marriage over this?" Our marriage at that point was very good. The problems that we had been having six or eight months before had disappeared. That's the period when she was still seeing him. But she had cut it off a few months before I found out, so it was already over. Our marriage was good, and, then, my kid. What am I going to do, just throw both of them out? I'm really close to my kid. And there's another interesting thing. She's the person I'm closest to. Whenever you have something tragic happen to you, you want to be with the person you're closest to, even if the person you're closest to produces the tragedy. It's a real strange thing. And I find her really attractive, so that's another factor. So, I don't know. I wished I had thrown her out for a week. But then I said to her,

"Okay, but don't expect fidelity from me," and she realized she could-
n't then. She owed me one. I even teased her about it. I said I have so
many affairs coming because I had been faithful up to that point. It
wasn't that I objected, that I thought it was morally wrong or terrible
for her to be unfaithful. That wasn't it. But the whole idea that I'm
home taking care of the kid, and she's out screwing this guy!

One time she was out late in the morning and I called the police. I
thought, "Where the hell could she be?" She said she was out with the
girls and I fell for it. It's unbelievable! I was suspicious at times, but she
always seemed so innocent. You know, its incredible how stupid I was,
and I'm not going to be that stupid again! I would not say I wouldn't
have had an affair if she hadn't done that. I probably would have had
one anyway. I just never pursued it before. Now if an opportunity
comes up, I'll do it. I feel I've got the right to now.

Jon was suprised at his gut reaction to his wife's affair. The thought of her
making love with someone else enraged him and made him want to throw
her out. His decision not to do this was based on several considerations. His
wife is very physically attractive and he knows it. Her lover is homely and
uneducated and does not present a threat to the marriage. She only wanted
the attention because she was not receiving enough at home—an excuse that
Jon does not reject. She had already cut off the affair several months before
and they had been getting along very well since then. Perhaps most important, he values his family life and does not want to lose it. Beneath his surface
acceptance, however, is the anger and the feeling that he is now justified in
doing what he wanted to do all along: have sex with other women.

Women vary a great deal in their reactions to partners' infidelity. Gloria
is the divorced businesswoman we met in Chapter 7. She describes her reactions to her husband's infidelities.

Gloria

My ex-husband was always very sexually active outside the marriage,
but I was unaware of this for a long time. I guess I was living in a vac-
uum. However, I saw men at work who were having affairs, and how
they behaved, so I knew the tip-offs and recognized them when my
husband began having an affair with his secretary. I think this was a
deviation from his normal pattern, which was one-night stands. He
would talk about his secretary in a manner that showed a little too
much concern. I sensed he was getting more and more distant and less
communicative. He was drinking more. I never said anything to him
about it. I figured he was under pressure and this was one of the ways
he blew off steam. Then I found out he was sleeping with the house-
keeper too, and this forced a confrontation.

He wouldn't admit to any of this stuff, and he refused to see a counselor. He just wanted a divorce. At that point I moved out and the secretary moved in, and I thought, "Good!" because I knew it wouldn't last very long if they lived together. Once you live with someone the romance dies. Dirty laundry and dishes and morning breath tend to destroy all illusions.

She wanted to marry him, so when I would call the house to discuss the separation with him, she would be very nasty to me. I really felt no malice toward her; she was just protecting her interests. And then she found out he was three-timing her too, with a cute 19-year-old waitress at a local restaurant. At that point my husband was trying to do me in in the divorce settlement by hiding his stocks and business interests. Being his secretary, she knew about that and called and asked for a meeting. I complied and when we met, she told me the story of the waitress. She said she also found numbers of a lot of other women in his bureau drawers. I asked her what had she expected—that he would change? If he was two-timing me, why wouldn't he do the same thing to her? Anyway, she had brought the xeroxed documents of his latest shady business dealings. He tried to contest them when we got to divorce court, but he didn't have much luck. I had the goods on him. So both she and I got back at him in a very pointed way. It cost me three years and $30,000 in attorney's fees to do it, though.

Gloria was willing to ignore what she thought was an isolated case of infidelity. Only when she found out that he was sleeping with the housekeeper too did she force a confrontation. Even then, she was apparently still willing to discuss it and try to work it out with a therapist, which he refused to do. Ultimately, she and the secretary were able to avenge his treatment of them.

Roger is a 40-year-old surgeon with an annual income of around $600,000. During his long training and the years it took to establish his practice, he was completely caught up in his work and was usually so fatigued when he came home at night that he had little to give his family—although he tried to be as good a husband and father as he could. He was 37 by the time he was fully established in his profession and he began to wonder whether it had all been worth it. His marriage had improved in the last few years, but conflicts over the years had created tensions and he and his wife led separate lives in some respects. In the following passage he describes how an affair with his secretary gave him a new lease on life.

Roger

I had been in a funk for some time: really starting to feel depressed, physically slowing down, uninterested in a lot of things. A few years ago I started thinking, "Is this what you worked so hard for: more work, the same old routine?" It didn't seem worth it. But in the last couple of years, that's begun to change. I can accomplish a lot more on automatic pilot now and still do it well. I'm realizing I have money. I can have fun! I'm not a student now, or a junior partner trying to establish a practice. I'm a real person! If I had known back then that it was possible to have this much fun, I would have done it then, but I didn't have it all together.

When my secretary was first hired, she said something about her husband being gone a lot, and I started getting this quivering between my legs. But nothing ever came of it until the other day. We chatted briefly after work, and she made a few lightly suggestive comments, so when I came in the next day, she gave me a big smile and I asked her to have lunch with me. It was like a great big flag came up and said, "Hey, here I am!" So by lunch we were already making plans to get together. The problem is, we have no place to go. She thinks motels are tacky, so we're trying to arrange with friends to use their place during the day. The first time we had a picnic in the country—by a little stream. It was great!

Her motivation is that she's bored. Her kids are grown up and her husband is kind of a clod with a nowhere job. Her marriage isn't exciting to her at all but she has never made a move to get out. She's convinced that my marriage must be bad or I wouldn't be messing around with her. She wants to be Number One in my life and I've had to make it clear to her that she's number three on my list: my family, my career, and then her. I don't feel the same way at all that she does.

All my life I've wanted to have affairs but I think I haven't acted on this more out of a sense of inadequacy than from a sense of guilt. For a great part of my marriage my wife didn't feel that I gave her enough love. This made me feel inadequate. She constantly complained that I didn't have enough time for her, enough energy, and I couldn't do anything about it. I took the energy I had left and I gave it to her and it was seldom enough. This made me feel like a cold, unloving person and that not many people would be able to put up with me. I felt that she was the only person in the world that would work for me because I was simply inadequate. It was a circular process: I didn't feel good enough about myself to give her enough to make her feel good enough to give me anything. She got love from the kids, who were also driving her crazy and I had nothing but my school, which was giving me absolutely nothing.

With my girlfriend it's different. She gets so excited about me, it's really an ego trip. For the first time I feel that I really have valuable personal qualities that allow me honestly and sincerely to feel and say things that make another person feel good. I can give and receive emotionally. I thought I would have a horrible guilt trip about this and I haven't. It's just been fun, pure fun! I have much more confidence and a lot more energy, and I feel just enough guilt that I'm more attentive to my wife. She says I'm great now because I'm much more affectionate. Our sex life had improved over the last few years, but since I started having an affair, it's been even better. I still love my wife more than my girlfriend, but sex with my wife is not as exciting in the same way because it's not new. On the other hand, it's very gratifying to come home to that security, go to bed, and get up and go to work the next day. It feels right.

I guess that's one of the reasons that I have no desire to split up my marriage. It's a cold, cruel world out there. I can't imagine a world that could be as satisfying as what I have. I've just never met anybody who's changed my mind about that. My wife and I have been through an awful lot together—just the sheer weight of time and experience. It's true that I probably couldn't have done it without her and the kids. So I feel she's entitled to share it with me now.

About two months after this interview, Roger's wife came home very late. While awaiting her return, he made several phone calls and established that she was not where she was supposed to be, and none of her friends had seen her. He confronted her with his suspicions and she finally confessed that she had been skiing with her lover and had gotten stuck in a snow bank where they had stopped to make love. He was very angry and his anger only increased when he discovered that her affair had predated his. Although she denied that she had had other lovers, her manner led him to believe that she had. He had been faithful for seventeen years of marriage, always feeling guilty and inadequate because he was not able to give her enough emotional support. The thought of this enraged him and made him feel justified in not confessing his affair at this time. Their emotional confrontation continued all night and finally climaxed in passionate lovemaking.

For the next few months Roger felt that this experience had brought them closer together, and their sex life was definitely better than ever before. But he became even less willing to end his own affair. About one year after their confrontation, he and his wife separated and eventually became involved in a bitter dispute over the property settlement. Looking back he observes:

I thought at first that having affairs and then confronting all the problems we had had strengthened our relationship, but obviously it didn't. The whole thing began to unravel after I found out about her affair. My affair was making me feel more confident and I was no longer willing to put up with all the shit I had taken all those years. About four or five times in our marriage we got into arguments and it escalated to the point where she would say, "Okay, I've had it! Just get your stuff and

get out." I would always back down because I was afraid she was
right: there really was something wrong with me and I would never get
anybody as good as her again. Well, I don't feel that way anymore, and
she couldn't play the martyr and make me feel guilty anymore. So the
next time we had an argument and she said, "I've had it!" I didn't
back down and that was it. I moved out. Later I found out that she had
talked to an attorney before that, so she knew exactly how much she
could get in a settlement, and she wasn't going to back down either.

Fear and guilt played an important part in keeping Roger sexually faithful
and willing to compromise over the years. His lover made him feel confident
and lovable, and this undermined his wife's ability to control him through
guilt and fear. When he discovered his wife's affair, and that she had probably
had others over the years, his wife lost her moral leverage. Her ability to make
him feel guilty was undermined. He would no longer acquiesce to her demands
and complaints, and he felt completely free to satisfy his long-suppressed
desires for sex with partners who made him feel good about himself.

When women and men forgive a partner's adultery, they do so for similar
reasons: to preserve what is otherwise a good relationship, for the sake of the
children, and because they do not think they could get a better partner anywhere else. But the ultimate sexual desires of men and women differ. The ultimate desire of most women is to have a long-term, sexually exclusive
relationship with a man who offers high levels of both emotional and material investment, whereas investing both materially and emotionally in one
woman is not the ultimate fantasy of most men. On the contrary, this type of
relationship represents a basic compromise of the ultimate male fantasy,
which is to spread his investments among several women in return for their
sexual favors. Consequently, when men discover that their wives have been
unfaithful, they are more likely than their wives to feel that they have been
paying too high a price in their marriages—after all, all this investment and
monogamy stuff wasn't their idea in the first place! They begin to feel that all
the investments and compromises they have made in order to keep the marriage together have been for nothing, and they become less willing to make
these compromises and investments in the future—particularly the compromise of their desire for sexual variety. This male reaction is another reason
why women's infidelity is more likely to lead to breakups than men's infidelity. But there is an explanation that goes deeper than all of these reasons
and subsumes them.

In a provocative article, Martin Daly, Margo Wilson, and Suzanne
Weghorst argue that men are innately more *sexually* jealous than women.[13]
Throughout history men have attempted to control women's sexual behavior
through laws and customs, physical violence, clitoridectomy, infibulation,
and physical isolation. Crossculturally and historically a married woman's

sexual infidelty has been considered a greater breach that that of a man, and the husband of the unfaithful woman is considered the victim. Whether the woman's lover is married or not is relatively unimportant. Police records in the United States suggest that male sexual jealousy is the primary cause of most homicides. Similarly, psychological and psychiatric studies in the United States indicate that men's jealousy focuses on the act of intercourse itself. Jealous men tend to run graphic, tortured fantasies of their female partners having sex with other men and these sexual fantasies often provoke fantasies of retaliatory violence. This reaction can occur even in educated middle-class males with no history of actual violence.[14] In comparison, women's jealousy focuses more on the threat of losing the relationship, and on their partner's investing time, money, and affection in someone else. These sex differences in the quality, experience, and reactions to sexual infidelity appear to be cross-culturally universal. There are some non-Western societies whose official rules concerning adultery treat men and women equally, and this is also the case now in the United States. But even in societies where adultery rules treat the sexes equally, and retaliation by either sex is discouraged or punished, men are more likely than women to focus on the act of intercourse as the core of the transgression and to react with physical violence. After an exhaustive analysis of diverse bodies of literature, Daly and Wilson conclude that men are more biologically predisposed than women to guard, defend, and control the sexual behavior of their mates. A brief introduction to the concept of paternity confidence explains why men act this way.[15]

In most species, females are more certain than males that their offspring are truly theirs. This is particularly true of species in which the mother carries the young inside her before birth. Most male mammals, however—for example, dogs, stags, or stallions—can never be certain that they are the fathers of offspring born months later, because other males may have succeeded in inseminating their mates before or after they did. On the other hand, these males invest nothing directly in the offspring, but instead try to insure their paternity by keeping other males away while they are breeding with the females who are in heat. In those species where confidence in paternity is low, males have evolved an amazing and often amusing variety of tricks and tactics to beat out other males in the mating competition and to increase their chances of being the only ones to inseminate their mates.

Human males face a slightly different problem because women do not come into heat but are potentially sexually receptive year around, and their periods of fertility are not marked by any obvious outward signs, as they are in most species. Consequently, men face a huge problem in trying to make certain that a child is theirs—particularly if they feel they are investing a great deal in a woman and her offspring. A woman always knows her children are her own, even if she is not sure who the father is. A man never knows with the same degree of certainty. It is something he must take on faith if he trusts his mate. Alternatively, he may try to guard his mate, keep other males away, and retaliate when he feels that his exclusive access to his partner is threatened.

Daly and Wilson suggest that there is a deep-seated, biological reason why men are reluctant to invest in women whose behavior makes them less certain that any children produced would be theirs. Men's desire to insure paternity also explains the value that so many societies have placed on female virginity, and the fact that female promiscuity is almost always considered more reprehensible than male promiscuity. Even in societies like Samoa and Mangaia, which permitted both sexes a good deal of sexual freedom, a man who had many sexual conquests was admired and envied—particularly when his conquests included many virgins (see Chapter 10). In contrast, a woman who allowed herself to be seduced by many men was considered foolish and was the object of ridicule or punishment. Men who have sexual access to many women are often admired because this access is taken as proof that they have the social status and skill to persuade these women to have sex with them. In comparison, any woman can have as many men as she wants, as long as she is not too choosy about the quality of investments they make. The sexual double standard is really just another example of the basic law of supply and demand: some assets are more valuable than others. Those who can acquire the most valuable assets are considered clever or powerful. Those who give away valuable assets too cheaply are considered foolish. Male sexuality will always be "cheaper" than female sexuality because men want sex more and will give it away. Women want sex with investment.

Daly and Wilson's argument does not imply that in modern societies like ours a sexual double standard is either inevitable or desirable. But it does suggest that a kind of informal double standard may persist in these societies even when their formal rules and laws treat the sexes' sexual behavior equally. It also suggests something else—that men who state that they do not care whether their female partners have sex outside their relationships either do not understand women's sexuality and the risk they are taking of losing their partners, or they are not investing very much in their partners and so are indifferent to these risks.

Although women's adultery is more likely to lead to divorce than men's adultery, most wives are hurt and angry when they discover their husbands have been unfaithful. Patricia has been married for fifteen years and has three children. She is presently finishing her training to be a physical therapist. She describes her reaction to her husband's affair.

Patricia

I don't think an outside relationship would mean very much to my husband. I'm the end of the line for him; he hasn't got the energy or the desire to get involved in something on the outside. I guess if he were at a convention he might fall into bed with someone. Well, that happened, and it bothered me; it sure did bother me. It was with a person that he met at a conference, and he followed up seeing her in New York. At that time he was going to New York weekly, and was staying with a friend of mine. I called up one night and he wasn't there; he was in the Bronx,. I knew this person he met was from the Bronx, so I put two and two together. That's how it came out.

That was about seven years ago. Theoretically, I think extramarital affairs are fine as long as they don't interfere with the marriage, but I felt crummy when it happened. I felt he owed me an apology and he didn't think that he did. I guess he didn't owe me one. What he did on his own time was his business, basically, as long as it didn't interfere with our relationship. I don't think it interfered with our relationship. I never saw this person as a threat. If he got involved with somebody that I saw as a threat to myself, that might be a different case. He promised to stop seeing her because he wasn't involved with her. I met her one time at a party and I felt on top of the world because she wasn't that great, and I had my husband and she had no one.

It would take something monumental to make us get divorced at this point, not because we're so bound together, but because it would be such a hassle to extricate ourselves from this family relationship. I grew up with a very strong sense of family that I love and appreciate. I think the family is a very special thing, and my husband is wonderful with the kids and my parents. If I got divorced tomorrow, where would I meet somebody like that? I couldn't even imagine. To do the bar scene would be absurd at this point, but where else would you meet people? First of all, the competition would be with 19-year-old Christie Brinkley types and I'm 35, so there's no way I'm going to compete with them. Second of all, it just doesn't seem feasible. I don't have the free time to sit in bars. Also there's the security factor. It would be a real concern of mine that if I did go home with somebody, he could turn out to be a Jack-the-Ripper type. You read Looking for Mr. Goodbar, didn't you? There are a lot of crazy people out there.

Patricia was willing to forgive her husband's infidelity because, all things considered, he had been an excellent husband. He is very involved with their children, who in turn are very involved with both sets of grandparents. Her husband promised to break off with his lover and never see her again, so Patricia is not sufficiently angry or threatened to destroy this intimate network of family relationships over this one incident. In making this decision, she is also aware of her options. She does not feel that she could replace him in the current dating-mating market, and the thought of trying to compete in this market at her age is not appealing. She is also not yet self-supporting, and even when she is, she knows that she could never maintain the standard of living after a divorce that she and her children have enjoyed up to now. Her feeling that she could probably not replace her husband's material and emotional investments with something equal or better influences her reaction to her husband's infidelity, and her decision to forgive and forget.

Replacing Male Investments

The divorce rate has almost tripled since 1960 and has now leveled off at around 40 percent, depending on what part of the population one examines. But the rate has leveled off largely because more people are postponing marriage and remarriage; this tendency limits the number of married people who could divorce.[16] Given today's high divorce rate, some researchers have begun to use a market model to study marital breakup. Traditional models assumed that married people were outside of the dating-mating market. The factors that led single people to marry were assumed not to operate for those already married because they were not available as potential partners. The new market model assumes that married persons are subject to the same attractions and temptations as single people. In other words, if a more attractive person shows up, and this person is available, a married person might be just as likely as a single individual to date and marry the new attractive person. There are still people who hold their marriages sacred and inviolable, and who are not available, even if the attraction is very great. But the market model of marriage explains the behavior of a great many people today.

Applying a market model, sociologist Richard Udry found that how people rated their marriages did predict to some extent whether their marriages were likely to last.[17] But a much better predictor of breakup was a person's perceived alternatives. In other words, some married individuals might have good marriages by other couples' standards, but if they think that they do not need their spouses anymore, or that they can replace their spouses with someone better, they are likely to break up. Sally is a case in point. She is 27, divorced, and works part-time. When she finishes her degree program, her starting salary should be about $30,000. Her ex-husband was progressing rapidly in his career, so she could not complain about his potential for material investment. It was his ability to invest emotionally that was sorely lacking. His devotion to his career caused him to neglect the emotional aspects of marriage. But like most men, the communication and emotional support his wife desired did not come easily to him. Even if he had not been so dedicated to his career, he still might not have known what his wife wanted and been able to give it to her.

Sally

The biggest problem in the marriage was that he was never at home.
He was involved in training personnel, so he might have a class until

nine or so, and when he came home, he was exhausted. He might be physically there with his body, but he was either napping, or taking a bath, or watching TV. His job was real exciting for him and it took a lot of energy, so when he was home, he was pretty tuned out to me. A lot of times he would be so busy with other things he wouldn't even show up for dinner. Sometimes I would call him at the office and tell him it's seven o'clock and dinner is ready and he would say, "Oh, I forgot to tell you: I'm kind of involved here and I won't be home." I would just think, "Oh! Now what?" It was hard for me to accept that he would just forget to call or come home, and when I found other ways to use my time, he seemed really happy. He wasn't this way in the first part of our marriage. He needed nurturance then too, but by the time we moved from Resort City, I was working six days a week and my day off didn't coincide with his. He said that was great because he could go and do all those things on his day off that I didn't like to do: meeting people, making contacts. I was pretty upset because right then I knew our relationship was going nowhere.

I gravitate now toward people who are more expressive of their feelings. My ex-husband couldn't deal with feelings at all. When I found out my father was terminally ill, my ex had been gone for a week on a job, so I was waiting all day for him to come home so I could tell him. When he heard it, he said, "I've got to go to this meeting in fifteen minutes. Is there anything I can do? Do you feel bad?" I said, "Wouldn't you if it were your father?" He said "okay" and left. Later he said that I should have asked him to stay home. Maybe I should have, but somehow I don't feel responsible for being totally on the ball at that moment. It was like I really needed him just to stay home and hold me. My friends told me my husband just has no experience with intimacy. He didn't grow up around it, he doesn't have any training in it, and he doesn't know how to do it. I think they were right, and I think that's really what broke up our marriage.

I wondered sometimes, all those late evenings, whether he was really just out with the boys? But I checked it out with other people, and it looked like he always was where he said. He was so uncomfortable anyway with things that were intimate that I felt that he had enough trouble with me, let alone another woman. He just never seemed to lean toward that. I think he really was married to his career. I did have other relationships though—after it got bad and I felt really neglected. I didn't like it, being involved with two men at the same time. I felt very weird about it. But it did help me make a decision because I could see that it could be different. There are caring, loving men in the world. There are alternatives.

After we moved here and I entered school, things really began clicking for me. I met a lot of supportive people and felt nurtured for a change. So when he wanted to move again, I just said, "What's in it for me? We don't get along anyway. I am not leaving a house we bought three months ago, pulling up everything I have put together here and starting all over again. It's just not worth it."

It's ironic because after we separated, my husband was living in another city and I flew in there on my way to visit my parents. He met me at the airport with roses and said, "I want to give you all the love I never gave you. I am sorry about the last three years but I have just seen the light. I have just found out what life is all about." I said, "Oh, shit!" I sort of knew it was coming because he was in a men's consciousness raising group and I knew that's what he would hear from the group. I just said, "No, I am dating a few guys at home. I am happy; my life is good. I do not want to get back into that relationship." I laughed, and he was standing there crying. It was awful. I couldn't stand what was happening either. I couldn't stand dating these other guys and my husband calling me. I wasn't getting anything done. Too much was going on inside me. It was too late. It was over.

Sally was seriously dissatisfied with her marriage for several years. But only when she believed she could replace her husband's emotional and material investments did she decide to get out. Her lovers and new friends convinced her that there were alternatives to the emotional deficiency of her marriage. Going back to school and working on a degree that would increase her earning power helped to convince her that she could survive without her husband's income. She also did not want to give up the house she and her husband had just bought, and she received this house in the divorce settlement.

We have seen that modern technology, convenient contraceptives, and the decline of the sexual division of labor allow contemporary men and women greater freedom to decide what they really want in marriage, and to leave if they are not satisfied. This means that modern marriages that last are probably much better than most marriages in previous eras.[18] But these freedoms have also made modern marriages more vulnerable to disruption. In Chapter 9, we will see that women and men differ in their vulnerabilities in marriages, and in the times when they are most vulnerable.

Who Does the Diapers and the Dishes?

The Domestic Division of Labor

> In sociology . . . it is easy to forget that the basic facts of family life con-
> sist in the coming together of people with physical bodies to mate, to
> reproduce, and to rear the young. . . . Just as the sexual script, so the par-
> enting script in the new family sociology seems to be modeled on what has
> been a male pattern of relating to children, in which men turn their father-
> ing on and off to suit themselves or their appointments for business or sex-
> ual pleasure. . . . In my judgment, by far the wiser course to such a future
> is to plan and build from the most fundamental root of society in human
> parenting, and not from the shaky superstructure created by men in that
> fraction of time in which industrial societies have existed.
>
> —Alice Rossi, *A Biosocial Perspective on Parenting*

ECONOMIC ANTHROPOLOGIST MARVIN HARRIS explains the women's movement of the 1960s and 70s in terms of the gradual erosion of the family as an
economic unit.[1] With the rise of industrial cities, children became economic
liabilities rather than assets because they were no longer needed for domestic labor, as they had been in rural settings. In urban societies, children may
not be present or willing to care for parents in old age, and developing technology required more education for adult work, so the cost of children, both
real and as investments for the future, increased. Progress in medicine led to
reduced child mortality, so couples could have fewer children and be relatively sure that they would survive.

In the last two centuries in Europe and the United States, the decade from
1940 to around 1950 was the only one when the birth rate was not declining slowly and steadily. The baby boom decade was partly the result of the
fact that 14 million World War II veterans received insurance and housing
benefits that greatly reduced the costs of marriage and children, therefore
increasing the marriage and birth rates between 1940 and 1957.

The influx of women into the labor market and a radical decrease in the
birth rate began in 1957—seven years before the pill became widely available—and this preceded the women's movement. The increase of working
women depressed the birth rate because group child care was not adequate
and because the cost of children rose. At first, married, middle-class women

worked so they could buy luxury items, but the inflation of the 1960s made a second income necessary for many couples if they were to manage a middle-class lifestyle. Married and single women continued to work because of inflation and because there were fewer men with incomes sufficient to support families adequately. According to Harris, women rebelled because they were trapped in boring, dead-end jobs at work with lower pay than men, and saddled with domestic tasks and chauvinistic husbands at home.

It is a mistake to think that the role of housewife and mother was always as powerless and devalued as it is today. In a detailed analysis, historian Susan Strasser documents that before food, blankets, and clothes were mass produced, a woman could take pride in her ability to provide these essential goods for her family and could earn respect for her fine quilts, clothes, and culinary achievements.[2] Her domestic activities were economically essential, and they often brought her in contact with other women. For example, as late as 1893, only the wealthy used canned goods. Food preparation was therefore a major and necessary activity. An average of one hour a day was spent on oven care alone. An increase of wage labor allowed more people to buy goods formerly made at home, and the improvements in technology allowed these goods to be produced more cheaply. By 1900 more women had entered the labor market leading to a greater need for manufactured goods. More efficient heating, and the introduction of the washing machine and later the dryer, further reduced family members' interdependency in maintaining the household and increased the social isolation of housewives.

Home technology and manufactured goods devalued the role of housewives because they reduced the importance of household tasks. The housewife who did nothing else could teach nothing else to her children, and in any case, schools had already assumed the major part of education for most families. Strasser argues that women's suffrage in the early twentieth century and the women's movement in the 1970s for equal opportunity and income in the labor market can be viewed as responses to this gradual erosion of the importance of traditional family tasks.

Cross-culturally, wherever family and kinship ties have economic and political importance, children are economic assets, and the tasks performed by women are economically indispensable—women enjoy respect and exercise power, although they may operate in a separate sphere from men and exercise power through different channels. This is true even in societies that are supposedly bastions of male chauvinism—such as rural Guatamala and Greece, and patrilineal tribes in Africa.[3]

Wives' Vulnerability

In modern society a wife who is completely financially dependent on her husband is in an extremely vulnerable position because her services can be bought relatively cheaply, whereas his paycheck is indispensable. If she has no marketable skills and he leaves her, her financial situation can be bleak indeed. She may have no alternative but to acquiesce to traits she finds undesirable for the sake of security. Young women are aware of the risks involved in depending on a man—particularly if they believe their mothers were in a degraded position. In the following interview Sharon explains that she wants financial independence so she will never have to put up with what her mother did. Sharon is a college senior and plans to have a professional career:

Sharon

My mother didn't work. I don't know why. Maybe she didn't have to; maybe everything was given to her— by her parents before she was married and by her husband after she got married. I think if you never have to think for yourself, you don't have any drive. I want to have a nice life for myself, contribute, and not be dependent on someone else for everything. I can be independent. I will never put up with the shit my mother put up with!

I never felt my life was normal or that I was normal because my parents don't get along well. My father goes out playing golf and drinking at the country club until late hours. I felt bad for my mother because she was not having any fun other than to go to the grocery store and stuff like that. I felt they were going to split up last summer but it got better when winter came.

It is going to start all over again this summer. I don't think they are the typical family. There is a lot of hostility in the house and lack of respect for my mother from the kids. Everybody goes their own way. There is no organization. My brothers are always fighting; my father is getting mad and yelling at my mother, belittling her. My siblings talk back to my mother too, and call her names like "bitch" and stuff like that. She doesn't use that kind of language at all, doesn't get mad, but she just threatens to leave and nobody takes her seriously. Of course, she doesn't have a car and has no way to get around. There is no joy in the house, just bad atmosphere.

I think part of the problem was that there was never any discipline; the boys were never made to pitch in and help with the chores. My father, when he was home, was out there in the corner in his easy chair reading his paper. I believe a man's first responsibility is to be successful in his job, but he's also got family responsibility. He's got to devote some time to them instead of just coming home and sitting down and reading the newspaper, eating dinner, and watching the ball game. While the kids are young there's time during the day and weekends he should spend with them. It's important when they are growing up.

I don't see my future husband playing a big part in raising kids, although it would be nice if he would. I think the first few years of a kid's life are very important to give the kid a sense of security and confidence. In the future I don't know whether I'll stay home with the kids when they are little. My mother did, but I'm trying to resolve that for myself now.

Julia is 35, divorced, has three children, and now works full time. She was raised in an Italian-American family with a traditional division of labor: her father brought home the money; her mother managed the household and received respect and support for her efforts. Julia's marriage was not like this. She was vulnerable to abuse because she was financially and emotionally dependent on her husband and he did not value her efforts.

Julia

I had no help from my husband with what I had to do at home or with the children. He should have been there to help with their homework in the evenings and that sort of thing. The kids wanted some of our time, like to play games or do things as a family, but we had no family. We got so that we never had dinner together because my husband would never come home at a certain time. Eventually he said, "I don't want dinner; feed the kids, and I will eat when I come home." It sat in the oven. Sometimes he came home, and sometimes he didn't. So I finally got to the point where I just made a smaller dinner for the children because they didn't appreciate the traditional meal anyway. Then there was no family relationship; we never sat down as a family and talked to each other.

My husband never consulted me about major purchases. With the refrigerator, I got a little of the say-so, but I never made a decision pricewise. I resented that too. I wanted to learn how to shop for a car and make the decision. I always got the car that he finished with; he always got the new car. That drove me nuts after a while; it really did. [Laughter] I got the car with the problems, and it made my life more difficult. Once I had to have it fixed and I was without a car for five days. He said that it was my fault because I must have misused it. He used to show me the budget and say this is what I make and I can't take out any more than that. I didn't feel he gave me enough grocery money and enough for my personal needs. Finally, he gave me my own checking account and an allowance to pay for groceries and so forth. But as inflation went along, that amount of money no longer bought what I needed. When I asked him for more, he wasn't willing to give it. He said, "No matter how much I give you, you are going to go through it, so you are going to have to learn to live on that budget."

My husband was a very power-driven businessman. When he wasn't working, he liked to be with his men friends because they made him feel good about himself. He just couldn't handle me and the kids— the emotional support that we needed. Even when I was sick he wouldn't pamper me. He would say, "Okay, go to bed if you're sick." I think he thought I was a hypochondriac, and I was doing that for attention, although he never gave me the attention. So I accepted it, but there were times when I would be in bed sick, and he would come home, and never come in that room to see if I needed anything. This is when I would really be sick, not just a cold. One time I had to call my mother to ask her to call him to get him to come into the bedroom to help when I was really ill. Does that tell you anything?

I need for the man in my life to want to be with me, to be a friend and a companion who wants to share time with me—not just put me in the house and expect me to shut up and work. He never said, "Gee, I think that's neat that you are home cooking dinner for me when I come home." I got just the other side of the story: "I don't really want to be here for dinner; it really doesn't matter if you cook for me; what you're doing isn't really important; I expect that from you 'cause you're my wife; I pay your bills and I expect you to take care of my children, cook dinner, and do the laundry. But that doesn't mean that I have to be here to share it with you; that's your job."

Julia felt degraded because her husband rejected her emotionally and humiliated her financially. She was also vulnerable because being a housewife isolated her from the community. Prior to World War II, most people still lived in small towns, and women were surrounded by relatives and friends. Even in large cities women often had kin nearby, knew some of their neighbors well, and were able to share knowledge and help each other with domestic chores. This is still true of some ethnic neighborhoods today. The middle-class movement to the suburbs and the rise of apartment living destroyed this pattern. People are more mobile now, and are therefore less likely to have relatives nearby or to establish helping relationships with neighbors or friends. Contemporary women are thus much more isolated and vulnerable than their grandmothers were.

In the last twenty years a huge popular and academic literature has accumulated on the domestic division of labor. The dominant message in most of this literature is that the role of housewife traps women in a boring, degrading existence which has many costs and few rewards. The traditional division of labor is viewed as obsolete, reactionary, and oppressive, while dual-career marriages in which domestic chores and child care are shared equally are viewed as egalitarian and fair—the so-called equal-partner marriage.[4] Criticisms raised about traditional marriages and advocacy of equal-partner marriages are understandable reactions to the vulnerability of the modern housewife. But those who proclaim the virtues and essential rightness of equal-partner marriages make several assumptions, all unfounded.

The first assumption is that the division of labor in marriages is determined by husbands' and wives' attitudes toward sex roles, and a major determinant of these attitudes is the type of household in which a person grew up. Individuals whose mothers do not work supposedly grow up with more traditional attitudes and have a more traditional division of labor in their own marriages. Contrary to this assumption, in my sample of medical students, women whose mothers worked were more willing to work part-time or take time off from work while their children were small than were women whose mothers stayed home. None of the women whose mothers stayed home stated that they would be willing to stop working completely, and most wanted to continue working full-time while their children were small. Neither are sex-role attitudes good predictors of how couples actually divide up household tasks. One study showed that even women who were in the forefront of women's liberation in their attitudes did about as many household tasks as did more traditional women, and all of these women did a lot more of these tasks than their male partners did. Apparently, there is no simple correlation between the values individuals were raised with, their attitudes toward sex roles, and their actual division of labor in adulthood. The ideas that people reproduce their parents' marital roles, or that their attitudes toward sex roles determine their actual division of labor, are simplistic and misleading.[5]

A second assumption is that wives who work outside the home are more satisfied with their marriages. On the contrary, some studies show that working wives are no happier than nonworking wives; others show that working wives are less happy with their marriages. On the other hand, working outside the home can increase a woman's satisfaction with herself. Working and earning a paycheck gives a woman more prestige and respect in the community and more bargaining power at home. As her earning power approaches or passes her husband's, she feels she has more right to demand that he take on more household tasks and, in fact, research indicates that she is more likely to have her demands met: the more a woman earns relative to her husband, the more domestic chores and child care he is likely to perform. But this woman is not necessarily happier with her marriage, because as her income and occupational status increase relative to her husband's, the total gain from his income and occupational status, over and above what she could obtain on her own, is declining.

In the wake of the women's liberation movement, many authors predicted that when wives acquired their own earning power, they would be less concerned with their husbands' status and income. This does not appear to be the case. A major cause of wives' dissatisfaction and depression in dual-career families is their perception of their financial situations: no matter how much wives earn themselves, this perception is based on their husbands' earning power, not on their own. Wives tend to compare their husbands' ability and financial success with that of their friends' and colleagues' husbands, and with that of men they meet at work. Among working wives, sociologist John Scanzoni found that the higher the wives' peers ranked the social position of their households, based solely on the husbands' attainments, the lower the wives' aggression toward their husbands. Higher-status husbands who provided higher levels of both material and emotional rewards to wives received in return lower levels of aggressive behavior, and were less likely to divorce.[6]

A third assumption is that husbands have nothing to lose by supporting their wives' careers: if men could only shed their reactionary, chauvinistic attitudes toward sex roles, they would enjoy equal-partner marriages more than they enjoy traditional marriages. This assumption is demonstrably false. Men who perform more domestic tasks tend to experience more marital conflict and are more depressed. These husbands often envy men with better jobs whose wives do not work. It is not men's attitudes toward sex roles that make them feel this way; rather, it is that when their wives work, the men lose a good part of their support system. Working wives simply have less time and energy for their husbands' physical and emotional needs, and less time for domestic tasks. Wives with demanding jobs pressure their husbands to assume more domestic chores and child care—tasks that afford little prestige and status in our society. Thus, while working wives are gaining status in society and bargaining power at home, their husbands may be losing in both areas. The potential for conflict in equal-partner marriages is therefore very great. Although Scanzoni is a supporter of equal-partner marriages, he recognizes their potential for conflict and divorce.

> Because the equal-partner possesses a high degree of individualism that predisposes her to bargain very strongly on behalf of her own interests . . . because her income disadvantage is narrower (some wives earn as much or more than their husbands), and finally because she no longer recognizes any fixed rights or inherent authority which he can plead, the potential for marital dissolution may be quite high. In view of recent evidence showing general increases in the level of sex role egalitarianism, or individualism . . . it is likely that part of the sharp increase in divorce rates over the past 15 years can be attributed to the development of the equal-partner marriage.[7]

Drawing on her own informal research and personal experience, Gloria, the divorced business woman we met earlier, describes some of the problems in dual-career marriages.

Gloria

Most men with ambitious careers can't be good family men even if they are monogamous. After a hard day at the office they don't have the energy for intimacy and warmth—if they even have the capacity for it. Most of their energy is directed at work. I have talked to a lot of businessmen about this and not one has told me there isn't a clash between their careers and their personal relationships. One very aggressive, extremely successful man told me that he had never been one to sit home and hold hands anyway. He said he provided a good life for his family, but his business came first. He saw the conflict between high achievement and family life and he had consciously made that choice. He was realistic. I have never talked with his wife but I can guess that she enjoys all the material benefits but suffers on the emotional side. That's the standard picture.

I don't think that dual-career marriages can work if both careers are demanding. It's like bringing together two bombs in the house. They both want this home, this haven to come home to, and neither can provide it. They can't lean on each other because they both need that traditional thing, that supportive, stroking person that listens to all the problems. Some career-oriented men try to listen to their wives and share their concerns, but it sure helps if she is not operating in a competitive job. If women think they can do this superwoman thing, they're crazy. They won't have the energy for their husbands or children. It won't be any different for them than for men in the same type of occupation. The odds against that kind of marriage lasting are at least two to one. But if you are writing this in your book, nobody is going to believe it. This is a fantasy that has developed out of the change we're going through. The women that I have talked to want to think it's possible, but they are all getting divorced. They believe that they just had the wrong partner, and they'll succeed with the next one.

Evidently, women and men still have different goals in marriage. Women prefer partners who are ambitious because they want their marriages to offer financial and social advantages. As Blumstein and Schwartz concluded:

> When husbands and male cohabitators are not ambitious, their relationships are less likely to last beyond the first few years. Heterosexual women want their male partners to be ambitious. If the man indicates that being successful is unimportant, his partner may see him as less worthy. A husband feels just the opposite about his wife. Her lack of ambition does not seem to bother him. On the contrary, we find that new marriages where the wife is ambitious are less stable.[8]

Blumstein and Schwartz claim that it is not that an ambitious wife necessarily grows dissatisfied with her marriage and seeks greener pastures: "Rather, it is her husband that does not want to live with such an ambitious woman." As we have seen, there is some truth in this claim. When women are ambitious and career-oriented, they may be less able to give their husbands the support they desire. The men then become dissatisfied with the relationship. Financially independent women have extremely high divorce rates. Blaming only the husbands for these rates smacks of the hackneyed "men are threatened by ambitious women" theory we examined in Chapter 4. This theory is a smokescreen that serves to conceal women's very real preference for men who offer significant socioeconomic advantages and their very real dissatisfaction with men who do not.

Richard Udry found that when either sex perceives few feasible alternatives to their marriages, they are less likely to divorce.[9] But marked differences appeared in men's and women's perception of alternatives. Women assess their physical attractiveness, their education and earning power, and the probability of finding a suitable replacement for their husband when contemplating a breakup. In fact, the higher the wife's income in relation to her husband's, the higher her perception of alternatives and the greater the potential for divorce. Men factor in only their own economic resources and earning power; those who felt secure financially evidently believed that this was sufficient to carry them through a divorce and post-divorce adjustment.

Evidently, a man faces a real threat in his marriage if his wife's earning power begins to equal or exceed his own. The threat is even greater if his wife is also physically attractive, because her chances of acquiring an acceptable replacement for him on the dating-mating market are largely determined by her physical appearance. Some advocates of the equal-partner marriage continue to deny that women prefer husbands who offer meaningful socioeconomic advantages. These authors blame the problems financially successful women have in finding and keeping suitable partners on the frailty of men's egos or on oppressive male chauvinism. Presumably, these authors ignore what the evidence tells us because they fear that acknowledging these female tendencies would impede women's fight for sexual equality. But the issue of equal political and economic opportunities for women must be separated from the issue of relative earning power in heterosexual relationships. The man who cannot offer his female partner meaningful economic and social advantages—whether because of his low income or her own earning power— runs a real risk of losing her, or never attracting her as a partner in the first place.

Fred is 38, divorced, and a successful financial analyst. His annual income is around $90,000. He personally experienced the effects of relative earning power on marital stability. His ex-wife was very physically attractive. After he helped her get through medical school, her earning power was double his own.

Fred

Prior to getting married, we had a verbal marriage contract that stipulated that she would maintain a low-profile career and be supportive of my career. I had seen other professional couples trying to match careers and having difficulties with it. I knew that I wanted to take my own career seriously and I didn't think that there would be room for two. At the time she agreed.

After we moved, she started working in a job that she really hated. She'd come home and complain to me, and I felt bad for her. She was considering going back to school and getting a Ph.D. in literature, but I insisted that all she would accomplish is a lot of agony in grad school and find herself jobless when she finished, so I suggested that she go to medical school. The more we talked about it, the more she decided it would be a good idea.

Before she entered med school she worked, bought furniture, and baked bread. She was cooking the meals. After she began school, I did the shopping, cooked all the meals, and did the vacuuming. We shared laundry, and she dusted. Gradually, I took on more of the household tasks. She was always in a crisis; she was terribly depressed and stressed. She was convinced that she was unable to come even close to measuring up to standards because everyone was much smarter and more capable. She was even afraid to speak up in class, so she began seeing a woman therapist for assertiveness training.

She did superbly in med school. At the end of her first year, she was first in her class. She didn't believe her grade report so she called the registrar to see if they had made a mistake. There was no mistake. During this time I felt like I was getting no support from her. I was going through a lot of stress. The people I was competing with were the best students from the best graduate schools. It was a level I never anticipated I would be in, and it was only getting more difficult by the day. I felt the crises she was bringing home were damaging to my career and to my peace of mind. The guys I was competing with were going home to supportive wives who didn't work or had low-pressure jobs, and who made a nice home and had a good time when their husbands were available.

I felt that the relationship wasn't working out the way we had discussed it when we agreed to get married, but I thought that it would be unfair to discuss this because she was going through a lot of difficulty herself, and I felt obliged to support her. I felt very strongly that she needed to do this in order to find a role for herself that was consistent with her abilities and needs. I saw it as an investment that someday, when she was fully trained and well-situated professionally, I would get the reward of having a wife who remembered that I helped her attain that. And I was willing to work at a job that I hated in order to make it possible, but it was very costly. I wasn't getting anything out of it at all.

Fred's willingness to share household tasks did not necessarily make his wife more satisfied with him as a partner. In fact, as he helped her to elevate her status and earning power and reduced her vulnerability, he was damaging his own career and increasing his own vulnerability. As her status and earning potential sailed past his, his occupational status and paycheck became dispensable. He also became dispensable as a mate because she was very pretty and had a good chance of finding someone as good or better on the dating-mating market. When such a man appeared, Fred's marriage disintegrated.

Fred

It was about a year after she began her practice that I had some inkling that something was wrong. One night when I was having a beer with one of her medical partners, he said, "If I were you, I'd watch out for Alister," who was one of their partners. I thought it was either a one-time thing, or at most sporadic. My wife maintained that nothing was going on with him at that point, but that people were suspicious because she was good friends with him. I thought so little of him as a man that I figured it was a very safe thing. It was widely known by mutual friends that he wouldn't get himself involved in certain situations because he wasn't a good enough doctor.

About that time I was given the opportunity to go back East and work in a large consulting firm for a year. I was opposed to her going along because I didn't want to be responsible for interrupting her career, or damaging it by pulling her out of it after several years of hard work. In retrospect, I realize that I also didn't want her to come along because I thought that if I went away for a year or so, it wouldn't hurt the marriage, and it would give her a chance to become less insecure and needy. Then I would collect the bonanza of having an independent, secure wife who had a career and from whom I could get an equal measure of support because she would feel good about herself.

She didn't argue the point. She didn't want to go either. She already had a good practice established. We reassured ourselves that there was no problem with the separation. We had a strong and healthy marriage. We'd take turns commuting to see each other. I sent her flowers. In fact, I spent over $400 on flowers that year. I sent little notes to stay in touch. I called her every day. We never discussed dating or extramarital affairs. I assumed we'd both get laid occasionally. Now I realize that she was already involved with Alister.

I was home for a weekend when I found her birth control paraphernalia, and it was clear that it had been recently used. She didn't need it with me because we had agreed early in the marriage that we did not want children, so I had gotten a vasectomy. I didn't confront her then because I thought that it was a harmless affair and that it would pass. I had a lot of faith in our marriage. I really thought it was extraordinary.

When I went home in February, our sex life was totally dismal. It was stiff, uncomfortable, and distorted. She made a few clumsy efforts to fellate me, but it was hideous. It was like trying to get somebody to stick a turd in her mouth. I also started finding evidence of his living in the house. At the end of May, I confronted her with my suspicions. She cried and said, "We never have talked about things like this. I don't want to talk about it now." She said she would take care of it and start seeing a therapist.

From that point on I was really distraught about the situation. I started dating other women back East, drinking a lot, and gained a whole lot of weight. I went home in November and arrived sad and depressed. I was determined to confront her with all this shit, which I did the first time we saw the therapist together. She finally admitted, "yes," she was having an affair: Alister had already been to the therapist with her, for Christ's sake! They had even spent the weekend together when she went to visit the therapist. That didn't come out until a few weeks later.

Basically, what she did was tell Alister that somehow she was going to get the situation straightened out with me, while she told me she was going to get the situation straightened out with Alister. She was hedging her bets and keeping us both on the line. When I returned home, she said it was all over with him and she was just going to stay friends. I actually put up with socializing with him occasionally in small get-togethers. I didn't like it, but it didn't bother me that much. I was still convinced that he was such a wimp, even though his family is very wealthy.

Finally, there was a confrontation, and the therapist said to her, "Look, you really have to make a decision; you can't take it anymore; you're destroying yourself." She decided to move out of the house for three weeks and think things through. Then we had a conversation with the therapist, and I said, "Look, you want a divorce; there is no way we can live together like this," and she said, "Yeah," and I said, "It's really your responsibility to file for it and get it over promptly." Then she came back a month later and moved her half of the furniture out of the house, and she had the nerve to ask me to help her get her things packed.

Blumstein and Schwartz suggest that men who deny they are sexually possessive, and women who are vehemently possessive, are projecting their own sexual psychologies onto the other sex. Men would be *more* sexually possessive if they knew what sex means to a woman, and women might be less possessive if they truly comprehended men's ability to dissociate sex from serious involvements. Fred made at least three serious mistakes—all because he projected his own male psychology onto his wife. He assumed that because he was capable of casual sex, his wife was also, so her extramarital encounters would be harmless like his. He assumed that when his wife had her own career, she would not need so much emotional support. He did not realize that all women want emotional investment from the people they love—usually more than men want to provide. When his wife became financially independent, she did not need less emotional investment; she simply transferred her needs to someone else. Finally, Fred never took his adversary Alister seriously. Fred never thought much of Alister as a man because he was boyish, frivolous, and not highly regarded professionally. Fred grossly underestimated the aphrodisiacs of great wealth and boyish charm. As a self-made man, Fred thought Alister had to have earned his wealth to merit respect. Fred did not understand that, to attract women, a wealthy man only has to spend it.

For her part, Fred's wife showed the pattern that women exhibit in such relationships. She was attracted to a man who could greatly elevate her status: first to Fred, who had a successful career and helped put her through medical school, and then to Alister, who was a physician and came from old money. Sexually, she found it impossible to be polygamous. Once she was in love with Alister, she could no longer make love to her husband. Her efforts at fellatio were "clumsy" and "hideous." But they were not so in the first part of their relationship. When she finished her medical training and began her practice, she no longer needed her husband's financial support. When she finally succeeded in getting a commitment from Alister, she no longer needed her husband's emotional support.

I also interviewed Fred's wife. When she was making the decisions he describes, she did not feel as calculating or in control as my analysis may imply. She only knew that although she still loved her husband, she no longer found him sexually attractive and she was not *in love* with him. She was *in love* with Alister and found him immensely sexually attractive, but she was uncertain about his intentions. Clearly, she did not want to break completely with Fred until she knew that Alister might marry her. Being "in love" for a woman usually means that she would like to have sex with a man because she wants his emotional and material investments. When she "falls out of love" with a man, she no longer feels like doing this. Sex differences in desires, emotional alarms, and perceived alternatives emerge in people's sexual behavior and decisions in relationships whether or not they are aware of them.

The marriages of working-class men are more vulnerable than those of higher-status men because it is more likely that their wives can achieve status and incomes superior to their own. Five women with working-class husbands in my sample were contemplating leaving their husbands or had already done so. All of these women had obtained white-collar jobs and were moving up—both in their occupational status and earning power and in their standards for men. Betty is 30, very pretty, has two children, and works as a secretary in a high school. Her lover is a teacher there. Her husband is a construction worker.

Betty

I stayed home and was a good little wife and mother for eight years. Before I went to work, my husband always wanted me to get a job because we were having financial problems. It got to the point that he was pushing me out of the house. Meeting people was very traumatic for me. Now that I'm out I love it! The house isn't always clean, and the laundry isn't always done. He has to wash his own clothes and he doesn't like that. But, more important, he sees how it has changed me and what it has done to our marriage. Now he doesn't want me to work anymore.

I love my husband, but after eleven years of marriage, the passion is gone. He's a good husband. He does the repairs, loves the kids, pays the bills, and treats me like an equal. In fact, I make all the major decisions. But I don't respect him, because for years I was the perfect wife. I loved him and took care of him like nobody could, and he neglected me for so long that it hardened me and made me bitter and destroyed my love. He feels very bad about that now. He can see where he went wrong. The other night he was trying to tell me what a perfect husband he's been, always bringing home the paycheck and giving love to his family. I reminded him of those nights he used to leave me sitting at home when he went out with the guys. I was there with two kids and dinner fixed and he didn't show up and he never called. Let me tell you, my affair made all of that easier to bear.

About two years ago I met this special man at work. It seemed like he was interested in me as a person. He would always say, "Come over here and talk to me," and I was just so crazy about him I could hardly stand it. We began to see each other, usually at a friend's apartment because he is married too. I was so much in love with him I would have given up everything. I would've walked out on my husband, my kids, and my home, and not wanted any support, or even half of what we own. I know I am neglecting my children emotionally now. I'm not the kind of mother I should be. My family is not a priority anymore. I've really changed since I started working. I've got so much going on in my life. I've met new people—new men. I'm not the wife I used to be.

After I started seeing my lover, I couldn't have sex with my husband anymore. I didn't have the need and I'm not the type of person that will go to bed with my husband just because he needs it. We were having sex once a month, and he would tell me, "I'm going to go out and get it if you don't give it to me," but I never worried about that because I never had a reason to suspect him. Eventually he moved into the guest bedroom. That's pretty bad. [Laughter].

The last time I saw my lover we only had a half hour together. I told him I loved him and wanted him, and all he said was, "That's pretty serious." I could have died because I wanted to hear, "I love you too." I told him I was ready to leave my husband and asked him if he was happy at home. He said, "Just because I'm seeing you doesn't mean I'm unhappy at home. Maybe there is something lacking there and I need you, but that doesn't mean I'm going to get a divorce. I waited until I was 33 years old to get married and I'm going to make the most of it." That's when I knew I had really blown it. He told me if I got a divorce, he wouldn't see me anymore because he didn't want me to be put in the position of waiting for him when he knew nothing would ever come of it. We were supposed to see each other later in the month. His wife was going out of town, so it was the perfect opportunity to meet. We'd have the house to ourselves. But that fell through and I didn't think we would ever see each other again.

Gradually things have gotten better with my husband and me. I guess it's because I'm not into this relationship with this other man right now, and I'm realizing that I have to work on my marriage because it's secure. I need my husband. I can't make it on my own. With my salary there's no way I can support myself and my kids in the style I am accustomed to. Maybe that's very cold, but I need my husband. And I don't care if I ever meet another man again, so I might as well stay married.

Like other women we have seen, Betty craves love and romance, but cannot be sexually polygamous: when she is seeing her lover, she cannot make love to her husband. In contrast, her lover is typically male. He can make love with Betty, enjoy her companionship, and still remain devoted to his wife. He sees no contradiction in this. When Betty became a secretary in a local school, she perceived new alternatives to her marriage: financial independence and new possibilities with men. She fell in love with one of the teachers, who for her represents a step up, and began to neglect her husband and children. Her romantic fantasy is crushed, however, when her lover is unwilling to make a commitment. She realizes that she has miscalculated and tries to recoup her losses by working on the marriage. She is hedging her bets, waiting for her lover to beckon, but holding onto her security. She defends the morality of her actions by citing her husband's previous neglect.

Women with high status and income relative to their husbands are more likely to experience marital conflict and breakup. But studies indicate that dual-career couples reduce this risk in the following ways. First, less conflict occurs when the husband's status and income remain substantially higher than the wife's. Second, many working wives reduce their career involvements and assume more domestic responsibilities. Third, even when wives' occupational status and income rival their husbands, they experience less conflict when they work in "traditionally female" occupations—for example, nursing. Finally, dual-career families can run quite smoothly when no children are at home.[10] This brings us to a fourth assumption of the equal-partner ideology: if husbands perform domestic chores and child care, wives will be as satisfied with their performance as husbands are with their wives' performance of these tasks. On the contrary, studies show that no matter how many of these responsibilities men assume, wives are more critical of their partners' performance than husbands are. Wives appear to be particularly critical in regard to child care.

In a study of professional men and women in dual-career marriages, Colleen and Frank Johnson found huge differences between the sexes in reports of strain and conflict.[11] Almost two-thirds of the wives' 161 reports of strain centered on problems of child care. Wives felt guilty and anxious about not being able to handle the emotional needs of their children, and not being able to watch their children grow. Financial or marital problems accounted for less than 15 percent of wives' reports of strain. In contrast, husbands' reports of strain were few, and when made, were vague and unemotional. Husbands tended to deny or minimize their wives' concerns about the children with statements like: "It is nothing to worry about. It's just a stage he's going through." Or, the men suggested solutions based on management principles involving logistics, optimization, and efficiency: we must identify the problem, examine the options, consult all levels of management, including the children, and arrive at the most acceptable solution. Mothers' anxiety about their children was not allayed by these "logical" solutions. These sex differences in the amount and source of strain were not affected by the amount of support husbands were giving their wives—which was, according to the authors, impressive in the majority of families.

This and other studies suggest that regardless of whether women have ambitious careers and equal-partner marriages, women are more sensitive to and concerned about the quality of child care, their children's emotional development, and the emotional quality of family life than men are. Most women feel a deep emotional bond with their children. While they may want their husbands to become more involved with the children, most women still feel they can do a better job than their husbands in dealing with their children's physical and emotional needs. Why does this sex difference persist, and why, given that joint legal custody is now presumed in most family courts, do the majority of divorcing women continue to *choose* to retain physical custody of their small children?[12] Some authors persist in claiming that this sex difference in parental tendencies is caused solely by sex-role socialization. The evidence does not support these claims.

Drawing on psychoanalytic theory, sociologist Nancy Chodorow offers a sex-role explanation of sex differences.[13] She argues that sex differences in personality and behavior develop out of the universal fact that women tend to be the primary caretakers of small children. Both boys and girls initially identify with their mothers (or female caregivers), but, in order to establish a masculine identity, little boys must soon reject this identification and reject female qualities in themselves. In contrast, little girls can remain identified with their mothers. Consequently, males grow up being more assertive and achievement oriented, and less nurturant and dependent on relationships than females. Chodorow believes that these sex differences are passed from generation to generation through the traditional institution of motherhood and are stunting for both sexes. To remedy the harmful effects of this process, Chodorow maintains that all boys need fathers who are more involved in child care, and girls need mothers who work outside the home.

Alice Rossi, past president of the American Sociological Association, offers an explanation contrary to sex-role theory. Rossi maintains that men and women have different biological predispositions for parenting. To support her argument, Rossi draws on research in neurology, endocrinology, and developmental psychology, and points out that, according to Chodorow's scheme, boys raised by single fathers should be less assertive, independent, and achievement-oriented, and more nurturant and emotionally expressive, because these boys do not have to reject their primary caregivers. Studies of single and coparenting fathers do not support Chodorow's theory. Rossi further argues that many sex differences appear in infancy— long before the age of three, when according to psychoanalytic theory, boys reject their mothers as objects of identification. These basic sex differences in behavior and aptitude appear to establish a basis on which socialization acts to exaggerate some differences and diminish others.[14]

Sex-role explanations of sex differences also ignore hormonal and neurological evidence. Laboratory experiments with monkeys and medical evidence from humans indicate that male sex hormones tend to masculinize the behavior of both males and females. Females that are subjected to male hormones while in the womb show higher levels of physical activity and aggression. Women who have abnormal levels of male sex hormones due to medical conditions also exhibit these tendencies, and can even show male patterns of sexual arousal and desire until their conditions are corrected medically. Sex researcher John Money, for example, studied young women who had had abnormally high blood levels of male sex hormones all their lives. These women had sex drives like those of men: they were frequently aroused sexually, and they were aroused by visual stimuli like pictures or the sight of strangers, even to the point of feeling a pressing need to masturbate and desiring intercourse with strangers. When these women voluntarily had their conditions medically corrected, they did not lose sensitivity of the clitoris, or their interest in sex. But, as Money recounts:

> What they lost, therefore, was that autonomous, initiatory eroticism of the phallus which seems to be so basic in the eroticism of men. The women were all unequivocally pleased to be relieved of clitoral hypersensitivity; it was the pleasure of being able to feel like a normal woman, several of them explained.[15]

Moreover, numerous studies have shown that men's and women's brains are organized differently. The right hemisphere is dominant in emotions, facial recognition, music, visual tasks, and identification of spatial relationships. Language skills are dominant in the left hemisphere. The brains of four-year-old girls show more advanced cell growth than do boys in the left hemisphere, and boys, more in the right hemisphere. These anatomical sex differences are reflected in sex differences in language skills and spatial perception from a very early age. Men show a more definite separation of function between the two brain hemispheres and have a larger percentage of space in the right hemisphere devoted to visual-spatial functioning. Further, the corpus collosum—a large bundle of nerve fibers that joins and communicates between the two hemispheres—is larger and more bulbous in women. There are thus two possible reasons for females' having greater verbal access to their emotions. First, in men, more space in the right hemisphere is devoted to visual and spatial functions, leaving a smaller proportion of space for mediating emotions than in women. Second, in women different functions are less localized and confined to one side of the brain because they enjoy better communication between the two hemispheres through the corpus collosum. For example, women with brain damage from trauma, epilepsy, or stroke are more able than men to substitute other areas of the brain to function in place of the damaged area. All of these characteristics suggest that the organization of the female brain is less rigidly specialized and localized than the male brain, and this sex difference provides a basis for women's greater language skills, fewer speech and reading disorders, greater sensitivity to context and peripheral information, and greater access to emotions.[16] In other words, women are more intuitive, in touch with their emotions, and emotionally expressive than men are, and this sex difference has a biological basis.

Along with other experts, Rossi believes that these sex differences in assertiveness, emotional expression, and nurturance were produced by natural selection. Over 90 percent of human evolution took place in small, nomadic hunting and gathering bands that had no domesticated plants or animals. Among hunter-gatherers, mothers had almost constant physical contact with newborn infants during the first year, and nursed children on demand for four to five years. The prolonged dependency of human infants and the restrictions imposed by pregnancy and nursing led to the sexual division of labor. Men specialized in hunting larger animals, and women gathered wild plants, caught small animals, and reared small children. Over hundreds of thousands of years of evolution, these differences in reproductive biology and specialization caused men and women to have different inclinations toward parenting. Women are more innately predisposed than men to learn and develop the nurturant skills and emotions necessary for the care of infants. Males can be taught to care for infants adequately, but females learn these skills more readily. Identical training will not make males and females equally skilled in child care. To accomplish this, males would have to receive compensatory training.[17]

Women tend to have lower rates of career advancement and productivity than men with comparable training. While sexual discrimination at work and husbands' refusal to assume domestic tasks contribute to these lower rates, a more important cause is the fact that many wives voluntarily choose to make their careers secondary to the needs of their children and to their husbands' careers. These women are not victims of outmoded sex roles. They are making conscious, rational decisions given their priorities and options. These decisions are influenced by many factors, but the most important influences appear to be a woman's earning power relative to her husband's, and her perception that her children will benefit from this decision. For example, among my sample of medical students, one-fourth of the women and three-fourths of the men preferred to work full-time when their children are small.[18] Three-fourths of the women preferred to work part-time or take time off from work while their children were small. Only one-fifth of the men preferred to work part-time and none of the men wanted to take time off from work completely. In explaining why they preferred to curtail their work commitments, women mentioned the constraints imposed by pregnancy and childbirth, that infants and small children needed care and attention that hired persons or husbands were less likely to give, and that they, as mothers, would be missing something important if they worked full-time while their children grew up. The fact that these women are succeeding in a highly competitive, lucrative, and traditionally masculine field does not erase and may not even reduce this sex difference in parental tendencies.

One-fifth of the women medical students reported that they would prefer to share domestic chores and child care equally with their husbands. But over half of the women in the sample had a sliding scale for the division of domestic tasks. If their husbands earned twice what they did, they would assume primary responsibility for these tasks—using maid service and supplemental child care as they deemed appropriate. But, if their career advancement and incomes were more equal to those of their husbands, they would expect the men to share domestic responsibilities more equally. These women were still single, so their statements are hypothetical. But studies show that the principle of a sliding scale does operate: the more a man's status and income exceed his wife's, the less likely he is to perform domestic tasks.[19]

Barbara is 34, married, and has two children. She is highly intelligent, well-educated, and was the managing editor of an academic journal when she decided to take time off from work to be with her children.

Barbara

I was a radical feminist when I was in college and even burned my bra in a demonstration. I'm still a feminist but my thinking about sexual equality has changed over the years. One of the things that caused me to change was my experience in Israel. My husband was in the [1973 Arab–Israeli] war and I knew he could easily be killed. I saw how important and necessary family ties are there and I felt I was part of his family. I think the actual danger and seeing the men go off to fight evoked these feelings in me. I desperately wanted to conceive a son for him during this time. In that situation, arguments about sexual equality seemed trivial.

After we returned to the States, I worked full-time and enjoyed my job. But when my son began to have problems in school, I could see he needed more attention and I decided to take off work for a while until my children were older. His problem straightened out almost immediately. My husband is a good father, but I knew he wouldn't give the kids the kind of care they needed even if he wanted to. He's just not sensitive to the same kinds of things I am. I don't think that there will ever be complete sexual equality in the sense that men and women are exactly alike and everything in marriage is split 50-50. I've seen women who've tried to have marriages like that and it usually doesn't work. These women may think they want their husbands to cut back on their careers to help more at home, but if the men do it, the women lose respect for them. I hate to say this because I really am a feminist and I support equal rights. But men and women are different in some respects and these particular aspects aren't going to change.

Barbara's decision was based on her perception that her children needed more attention and she was the best person to give it. Her decision was also facilitated by the fact that her husband is highly respected in his field and earns about $100,000 a year—roughly twice what she could earn if she worked. In taking time off from work, she felt that her family's standard of living would not suffer appreciably, but her children would benefit substantially. Most women still want to be married to successful men, have healthy, well-adjusted children, and enjoy a good family life. A great many women are like Barbara: if their career ambitions begin to interfere with these goals, they are willing, circumstances permitting, to cut back on their careers. In her book *The Second Stage*, feminist leader Betty Friedan acknowledges these female priorities. She writes that the women's movement was a reaction to a rigid sex role that defined women solely in terms of their relations to men as wives, mothers, and homemakers. In this reaction, some women took up a brand of feminism that denied the core of women's personhood that is fulfilled through love, nurture, and home.[20]

Different Vulnerabilities in Different Periods

In modern urban society, the following factors have weakened the traditional economic bases of marriage: the decreased importance of children as economic assets; the cheap replaceability of traditional female tasks; and women's increasing economic independence. Women's desire to work outside the home is an understandable response to monetary inflation and the sexual and economic vulnerabilities of the modern housewife. As women work and reduce their vulnerability, however, they simultaneously increase their husbands' vulnerability because they reduce the economic advantage of their mariages—as well as their own ability to provide the sexual, emotional, and domestic caretaking that most husbands desire. Consequently, many men oppose their wives' pursuing demanding careers and they resist increased sharing of domestic tasks.

Married men and women are vulnerable to different threats in different periods of their lives. A man is most vulnerable if his wife's income and occupational status are comparable to his own and she is physically attractive enough to find a suitable replacement for him on the marriage market. If he is successful in his career, his vulnerability declines over the years because his wife's chances on the marriage market decline as she grows older, while his chances increase. The younger man who cannot offer his wife a significant socioeconomic gain is most vulnerable, particularly if she is physically attractive. The older woman with no marketable skills is maximally vulnerable economically if her husband leaves her, and maximally vulnerable sexually to replacement by a younger woman. In the next two chapters we will see how some couples cope with these vulnerabilities and how sex differences affect marriages worldwide.

10

Are Men and Women Alike Around the Globe?

Sex in China and Samoa

The Don Juan of the village was a sleek, discreet man of about forty, a widower, a *matai*, a man of circumspect manner and winning ways . . . he noticed that Lola had reached a robust girlhood and stopped to pluck this ready fruit by the way . . . after three weeks which were casual to him, and very important to her, he proposed for the hand of the visitor . . . the rage of Lola was unbounded and she took an immediate revenge, publicly accusing her rival of being a thief and setting the whole village by the ears.

—Margaret Mead, *Coming of Age in Samo*a

You must get her alone. The best time is during rest break. Then no one will suspect. Get her to drink some beer or wine and then start kissing her. Try to take off her shirt. Don't ask her; just do it! If she lets you kiss her breasts, then you have a chance to have sex. But women are strange. Most of the time unmarried women will not want to do anything but pet.

—A Chinese man's advice to his younger cousin

SOME AUTHORS HAVE ARGUED that the patterns of male and female sexuality identified in the United States vary drastically across cultures and may be totally absent and even reversed in some societies. There is not space in this book for a thorough review of the cross-cultural evidence.[1] But we can examine opposite extremes on one behavioral continuum—sexual permissiveness. Differences in sexual behavior have traditionally been most pronounced among the upper classes of agrarian kingdoms, where men vehemently strive to control female sexuality.[2] Even in relatively permissive cultures, however, casual sex for women diminished their value as mates and thus damaged their reputations.[3] Polynesian cultures were certainly among the most tolerant regarding women having casual sex; the People's Republic of China was one of the most restrictive, yet both these cultures reveal the sex differences in sexual behavior that we have seen in previous chapters.

Margaret Mead is probably the single most important individual whose work contributed to the view that human behavior is almost infinitely malleable and, more specifically, that our Western notions of sex differences are the result of our own particular conditioning. Mead enjoyed an international reputation and influence both within and outside of anthropology, and she is probably the most famous female scholar in this century. Her works continue to be cited as evidence that the differences between males and females in our society are totally a product of our cultural conditioning.[4]

In his book *Mead and Samoa*, Derek Freeman accused Mead of biasing her description in favor of an idyllic paradise where free love, cooperation, and a casual, easygoing existence were the norm. He contends that Mead suppressed or ignored any information that contradicted this portrait, and accepted at face value questionable observations and reports that supported her view. The purpose of this distortion, Freeman claims, was to support the view of her mentor, Franz Boas, that culture, not biology, determined human behavior. The evidence for and against Freeman's claims have been amply analyzed elsewhere.[5] What is more interesting is that a close reading of Mead's account shows exactly the same gender differences in sexuality that are familiar to Westerners. These sex differences caused just as much trouble in Samoa, it seems, as they continue to do in our culture today.

Sexual Relations in Samoa

Mead's *Coming of Age in Samoa,* first published in 1928, is one of the best-known works in the ethnographic literature and has been read by literally millions of people, both students and the general public.[6] Her purpose in this study was to investigate Samoan adolescence and to determine whether the stress, confusion, and conflicts experienced by American adolescents were the result of biological changes accompanying adolescence, and hence universal, or were instead the result of particular stresses and cultural conditioning found in some societies and not in others. In her study of Samoa, Mead emphasized a pattern of casual premarital relations for adolescent girls:

> With the exception of the few cases to be discussed in the next chapter, adolescence represented no period of crisis or stress.... To live as a girl with many lovers as long as possible and then to marry in one's own village, near one's own relatives and to have many children, these were uniform and satisfying ambitions.... The opportunity to experiment freely, the complete familiarity with sex and the absence of very violent preferences make their sex experiences less charged with possibilities of conflict than they are in a more rigid and self-conscious civilization.... The Samoan child faces no such dilemma. Sex is a natural, pleasurable thing, the freedom with which it may be indulged in is limited by just one consideration, social status. Chief's daughters and chief's wives should indulge in no extramarital experiments.[7]

Portions of Mead's own data indicate that sexual relations were neither as casual nor as typical as her general description implies. For example, although a majority of her sample of adolescent girls were virgins, they receive only a paragraph in the chapter that describes the sexual careers of the others. Although she emphasized the girls' casual sexual relations, Mead noted the coexistence of an idealization of virginity—particularly for girls of higher social rank. In precolonial days, high ranking girls were ritually deflowered at the wedding ceremony by the chief of the bridegroom. If the girl proved not to be a virgin, her female relatives beat and stoned her, sometimes fatally injuring the girl who had shamed her family. Obviously, a young girl's virginity was considered a prize. Male virginity was not similarly valued. The Samoan man who had many conquests was viewed with respect and envy, and the more virgins he had seduced, the more prestige he enjoyed. Mead writes:

> But virginity definitely adds to a girl's attractiveness, the wooing of a virgin is considered far more of a feat than the conquest of a more experienced heart, and a really successful Don Juan turns most of his attention to their seduction. One youth who at twenty-four married a girl who was still a virgin was the laughing stock of the village over his freely related trepidation which revealed the fact that at twenty-four, although he had had many love affairs, he had never before won the favors of a virgin.[8]

Some young Samoan males also practiced night crawling (*moetotolo*), in which they would sneak into huts at night and attempt to seduce or rape young girls. If the girl cried out, or if the boy was otherwise discovered by the girl's male relatives, he could be beaten. Mead described two motives for *moetotolo*. If a boy felt a girl had led him on, only to snub him in the end, out of anger and revenge he would attempt to ravish her at night while her family was sleeping. The boy hoped that in the dark he would be taken for an experienced lover, or that the girl would be too embarrassed or overwhelmed to call out. The second explanation is that a boy who could not win a particular sweetheart by legitimate means attempted a *moetotolo*. As Mead notes, these explanations are not entirely satisfactory since some of the boys who were notorious *moetotolos* were among the most charming and attractive youths in the village.

Mead's general statements tend to obscure sex differences in sexuality, while her own descriptions of female virginity, *moetotolo*, and "Don Juans" and "Lotharios" imply the existence of a double standard. For example, in the following passage Mead never specifies a sex difference, but her language implies that the desire for many sexual partners and the prerogative of seduction are male traits. Men are the ones who must coax, declare undying love, and write songs and love letters in order to have many mistresses:

> A boy declares that he will die if a girl refuses him her favours, but the Samoans laugh at stories of romantic love, scoff at fidelity to a long absent

wife or mistress, believe explicitly that one love will quickly cure another. The fidelity which is followed by pregnancy is taken as proof positive of a real attachment, although having many mistresses is never out of harmony with a declaration of affection for each. The composition of ardent love songs, the fashioning of long and flowery love letters, the invocation of the moon, the stars and the sea in verbal courtship, all serve to give Samoan love-making a close superficial resemblance to our own, yet the attitude is far closer to that of Schnitzler's hero in *The Affairs of Anatol*.[9]

Mead's allusion to Arthur Schnitzler's character, Anatol, is apt. The character of Anatol perfectly exemplifies men's desire for a variety of sexual partners and their false promises of investment to have casual sex. Anatol seduces innumerable women — often from lower social strata — with romantic promises, champagne, dinners in plush restaurants, and his Edwardian version of a playboy apartment. Despite his own continual infidelities and deceits, he exhibits extreme sexual possessiveness and jealousy toward his partners. He defends his myriad seductions and infidelities with the claim that women are similar to men in their fickleness, infidelities, and desire for transitory affairs — a claim that is not substantiated by the women's statements in the play.

In the following passage, Mead is more explicit concerning the male desire for partner variety and the staus enjoyed by men who were especially successful in satisfying this desire:

> And native sophistication distinguishes between the adept lover whose adventures are many and of short duration and the less skilled man who can find no better proof of his virility than a long affair ending in conception.[10]

A few examples from Mead's book show that sex was not nearly so casual as she claimed—at least not for females. She writes of Moana whose sexual affairs had begun at fifteen, and in a year and a half her conduct had become so "indiscreet" that her parents feared it would "mar her chances of making a good marriage." The parents asked her uncle to adopt her and straighten her out. Unfortunately, her uncle was a sophisticated womanizer who, "when he realized the extent of his niece's experience, availed himself also of her complacency".[11] The incident might have gone unnoticed except that Moana's older sister, Sila, was also in love with the uncle, and when she discovered the affair, "her fury knew no bounds." Sila publicly denounced the uncle and accused him of incest, thus causing a huge scandal.

In another incident, a high-ranking girl from another village was staying in Lola's household. The Don Juan of Lola's village, Fuativa, was about forty, rich, and charming, with winning ways. While he was courting the visiting girl, Fuativa noticed that Lola had "reached a robust girlhood and stopped to pluck this ready fruit by the way." Fuativa seduced Lola easily, and "after three weeks which were casual to him, and very important to her, he proposed for the hand of the visitor".[12] Lola's pride was wounded but she still hoped that the wedding plans might miscarry. When she heard, however, that Fuativa had been granted sexual access to his betrothed to solidify the marriage contract, her rage "was unbounded," and she attempted to take revenge by publicly accusing her female rival of being a thief. Her plan backfired and she was driven out of her host's household.

Having casual sexual relations with multiple partners damaged Samoan girls' reputations, reduced their marital chances, and produced low self-esteem:

> [Sala] was stupid, underhanded, deceitful and she possessed no aptitude for the simplest mechanical tasks. Her ineptness was the laughing stock of the village and her lovers were many and casual, the fathers of illegitimate children, men whose wives were temporarily absent, witless boys bent on a frolic. It was a saying among the girls of the village that Sala was apt at only one art, sex, and that she . . . would never get a husband. The social attitude towards her was one of contempt . . . and she had experienced it keenly enough to have sunk very low in her own eyes.[13]

Mala was a social outcast. She stole, lied, and played with boys when it was improper to do so:

> [The boys] teased her, bullied her, used her as general errand boy and fag. Some of the more precocious boys of her own age were already beginning to look to her for possibilities of other forms of amusement. Probably she will end by giving her favors to whoever asks for them, and sink lower and lower in the village esteem and especially in the opinion of her own sex from whom she so passionately desires recognition and affection.[14]

These and the other cases Mead describes do not support her generalizations about casualness and the lack of male-female differences in sexuality. For girls, quantity and casualness of sex were associated with a bad reputation, decreased attractiveness, and low self-esteem. In fact, Mead reported that in native theory, sterility was the punishment for female promiscuity.[15] In contrast, for men, sexual conquests added to a man's reputation, and only the older, highest-status men had access to the young virgins, who were considered the most desirable.[16]

In her general characterizations of Samoan sexuality Mead denied basic sex differences, but her own data clearly show that they were quite evident. The Samoan idealization of virginity for girls of better families, the institution of *moetotolo*, the fact that Samoan men wanted to have many lovers, attempted by diverse and creative means to seduce women, and apparently gained status thereby, especially when the girls were virgins — all show a pattern of sex differences that is quite familiar to westerners.

To Mead's credit, by Western standards in the 1920s, the relative sexual freedom of Samoan adolescents and Samoan women and their apparent enjoyment of sex did seem remarkable. But compared to the sexual behavior of young people in contemporary America, Mead's observations do not seem at all remarkable—as we saw in previous chapters.

Mangaia is another Polynesian island "paradise" whose culture and language are related to those of Samoa. Donald Marshall reports that most Mangaian girls have had several lovers prior to marriage, and most Mangaian women are capable of having multiple orgasms during intercourse.[17] These findings might be interpreted as a lack of a sexual double standard and a general similarity between male and female sexuality. Yet Marshall's account provides ample evidence to the contrary. He reports that "Mangaian males very definitely believe that men tend to want sexual activity more frequently than do their women but that women tend to 'hold them back' from full sexual indulgence. Some husbands may beat the wife into submission."[18] Young males are possessive about their local girls and may fight with boys of other villages when attempts are made to take away their girls. The average girl has had at least three or four lovers between the ages of thirteen and twenty, whereas the average boy has had over ten (boys travel to other islands to expand their conquests). Boys compete to seduce as many girls as they can; the strongest contestants have a penis tattooed on their thighs or a vagina tattooed on their penises. Some of these Lotharios boast of having tried sixty or seventy girls and maintain notebook records of their exploits. The boys compare exploits, sexual knowledge, and techniques, and the compliance and responsiveness of different girls — as boys do in Samoa and in America.[19] Mangaians admire the boy who has had many girls, and compare him to "a strong man, like a bull, going from woman to woman." Men want to sleep with as many women as possible, and use gifts, food, persuasion, and serenades to achieve their ends. Women, however, who chase men and use gifts to entice them are considered "silly pigs."[20]

Mead was not the only anthropologist who was guilty of overemphasizing the differences between societies and ignoring traits that might be universal. For example, Bronislaw Malinowski emphasized the relatively relaxed and sexually egalitarian nature of sexual relations in the Trobriand Islands and tended to gloss over observations that contradicted this view. Young Trobriand women are described as enjoying sex as much as men and were free to choose their lovers. Nevertheless, Trobriand men give small presents to their lovers, and if they had little or nothing to offer, the women refused their sexual advances. As Malinowski noted, "this custom implies that sexual intercourse . . . is a service rendered by the female to the male." But Malinowski expected sexual relations to be treated "as an exchange of services in itself reciprocal," and he was therefore puzzled by this custom. He dismisses the practice by assigning it to arbitrary custom: "But custom, arbitrarized and inconsequent here as elsewhere, decrees that it is a service from women to men, and men have to pay."[21]

Sex differences in sexuality are also evident in the fact that men used magic as an aid in seduction and women did not. Similarly, adolescents could enjoy relatively casual sexual relations, but after marriage adultery was a grave offense, punishable even by death for wives, but not for husbands. Like Mead in her earlier works, Malinowski was apparently motivated to maximize contrasts with Western sexual conventions and also, perhaps, to find a "heaven on earth," where men do not have to pay for sex with signs of investment.[22] In Melanesia, Polynesia, the United States, and in fact anywhere that has been adequately analyzed, it is men who coax, declare undying love, serenade, and offer gifts, compliments, and other signs of investment in exchange for female sexuality.

Mead's *Sex and Temperament in Three Primitive Societies*, first published in 1935, represents the purest expression of her zeal for cultural determinism. In this study, Mead attempts to demonstrate the malleability of human behavior by examining sex differences in three New Guinea tribes: the Arapesh, Mundugumor and Tchambuli.

In her original Introduction, Mead had stated explicitly that her book was not concerned with whether there are or are not actual and universal differences between the sexes, either quantitative or qualitative, but rather was "an account of how three primitive societies have grouped their social attitudes towards temperament about the very obvious facts of sex-difference."[23] Despite her introductory statement of purpose, her message is clear throughout the book—Western notions of sex roles that assign different amounts of sexual desire and assertiveness to men and women are a product of our own cultural conditioning. In some societies both sexes exhibit these traits to the same extent, and in others our notions of sex differences in these traits can be reversed, with men exhibiting what we consider to be female traits, and women exhibiting what we consider to be male traits. The following quotation exemplifies this message:

> The material suggests that we may say that many, if not all, of the personality traits which we have called masculine or feminine are as lightly linked to sex as are the clothing, the manners, and the form of head-dress that a society at a given period assigns to either sex. When we consider the behaviour of the typical Arapesh man or woman as contrasted with the behaviours of the typical Mundugumor man or woman, the evidence is overwhelmingly in favour of the strength of social conditioning. In no other way can we account for the almost complete uniformity with which Arapesh children develop into contented, passive, secure persons, while Mundugumor children develop as characteris-

tically into violent, aggressive, insecure persons. We are forced to conclude that human nature is almost unbelievably malleable, responding accurately and contrastingly to contrasting cultural conditions.[24]

Mead argued that among the Arapesh in New Guinea, both men and women exhibited what we call female traits; among the Mundugumor, both sexes had male traits; among the Tchambuli, our notion of sex roles was completely reversed. Mead described the Arapesh as a cooperative, noncompetitive society in which neither sex was aggressive nor spontaneously sexual, and both had a maternal temperament. Women were viewed as the seducers in chance sexual encounters, and young men were warned against the advances of strange women who might deliver them into the hands of sorcerers. Mead's own observations belie this portrait. Although actual warfare was absent, violent brawls did occur, and they usually involved men fighting over women. When women or pigs were stolen by men from neighboring villages, men would avenge these thefts. Although Mead stressed equal levels of aggressiveness in men and women, and claimed that men were not honored for warfare or killing enemies, only men exacted vengeance, did the killing, and performed the necessary rites of purification. Similarly, despite her emphasis of equal and low sex drives for men and women, Mead's examples show that women used sex to obtain male resources, and some men promised marriage and other investments and then reneged on their promises after they had satisfied their desires.

Mead characterized Mundugumor men and women as mutually hostile, aggressive, sexual, and nonmaternal. Prior to colonization, however, warfare, head-hunting, and cannibalism were important activities for men, who constantly competed for the sexual favors of women. When Mead was there, the ideal was for men to have nine or ten wives, but only about one man in twenty-five achieved this goal. As in all polygynous societies, a greater number of wives indicated greater wealth and status for the man. Men customarily traded sisters for wives; men without sisters had to fight for women. Frequently, a boy's young bride caught the eye of his father or elder brother, who tried to usurp her and thus caused a power struggle within the family. There was a premium on female virginity, and kin attempted to protect the chastity of their female relatives. Men had affairs with married women, but they were not interested in marrying women who already had children. Because of the value placed on female virginity, and because men did not want to marry women with children, we can infer that Mundugumor men preferred younger women to older women as sexual partners and wives.

Mead portrayed the Tchambuli as a society in which our notions of masculine and feminine were totally reversed. Men gossiped, adorned themselves, and were more artistic than women. Although this society was both polygynous and patrilineal, Mead claimed that women had the real power because they engaged in the principal economic activity—fishing. She also claimed that the Tchambuli believed that women were more "urgently sexed" than men. A close reading of her own observations contradicts her simplistic portrayal of sex-role reversal.

The aesthetic, coquettish, and "dependent" Tchambuli men expected that every boy in childhood should kill a victim. For this purpose victims were purchased. These victims were usually infants or young children from other tribes, or war captives or criminals. Their heads became trophies for the boys to boast about. Men competed vigorously for women. The young men complained bitterly that older men used every bit of their power and strategy to cut out their young rivals and to shame and disgrace them before the women. Despite her claim that Tchambuli women were more urgently sexed than men, all of Mead's examples show older men using their superior status to capture the favors of young women. Mead states explicitly that the conflict over women in Tchambuli was a secret competition where young men and old struggled for the possession of women's sexual favors, and young men and young women were both likely to lose to the will of their elders. The men, who were supposedly dominated by the women, would beat the women if they violated custom or taboo.

In her early studies, Mead attempted to characterize each society in terms of a single, dominant pattern and tried to demonstrate that our conceptions of male and female traits could be found in both sexes or even reversed. These attempts caused a serious bias in her generalizations, but her specific examples and observations reveal sex differences that are quite familiar to Westerners.

In the twenties and thirties, racists and elitists were using pseudo-biology to justify discriminatory immigration laws, deportation, and eugenics measures.[25] Like many anthropologists in this period, Mead used cross-cultural evidence to refute this simplistic, erroneous, and dangerous use of biology. Given her targets, Mead's bias is understandable and praiseworthy, but this bias caused her to overlook or conceal cultural universals, and to impede legitimate biological explanations of these universals. In 1939 Mead freely admitted her bias in the following statement:

> It was a simple—very simple—point to which our materials were organized in the 1920's, merely the documentation over and over of the fact that human nature is not rigid and unyielding, not an unadaptable plant which insists on flowering or becoming stunted after its own fashion, responding only quantitatively to the social environment, but that it is extraordinarily adaptable, that cultural rhythms which they overlay and distort. . . may produce more unhappiness and frustration in the human breast than the most rigorous cultural curtailment of the physiological demands of sex or hunger. We had to present evidence that human character is built upon a biological base which is capable

of enormous diversification in terms of social standards . . . The battle which we once had to fight with the whole battery at our command, with the most fantastic and startling examples that we could muster, is now won. As the devout in the Middle Ages would murmur a precautionary "God willing" before stating a plan or a wish, those who write about the problems of man and society have learned to insert a precautionary "in our culture" into statements which would have read, fifteen years ago, merely as "Adolescence is always a time of stress and strain," "Children are more imaginative than adults," "All artists are neurotics," "Women are more passive than men," etc., with no such precautionary phrase.[26]

Mead published *Male and Female* in 1949. By this time she enjoyed an international reputation, the eugenics movement had been crushed, and she had an additional fifteen years of study and personal experience to inform her views. In *Male and Female* Mead argued that universally men, more than women, must compete to obtain adult status and the right to sexual favors.[27] She devoted an entire chapter to the thesis that the role of mother is more determined by biology than the role assigned to fathers, which is more variable cross-culturally. Mead regarded female orgasm as a potentiality that could be encouraged and developed in liberal societies like Samoa, but this potentiality could also be ignored by whole societies.

In contrast to female sexuality, Mead argued, male sexual functioning seems to work best when it is most automatic: a spontaneous response to bodily exposure, a special perfume, a woman's reputation for compliance, or simply a woman alone. Once male sexuality is complicated by ideas about sentimental love, moral qualms, and marriage, males' sexual responses are less automatic, less spontaneous, and less reliable.[28] In comparison, the female sex drive is more dependent on women's "fitful moods," "which are so differently spaced in different females that they cannot be referred even to any sex-wide regularities".[29]

In her introduction to the 1962 edition of *Male and Female*, Mead concluded that if she were rewriting the book, she would place more emphasis on man's specific biological inheritance from earlier human forms and on the parallels between homo sapiens and other species. It is to her credit as a scholar and a scientist that Mead was able to alter her views in accordance with the available evidence.

Sexual Relations in China

The Chinese Marriage Law of 1950 (revised in 1980) stipulated the appropriate criteria for mate choice: personal compatibility, political attitudes, and judgment of character. Inappropriate criteria were wealth, good looks, sexual attractiveness, and family connections. Sinologists Martin Whyte and William Parish interviewed 133 emigrants in Hong Kong from various cities in China.[30] Despite the official criteria for mate choice, Whyte and Parish's sample ranked criteria used by men and women in the 1970s as follows:

Woman considers:	Man considers:
1. Job and income of man	1. Class label and political record of woman
2. Class label and political record	2. Good looks
3. Family income, housing, connections	3. Family income, housing, connections
4. Urban registration	4. Pleasing personality, good character
5. Overseas connections and remittances	5. Job and income of woman
6. Pleasing personality, good character	6. Urban registration
7. Good looks	7. Overseas connections and remittances

In the early 1980s, anthropologist William Jankowiak conducted research for over two years[31] in Huhhot, the capital of the Inner Mongolia Autonomous region. Huhhot is a city of over 491,000 inhabitants. About 417,000 of these are Chinese, who are known as *Han.* Urban Mongolians are the largest minority in Huhhot (over 42,000). Jankowiak interviewed both Chinese and Mongolian men and women. Bill and I became friends while I was a guest professor at the University of California, Santa Barbara, in 1984. We were amazed at how closely Bill's findings from China matched mine from the United States, so we decided to collaborate on an article.[32] What follows is an update of our original article. Since his first fieldwork in China, Jankowiak has returned twice, and published a well-received book on China and a fascinating study of romantic passion in different cultures.[33]

The men and women Jankowiak interviewed all believed that physical attractiveness is more important for men in choosing partners than it is for women, and youth is a more important determinant of female attractiveness than it is of male attractiveness. Unmarried women over 27 are often referred to as "old girls" and such women are at a disadvantage in the marriage market. They see their chances as receding as they get older. This was a particularly difficult problem for women whose education was delayed because they were sent to the countryside during the Cultural Revolution. These women were often over 24 when they started college and because Chinese college students cannot marry while still in school, these women's opportunities for marriage were further delayed. A number of women informants in this situation reported being told quite bluntly by their male companions that they were simply too old to marry. Because of this male preference for younger women, women over 27 often have to compromise and settle for less than their ideal (namely, a man of equal or higher status). A female teacher, 29, recounts being introduced to the man who would be her husband:

> At first I was disappointed. He was short, somewhat handsome, and one year younger than me. He liked me right away. I have now known him for one month. He likes me because I do not look down on his peasant background. He told me I am getting older and that I would have trouble finding a suitable mate. After some thought, I agreed. In China, a woman must marry [her emphasis]. Even when you have no desire.

Another woman who knew the preceding woman explained, "This woman would love to give herself completely to her ideal mate, but she could not find him and so she settled for less." The fact that this couple's job statuses were approximately equal helped to offset his peasant background in her eyes. Now she says she likes him better and they seem to get along well. Another male informant, 28, said:

> My girlfriend is 29, so we must marry this year. I would like to wait another year, but she is already old. We must marry this year.

Similarly, a college-educated woman, 27, complained to the researcher: My mother is always crying around the house. She thinks that I'll never marry. I still have suitors; three in fact! They all bore me. I didn't use to worry about it. Recently, however, my younger sister told me I had too many wrinkles. Do you think so? Women— especially unmarried women—fear them.

Professional achievements did not seem to reduce the emphasis on female youth. Of fifteen professional women who were 45 and older, all said that it was better to be a young girl: that was the time of life they had enjoyed the most. When asked why, they replied that it was "just better" to be a young girl than an older woman. All of the women interviewed on this topic said they used oil to moisturize their skin and prevent wrinkles. One woman, 55, recently remarried a high official who had a reputation for philandering. She said she applied oil three times daily because she was worried about competing with other women. A female student, 25, admitted during a group discussion: "I fear growing old. That's why I put cream on. We all do it, you know." Older women informants reported that women's use of beauty aids and skin care predated the Revolution, so these practices did not seem to be merely the result of recent Westernization.

, About 40 percent of the women interviewed said they used cosmetics like lipstick and powder on dress-up days (a dance once a month). Women under

25 were more likely to use cosmetics. Skin care extended to protection from sun and wind. Of over 5,000 bicyclists observed on the streets, women were four times as likely to wear surgical masks during cold weather. When asked why this was so, women informants mentioned that they were more concerned than men were about the cold, but more important, they wanted to protect their skin from the weather because they worried about wrinkles. Men said they did not need to wear masks because they were men and did not have to worry about such things.

As late as 1980 cosmetic surgery and beauty products were reserved almost exclusively for actors and actresses. Since 1982 cosmetic surgery has become more generally available and a growing number of Chinese women have had fat and wrinkles removed, breasts enlarged, and eyelids given a double fold. A higher standard of living and a relaxation of restrictions have allowed these operations. Similarly, cosmetic sales amounted to $207 million in 1981, a 20.5 percent increase over 1980s record.[34]

The use of depilatories to remove body hair is also increasing among Chinese women. Every Sunday in Huhhot there was a market where more fashionable clothes—for instance, from Beijing and Shanghai—could be bought. This market was extremely popular. The young women dress up and many wear white gloves and facial powder; they circulate in groups, eyeing both the goods and the unattached young men. So, although certain standards of female attractiveness are indigenous to China and have persisted in the post-revolutionary period—like the use of oil to preserve a youthful complexion—others, like eyelid operations, presumably reflect Western influence. Consistent with what we have seen in other cultures, the core of beauty aids in China serve to enhance the signs of youth and health: a clear, smooth complexion, absence of wrinkles, minimal bodily hair, and a youthful figure. Women who possess these characteristics are considered more physically attractive and, as we will see, can use their attractiveness to obtain the partners they desire: men with greater resources, prestige, and earning power.

The Chinese emphasis on female youth and beauty appears to exist despite attempts to suppress it. For example, a content analysis of major magazines for the period between 1940 and 1983 revealed that whenever state control relaxed, attractive women began to adorn the covers. In the 1950s women were typically portrayed as sexless comrades in arms, standing beside tractors, holding guns, dressed in unisex quilted pajamas, and looking stalwartly off into the horizon. Between 1960 and 1962, a political thaw occurred and the percentage of young, pretty women depicted as individuals (rather than as sexless workers and soldiers) increased. After the downfall of the Gang of Four in 1976, dozens of new magazines appeared, and a majority of these featured young pretty women on the covers. In 1982 a number of older officials, both male and female, protested the flood of beauty in magazines. A magazine editor, however, told Jankowiak that the preponderance of pretty women on covers simply reflected demand: "We want to sell magazines and this is what sells them."

In addition to its control of the media and of production and sales, the state used more direct means to suppress an interest in female beauty and sex appeal. A female official, 27, stated, for example, that she had received a letter of commendation for wearing dull, drab clothes: "I am not leading a bourgeois life and they wanted to congratulate me for it." Despite this type of pressure, female informants tended to own more clothes and shoes than did male informants, who typically remarked that they had less interest in such things because they were men.

Chinese hypergyny

Despite the official repudiation of these criteria, Chinese men are more concerned about their partners' looks, while the women are more concerned about their partners' status and resources.[35] Several of our informants remarked that, ideally, in mate choice "like doors should match." In other words, people should marry individuals of approximately equal status, and most Chinese marriages tend to observe this. But if anyone does marry up, our informants believed it should be the woman (hypergyny) rather than the man (hyperandry). A number of informants reported that families generally oppose their daughters' marrying down because they assume that the men have "no real feelings" for their daughters, but merely want to use the connection to advance their material interests. As one mother said, "Pretty boys want to marry high officials' girls and afterwards they want to give the money to their own parents." For example, a Han female medical student, 30, was planning to marry a worker, 27, who despite his worker status was relatively cultured and was learning English. Concerning the woman's motives for marrying him, the boy said, "She knows that if she does not marry me, she'll never marry anyone." When asked, why? he replied,"It's quite simple. Anyone over 30 will want to marry a much younger woman." Regarding his motives, the boy admitted that the status advantages her family could offer were his primary consideration in marrying her. Her high-status family strongly disapproved of the match.

Most informants had a story to illustrate the inadvisability of men marrying up. For example, a male musician, who had not completed college because he was sent to the countryside during the Cultural Revolution, married a 31-year-old college graduate. Everyone familiar with the case thought that it was regrettable that she was marrying down, but because she was 31 and homely, she was seen as having no alternative. In a similar case, a female college graduate married a man seven years her junior. He was attractive but from a peasant background. After graduation he was to be reassigned to the countryside, so he agreed to marry her if her father would arrange for him to move to the city (her father was director of the committee for job placement). The girl's father strongly opposed the marriage. Both families considered this a desperate move on her part, but being 30 and average looking, the woman felt that she had to settle for this man.

Sex differences in partner selection and marital goals imply sex differences in causes of marital satisfaction and dissatisfaction. Part of the aversion to hyperandry in our informants' reports sprang from a recognition of this principle: most people believe that hyperandrous unions will be unsatisfactory because such unions run counter to the marital goals of the principals. This frustration of the different marital goals of the sexes is believed to be an unending source of marital conflicts. As one man remarked, "Whenever a woman has higher status than her husband, it is something that neither party can ever forget." Similarly, a male worker, 25, said: "I would never marry a woman of higher status than me. She would dominate me. She would say, 'Look at the things that my father gives us. What can your father give us?' She could shame me. "

These statements by men were corroborated by interviews with women. After the Cultural Revolution political ideology became less important as a criterion for women's partner selection, except insofar as it reflected the man's ability to obtain concrete advantages—better housing, employment, and urban registration, for example. But during the Cultural Revolution the normal female criteria for partner selection were turned upside down. Many college-educated and higher status women married workers or lower-status men because "bourgeois, exploitative" classes were under attack: to marry the son of a high-status family was risky at this time. But by 1981 it was obvious that the worker class was low in prestige and influence. Informants who knew of such cases reported that most of the women who had married lower-status men during this period were bitterly disappointed with their marriages. Interviews with three such women revealed serious marital quarrels and dissatisfaction stemming from the fact that these women had married down when they thought they were marrying up. As a college lecturer, 36, complained:

We have had too many changes in China! I picked a man who was a worker. We were told that workers were the future of China. Today I make more money than he does. Who would have thought that after ten years of marriage I would be more successful than him!

Chinese parents may also oppose their sons' marrying down if the status difference between families is great. Their opposition usually derives from their fear that the girl and her lower-status family will drain their own superior resources. Thus, parents may reject both hypergynous and hyperandrous unions, but the reasons in each case are different. In hypergynous matches the boy's parents find the couple's motivations more intuitively acceptable (even if the parents are unwilling to accommodate them) because they know from experience that men are attracted to young, beautiful women, and women are attracted to men with resources. They assume that it is more likely that a high official's son could be genuinely in love with a beautiful worker girl—and she with him—than a young, handsome, male worker would be genuinely in love with an older, homely, high official's daughter. Hypergyny thus appears to correlate with female youth and beauty because to some extent men and women have different goals and preferences in sexual relations and marriage. Informants' statements reflect an intuitive understanding and acceptance of this principle.

Indeed, all informants who were interviewed on this topic agreed that youth and beauty were more important determinants of women's options and bargaining power than they were of men's. Several middle-school teachers and college students reported that in middle school the prettiest girls stopped studying and seldom passed the college entrance exam because they knew they could marry high-status men. One college man said that it was for this reason that there were no truly beautiful women in Chinese universities. Similarly, a group of women college students expressed disbelief when the female research assistant informed them that there were many pretty women on American college campuses.

As pretty women use their beauty to marry up, men use their status to obtain sexual favors and more attractive partners. A high official's son, first in his class, was accused by the girls on campus of being arrogant and uninteresting. He laughed about this and said:

> Yes, but when I am feeling low, I go over to those girls and tell them I am interested in finding a woman who can really understand me. They get really interested in me but then I walk away from them. I don't want to get married until I am forty because I know I will be very successful then and I can marry a very pretty young woman. Until then I want to play around.

A male teacher, 46, remarked:

> When I first came to Huhhot in the 1960s, teachers were looked down on. I could not have my choice of women. Today we have very high status. I could find a very young, very pretty girl. When I go out at night, my wife thinks I am going to look for a girl. I would like to but I don't. She is still jealous and suspicious and nags a lot. We call this type of woman tang su, or pot of vinegar.

The common assumption of the connection between female beauty and women's marrying up was poignantly expressed by an uneducated young bachelor: "I would fear marrying a very pretty girl because she would not be loyal to me. In China we are wary of very pretty women because we know that only powerful men can have them." Although looks and status figure in partner selection criteria for both sexes, they are weighted differently. When asked whether a worker girl was pretty, a male college student, 25, replied, "No, she is a service worker. She has no culture." When asked further whether he would not consider a woman from an inferior class, he replied: "Oh, yes! Status is not that important; only a little. If she were really beautiful, I would marry her, but she is only average, so why bother?"

But class and background do set limits on women marrying up. A cab driver divorced his wife at 42 and married a beautiful peasant girl (some considered her the most beautiful woman in the city). Cab drivers enjoy relatively high status as workers because they have access to a car. In comparison, peasants are considered by higher strata to be distinctly inferior, so this woman's beauty had catapulted her into an urban residence and a greatly elevated status. Despite her beauty, however, her peasant background would preclude her marrying men of the highest levels—although many would desire her as a lover.

Sexuality in China

Evolutionary psychologists argue that in every society sexual access is considered a favor that women can bestow upon men.[36] Consequently, women are able to use their sex appeal to gain advantages in both sexual and nonsexual relationships, and they are usually put off by men's attempts to engage in more casual sexual relations. This is definitely the case in China. Several male university professors reported that female students would often flirt with them in private. The men affirmed that this flirting indicated a desire for a better grade rather than a desire for intercourse. Women teachers did not report that male students flirted with them for grades and favors.

Chinese women are wary of men's attempts to engage in intercourse that involves little or no commitment of emotion and resources. For example, a pretty college graduate, 22, reported that a high-ranking party member, 35, was propositioning her. He was an infamous philanderer but was jealous if anyone went near his wife, who was a beautiful artist. The young woman was very interested in him and had engaged in petting, but she said that she would never sleep with him because she was from a good family and would not have an affair, and the man would never leave his wife. Similarly, an attractive, married college graduate reported that whenever a man showed interest in her, she was wary:

If he likes me for my character and my abilities, I am pleased and want to exchange thoughts. But if he only wants to sleep with me, then I feel disgusted and I loathe him.

When asked whether young men had erotic dreams, a male college student, 25, said that he and his male friends frequently discussed their dreams. When asked who was the subject of these dreams, he replied that worker girls usually were because these young men knew that the higher-class college girls would not engage in sexual relations with them, whereas the worker girls represented a more likely possibility. In reality, a few worker girls and pretty peasants did attend private parties with high officials (most of whom were married) and engaged in dancing, necking, and petting with them. The men used these meetings to try to initiate sexual affairs with these women. These girls were not prostitutes but were paid indirectly through gifts, services, and other favors.

All informants agreed that male sexuality differed from female sexuality: men desired intercourse more frequently and they had a greater desire for a variety of sexual partners. Young male informants occasionally discussed techniques of seducing women, and they agreed that the best method was to be forward and unyielding. One college-educated man advised his younger cousin:

> *You must get her alone. The best time is during rest break. Then no one will suspect. Get her to drink some beer or wine and then start kissing her. Try to take off her shirt. Don't ask her; just do it! If she lets you kiss her breasts, then you have a chance to have sex. But women are strange. Most of the time unmarried women will not want to do anything but pet.*

Accusations of infidelity were common from both sexes and were a major cause of marital discord among both Chinese and Mongolian informants. Although men and women seemed to be equally suspicious and accusatory, informants generally believed that men philandered more than women. A student informant who had conducted a study of an Ann Landers-type column in the *People's Daily* between 1982 and 1983 said that 70 percent of the letters were from women complaining that their husbands or fiances were flirting or having affairs with other women.[37]

Both ethnic groups believed that Mongolians were more sexual than Chinese, and two-thirds of the Mongolian women informants reported liking sex. In contrast, most Chinese women reported that they were not interested in sex. Women generally controlled frequency of intercourse in marriage. If they felt the relationship was good, they would amicably acquiesce to their husbands' advances; if not, they rejected these advances directly or with various excuses. Both Chinese and Mongolian women informants reported that women's desire for intercourse dropped drastically after the birth of a child and that women's sexual desire ceased, or should cease, after menopause.

Cases of male sexual harassment of women are common in China and are colloquially classified as follows: speaking rudely to a woman (*tao xi*); acting obscenely or touching a woman (*wei xie*); getting a woman into bed (*you jian*). All of these categories are considered improper behavior. Nevertheless, a factory manager claimed that about 20 percent of his female workers had reported cases of sexual harassment. All of our female informants reported having observed or experienced personally at least one case of sexual harassment within the last three years. Observing for fifteen hours on five consecutive Sundays in the central market, the researcher saw about two cases per hour of harassment (about 800 people per hour passed through his field of vision). Some cases were only verbal and others involved touching. The victims were generally under 25. The offenders dressed and acted like workers or unemployed males.

Women alone on the street at night are seen as looking for trouble. Women informants reported being afraid to go to the movies at night or even to the outhouse. At nine o'clock one evening Jankowiak encountered a 33-year-old woman on her bike whom he knew and asked why she was not afraid to be out at night alone. She replied that it was all right for her because "young boys only want young girls." In two years Jankowiak observed only six women alone on the streets after 9 p.m.

Statistics on rape are a closely guarded secret in China but a policeman told the researcher that in his precinct there were sixteen rapes in one month. There are six precincts in Huhhot. If his figure is accurate, and representative of other precincts and months, Huhhot would have over 1,100 rapes per year. This estimate is probably exaggerated, and there is presently no way of accurately estimating the number of rapes, but informants clearly believed that it was unsafe for women to be out at night. This popular belief evidently reflects an actual threat—although the incidence of rape in Chinese cities is probably much lower than the incidence in many American cities. A lower incidence of rape in China than in the United States is consistent with evolutionary analyses of rape. Generally, rape is less common in societies where kinship bonds are strong and women are protected by their kin, where most males can attract and reproduce successfully with desirable mates, and penalties for rape are severe.[38]

One might object that sex differences in sexuality and partner selection persist in China because sex-role socialization has lagged behind improvements in women's economic and educational opportunities. On the contrary, our data suggest that these sex differences appear in contemporary China *despite* concentrated efforts to suppress them. Whenever this suppression is relaxed, these sex differences emerge more strongly. A comparison of sexual behavior in the 1980s with behavior in the 1990s makes this clear.

In the early 1980s, infidelity, voluntary singlehood, and divorce were still strongly condemned. Numerous Chinese married men admitted that they desired other women but they feared social repercussions. The restrictions on women were even stronger. One women professional remarked that her moral reputation and family image were at least as important to her career as her competence. Young women's activities were scrutinized and premarital virginity was still the ideal, although many couples had intercourse during their engagement. There was no dating culture, and when a couple began dating, they were considered engaged. If either party backed out at this stage, it was considered a blot on their character and they would be likely to have problems finding another partner.[39]

Playboys were criticized and held in contempt. Most young men simply did not have the opportunity to engage in casual sex. They lived in dormitories or with their families and had little money; the rules of courtship were strict, and a watchful neighborhood made anonymity impossible. Nevertheless, in the cities an increasing number of young men from high-ranking families were obtaining apartments—or access to friends' apartments—and had parties that involved necking and petting. One boy who was known to hold such gatherings was arrested in the October 1983 police roundups and sent to prison. He had made the mistake of inviting college girls from good families to these gatherings, and a high-ranking father had pressed charges. If the boy had invited only worker girls, he might have escaped punishment. By these moral strictures, a majority of American youth would be incarcerated.

Sanctions and punishments could also be indirect. Several men said that of the youth sent to the countryside, the ones who were selected to go back to school were those who were "wholesome" and had refrained from sleeping with peasant girls in the village. These men envied their friends who had peasant lovers, but they knew that if they did the same, they would never be allowed to return to the city. One man said the peasant women were more likely to engage in premarital or extramarital sex because they were peasants anyway, so they had nothing to lose by their behavior. Compared to urbanites, the cadres had no control over them.

The government also controlled male-female relationships by severely restricting divorce. Despite the 1980 reform in the divorce code, applicants were frequently subjected to long delays—often two years or more—and had to undergo interviews with government officials.[40] Typically, couples were forced to live together during this delay, and their work units, families, and neighbors pressured the couple to reconcile their differences and make the best of it. Custody awards also acted to deter divorce. If a woman wanted a divorce and the man did not, she might be forced to give the children to him and his family. On the other hand, a divorced man with two children could not have any more children—because of the official limit—so most childless women would not consider marrying him. As one man who found himself in this position remarked, "No Chinese woman wants to be a stepmother!"

Divorce and the marriage market in the 1990s

There have been three waves of divorce in China.[41] The first was in the 1950s. After the Revolutionary law forbade polygamy, men had to abandon multiple wives, and some wives chose to leave husbands because the new regime allowed women more freedom to choose their own partners. Also, as some peasants and workers gained power under the Communist regime by becoming cadres and village leaders, they frequently dumped their old wives for younger, prettier, and better educated women. This pattern is so well known it is now a popular theme in novels, and there is a common label for men who do this: *chen shimei.*

The second wave of divorce was in the early 1960s when there was a brief relaxation of controls on divorce. The divorce rate has been increasing steadily since the 1970s. This is the third wave. The economic reforms and liberal divorce codes instituted in the late 1980s allowed even greater financial opportunities, personal freedom, and ease of divorce. These reforms now allow divorced individuals increased opportunities to express their preferences: older divorced men can choose younger women; divorced women can search for higher status males—and can choose not to remarry if they fail to find such a man. This seems to be happening.

In the city of Wuhan, the local courts accepted more than 10,000 divorce cases in 1989—the highest number since 1949. Most of these cases were filed by wives, and this phenomenon has become so prevalent that it has earned the name "husband dumping." Greater availability and acceptance of divorce, women's financial independence, improvement of women's social and political status, and wives' dissatisfaction with husbands' economic performance were the most important causes of this divorce surge.[42]

A 1994 study of the singles population in Beijing showed that there are almost three times as many single men as women in the clerk category.[43] For workers in business services, the ratio of single males and females is about even, but in the highest occupational category, there are more single females than males. In fact, the professional class is the only occupational category where single women outnumber men.

Among teenagers there are only slightly more single males than females in Beijing, but by age 20, there are about one and a half times as many single men as women. By age 27, there are more than three times as many single males as females. This makes sense because Chinese couples are strongly encouraged by the government to only have one child and most Chinese want children. So virtually every woman who has the option is married during the years of her peak fertility—between the ages of eighteen and thirty. After age 27 the discrepancy between the number of single women and men rapidly declines and reverses. By age 33, there are about 1.5 single men for every single woman. By age 38, the ratio of single men and women is about even. By age 46, the ratio begins to reverse, resulting in ever greater numbers of single women compared to the number of single men. In later ages, this discrepancy is partly caused by middle-aged men's higher mortality, but this effect is minimal at age 50, and by that time there are already twice as many single women as men. This trend continues so that by age 64, there are 2.5 single women for every single man in Beijing. This pattern is virtually identical to our analysis of the American marriage market in Chapter 6.

In Guangzhuo, a major city bordering Hong Kong, the one million single adults—which is about one sixth of the city's population—is a serious social issue. Chinese experts believe that a major cause of this buildup is that people's standards are too high.[44] The ideal mates of many Chinese women are foreigners and Chinese businessmen who have the freedom to travel, and have connections overseas and hard currency. For many single men, their ideal mate is much younger than they are. Owners of marriage agencies stated that for men between 50 and 60 years old, their appropriate mates should be between 30 and 40. But when they list their prerequisites, many men who are between 50 and 60 say they want women who are beautiful and between the ages of 20 and 30. In a 1992 survey of marriage and dating agencies, 90 percent of the women wanted men with extensive education and professional positions; only 20 percent said looks were important and eleven percent listed "kindhearted." In a survey of men, 86 percent did not list educational background as important.[45]

Women migrate from poorer provinces in China to marry men in more affluent regions. Thousands of women have migrated from Hunan, Sichuan and Guangxi to Zejiang, where the average annual income is almost twice as high as in their home provinces. These women are often better educated than the men they marry in Zejiang, but the greater affluence and earning power in Zejiang apparently offsets the discrepancy in education, so the women still feel they are marrying up rather than down.[46]

Men who are successful entrepreneurs are a special social class in China. They are extremely wealthy compared to the average worker and they can regulate their own time. To join one of their country clubs costs more than ten times the average annual income. Such men have more opportunities to travel and meet attractive women, and Chinese women find them maximally attractive. One man who was 34 and owned several apartment buildings advertised in a popular newspaper that he wanted a beautiful, unmarried woman, between 24 and 30, who had good social and secretarial skills. Within three days he received around 400 responses, many of them from teachers, doctors, technicians, and government officials. The average age of the respondents was 25.7 years.[47]

In the marriage market of the 1990s, the successful Chinese businessman can trade his superior resources for casual sex with multiple attractive partners, and his wife cannot supervise and restrict his daily activities as she can in the average Chinese marriage. Not surprisingly, these men have a very high divorce rate.[48] As we saw in previous chapters, men with greater opportunities for casual sex are prone to exploit these opportunities, and this seems to be as true for Chinese men as for American men—despite almost 50 years of restriction and punishment of these tendencies in the People's Republic of China.

Relaxed restrictions in the 1990s have led to higher rates of premarital and extramarital sex in China, and both men and women are more concerned with the quality of their sex lives. In one survey, 41 percent of the women said that they wanted to orgasm "as much as possible" when they had sex, and 27 percent said they wanted to climax every time they made love.[49] Relaxed restrictions have also resulted in a flood of pornographic materials—although pornography is still illegal in China and the government confiscates millions of items every year and punishes offenders.[50]

The same sexual dynamics that we observed in the contemporary United States seem to operate as well in cultures as diverse as Samoa in the 1920s and China in the 1990s. Men strive for status, which they try to translate into casual sex with multiple partners. For sex and marriage, they prefer young, physically fit women who are in the years of peak fertility. The mechanism for men's sexual arousal and assessment of sexual attractiveness is primarily visual. Men promise material and emotional investments and then hedge on their investments in order to spread them among several women. Men who have the greatest opportunity to have multiple, attractive partners tend to do so.[51] For their part, women are attracted to men who have ability to invest, but they also need to see signs of willingness to invest: generosity, affection, and consideration. This is the challenge—to induce a man who has great ability to invest to love, cherish, and invest exclusively in her. But when women are successful in playing out their own sexual strategies, their male partners' emotional alarms sound and motivate them to counter their partners' sexual strategies and fulfill their own. And when men are successful in fulfilling their most basic desires, women feel threatened and launch counter strategies. This is a major source of tension and conflict in heterosexual relationships.

In the countries we have examined, when social restrictions on sexuality and marriage are relaxed, premarital and extramarital affairs blossom, divorce rates skyrocket, and men's and women's fundamental desires become even more visible in the ebb and flow of selection and rejection in the sexual marketplace. In the final chapter we examine these dynamics on a global stage, speculate on the future of marriage, and offer examples of how some couples create successful, durable marriages.

Conclusion

Coping with Sex Differences and Cultural Change

In the theoretical background, as opposed to the descriptive and normative content of this book, I would, if I were writing it today, lay more emphasis on man's specific biological inheritance from earlier human forms and also on parallels between *Homo sapiens* and other than mammalian species. I believe I underestimated the fruitfulness of comparisons between human beings and birds, for example, where the importance of vision, the requirements of shelter, and two parents for the care of the young provide more than a pretty figure of speech for explaining the facts of life to children.

—Margaret Mead, *Male and Female*

The two chamberlains, who were to carry the train, stooped down with their hands toward the floor, just as if they were picking up the mantle; then they pretended to be holding something in the air. They did not dare to let it be noticed that they saw nothing. So the Emperor went in procession under the rich canopy and every one in the streets said, "How incomparable are the Emperor's new clothes! what a train he has to his mantle! how it fits him!" No one would let it be percieved that he could see nothing, for that would have shown that he was not fit for his office, or was very stupid. No clothes of the Emperor's had ever had such a success as these.

—Hans Christian Anderson, The Emperor's New Clothes

ALTHOUGH A FEW CULTURAL ANTHROPOLOGISTS have sought to isolate a core of cross-cultural universals they could call "human nature," by and large, they have emphasized how much human behavior varies in different societies.[1] Cultural differences are the anthropologist's stock and trade. After all, if people were the same everywhere, there would be no need to travel to exotic lands to study them. A study right in one's own backyard could deliver the same information. Anthropologists have thus been inclined to look for the exotic and to gloss over or ignore the familiar. This bias is particularly apparent in the study of sex differences. In the pages to follow, we will see how differences in sexual psychology affect relationships on a global scale, and how people cope with these differences in their everyday lives.

Modernization

In the early 1960s sociologist William Goode described a worldwide pattern of changes in family and marital relationships.[2] Wherever urbanization and industrialization occur, they lead to increased participation in the labor force of both sexes, and different types of families converge toward a nuclear family unit. The influence of parents on children's choice of marriage partners declines, and the general influence of older people wanes. The sexual division of labor is weakened, which in turn weakens the economic interdependency of husbands and wives. The importance of the quality of the personal relationship between spouses increases, as the importance of the economic bond, and of relations with other relatives, decreases. Whether one views these changes as positive or negative depends on his or her personal circumstances and perspective. On the one hand, the changes allow individuals much greater freedom to move up socioeconomically by means of their own achievements, to choose their sexual and marital partners, and to leave unsatisfactory relationships. On the other hand, these changes correlate with higher rates of nonmarital sex, divorce, and functional polygyny. This means that both men and women are more vulnerable to rejection and abandonment by their partners, and functional polygyny tends to replace legitimate polygyny. In Africa, for example, there has been some movement away from polygyny among the educated classes, but this is not an unmixed blessing. Many Nigerian women currently in polygynous marriages fear that polygyny will be replaced by open affairs on the part of their husbands. This pattern has already emerged in urban Ghana— where legitimate polygyny is declining.[3] Many young women in urban Ghana are now attending school or working and are consequently postponing marriage. While doing so, they frequently become the lovers of older married men. This pattern of functional polygyny is also prevalent in the United States, as we saw in Chapter 6, and can work to the advantage or disadvantage of women, depending on the outcome.

The high divorce rates that accompany modernization increase the number of households headed by single parents. This is particularly true in advanced, socialist countries like Sweden, where state-supported child care, maternity leave, and medical benefits have reduced the economic importance of husbands and the costs of divorce. Sweden has an estimated rate of female single-parent households of 20 percent.[4] In the United States, the incidence of female single-parent households has increased by 81 percent since 1960. The odds are now that over 30 percent of children born today will live in such a family during their lifetimes. Increasing women's economic independence, however, has not eliminated sex differences in parental tendencies. Divorced women tend to retain physical custody of their children. This tendency results in the average ratio of five to one of female single-parent households to male single-parent households in developed nations. Most single mothers bear the major burden of supporting and raising their children. So a high divorce rate reduces the average male investment in children, despite laws that seek to guarantee equitable investment.[5]

Wherever women possess economic alternatives to marriage, and men possess sexual alternatives, rates of divorce, desertion, and nonmarital sex are high. We see this pattern among the Turu of Tanzania, the middle classes of advanced nations, and the impoverished classes of urban societies. In his classic study of poor black men in Washington, D.C., Elliot Liebow concluded that a man's inability to support a woman and her children was a major cause of disputes between men and women, of the fragile, transitory nature of their relationships, and of the high incidence of female-headed households and commonlaw relationships in lieu of marriage. Other studies of the urban and rural poor support his analysis.[6]

Social Experiments

In his excellent book, *Human Family Systems*, sociologist Pierre van den Berghe analyzes social experiments that have attempted to modify or eliminate the nuclear family unit, basic sex differences, and the sexual division of labor. One study reported the results of 26 group marriages. These marriages included individuals in the United States who were mostly young, middle-class, and highly educated. Fifty-eight percent of these group marriages lasted less than a year. Only 5 of the 26 groups were still intact at the time of the study, and only two of these had survived more than four years of communal living. None of the extinct groups had lasted more than four years, and only three had lasted more than two years. Of the 69 children born to these 104 individuals, 67 were from existing or preexisting legitimate marriages rather than from group marriage partners. Both children and adults recognized the relationship between children and their biological parents was special and distinct from other relationships—in other words, the nuclear family unit was recognized. Rampant promiscuity was not practiced; sexual rights and duties were bound by more explicit and formal rules than are found in most conventional marriages.

Van den Berghe concluded that group marriages are rare, do not last long, almost never produce children, and, regardless of how they start out, they eventually evolve into monogamy or polygyny, with a clear nuclear family structure recognizable within a larger group. This evolution is best exemplified by the Oneida Community, which is the group marriage experiment with the most longevity on record. The leaders of Oneida, all middle-aged men, began to usurp and monopolize the sexual favors of the young women and assigned the older women to the young men as sexual partners. The founder of Oneida, John Humphrey Noyes, increasingly demanded sexual privileges with the community's teenaged girls. He was eventually threatened with charges of statutory rape and the commune disintegrated shortly thereafter. Van den Berghe points out that economic communism evidently worked in Oneida; sexual communism did not. Although Oneidans explicitly set out to do so, they failed to eliminate the sexual division of labor, the sexual pair-bond, and parent-child ties. In fact, instead of sexual communism, polygyny and hypergyny evolved to replace conventional monogamous marriages.

Men in positions of power tend to practice polygyny: legitimate polygyny where it is allowed; functional polygyny where it is not. Jim Jones, the founder of Jonestown in Guyana, is another case in point. Originally based upon communistic principles, Jonestown soon became a dictatorship. Jones was the supreme leader of all his followers. He had a select group of top level counselors and workers—almost all of whom were female, tall, white, and attractive. Normal sexual contact between spouses was proscribed, deviations were reported to the leaders, and the most attractive young men and women were directed to Jones, who enjoyed them according to his whim.[7]

Similarly, the Synanon Foundation was ideally based on egalitarian and communistic principles, but a ruling elite soon emerged. Synanon's leader, Charles Dederich, explicitly described the lifestyle of this elite as rich, decadent, and opulent, "like a royal family," with the overwhelming majority of members in the position of peasants "doing the dirty work."[8] Dederich issued two proclamations that eventually led to his downfall and the break up of Synanon. First, he ordered that all men (excepting himself) who had been in Synanon longer than five years had to have vasectomies or leave Synanon. This order eliminated men who had any seniority from reproductive competition with Dederich. Women who wanted to have children would have to do so with Dederich or with new members, who would be at the bottom of the hierarchy doing the dirty work, and therefore be less attractive to most of the women. Second, Dederich ordered that all members had to separate from their present partners and choose new ones. This directive freed up the female partners of younger, lower-ranking males for takeover by the elite males. Ben, whom we met in Chapter 8, lived in a Synanon commune for almost two years. He reflected that although he had not noticed it at the time, the forced changing of partners had allowed the more senior males to exchange their old partners for younger, more physically attractive women.

The Israeli kibbutz is one of the most successful, longest-lasting, and largest-scale experiments in social utopia. The original founders decreed that the kibbutzim would be socialist, with communal ownership of all property and no private inheritance of property. Marriage was not to be formally recognized, so that women would be liberated for productive work, and children would be reared in communal centers where parents could visit them at designated hours. All economic and sexual inequalities were to be eliminated, and men and women would participate equally in production, the service industries, and child care. As in the Oneida experiment, economic communism worked quite well in the kibbutzim, but the attempt to eliminate sex differences and the sexual division of labor failed. Some authors have argued that the kibbutz does not prove the existence of basic sex differences because the founders had been raised with conventional sex roles and were inclined to return to them in spite of their best intentions. It was, however, among the new generation of kibbutzniks that the nuclear family and the sexual division of labor began to reemerge. Other critics maintain that sexual equality never had a real chance of flourishing because, although an attempt was made to integrate women into traditional male roles, no comparable attempt was made to integrate men into traditional female roles. Other experts, including an original founder of the kibbutzim, Joseph Shepher, reject these arguments and present evidence indicating that the new generation of kibbutz women *voluntarily* made these choices: they insisted on living with their husbands and children, and they gravitated to positions in the service industries because these positions allowed them closer contact with their children. The intricacies of this controversy need not concern us here.[9] We need only note that this social experiment, like all others, and like every known society in the world, failed to eliminate the sexual division of labor, the primacy of biological ties between parents and children and other relatives, and the nuclear family unit. In commenting on the failure of social experiments to eliminate these institutions, van den Berghe states the following:

> Their failure can be ascribed to the deadweight of tradition, the hang-ups of their upbringing, the pressures of the larger society or any number of ad hoc cultural explanations that social scientists are so quick to advance to salvage the cultural determinist thesis. The cultural determinists, however, cannot have it both ways. If highly self-selected groups of highly motivated people cannot make their behavior conform to their sexual ideology, try as they may, and at considerable cost to themselves, then their failure begs for a better explanation than that conventional morality triumphs in the end. This is doubly true if their actual behavior bears a striking resemblance to that of countless other humans in numerous other societies that have quite different values and ideologies.[10]

Proving the Case

There is no way of proving the evolutionary thesis without performing unthinkable experiments on human beings. Without such proof, the differences that exist between men and women can always be attributed to differential social ization by those who prefer to believe this. There are, however, different types of evidence that can be used to support an evolutionary view.

Biological Correlates

One can establish genetic or physiological correlates for sex differences. There is good evidence, for example, that sex hormones influence a host of traits, in other species as well as in people. In general, higher levels of aggression, assertiveness, and sexual activity correlate with higher levels of male sex hormones.[11] Richard Udry and J. O. G. Billy conducted a longitudinal study of 1,400 adolescents that produced some surprising results. Before puberty boys and girls start with the same levels of androgens (male sex hormones). During puberty males' levels of androgens increase by a factor of ten to twenty, whereas girls' levels hardly double. Boys' sexual activity is determined primarily by their androgen levels. Social influences seemed to have no effects except that the opportunity to have intercourse (as opposed to masturbating) determined the incidence of intercourse for white boys. For girls, androgen levels correlated with sexual interest and sexual activities other than intercourse (masturbation, petting) but did not correlate with the incidence of intercourse. Social controls like parental chaperonage, religiosity, and whether their best friends were having intercourse predicted white girls' having intercourse, but did not affect white boys' having intercourse. African American girls' having intercourse was affected by how physically developed their figures were. (African American boys were not mentioned in the study.)

Constructionists propose that pubertal development affects adolescents' sexual behavior, but it does so through social feedback. People see a boy or girl developing and changing in adolescence, and they respond with social messages and expectations about behavior that are part of the socially constructed script. The adolescents then alter their behavior to conform to these messages. According to this theory, sexual behavior should correlate with the adolescent's visible, physical development—for example, curvaceous hips and breasts in girls—rather than with hormone levels. Physical development, however, only correlated with incidence of intercourse for black girls and not with other types of sexual activity, like petting and masturbation, and did not correlate at all with whites' sexual activities. Udry and Billy concluded that pubertal hormones did increase sexual interest in girls, but whether their peer group was having intercourse, whether they were in love, and the strictness of parental supervision determined girls' rates of intercourse. Having ten to twenty times the androgen levels that girls have, adolescent boys show much higher rates of sexual arousal and masturbation, and when opportunity allowed, of intercourse. The authors concluded that, for boys, the effects of hormones overwhelm the effects of social controls.

These results, and those of every study done in the last 30 years, support the Kinsey team's conclusion that although cultural training, restraints, and opportunities affect the expression of basic sex differences, these differences are always present in motivation, desire, fantasies, and arousability.

Compared to the correlations about sexual activity, the evidence that relates hormones to sex differences in mate selection, and to sex differences in emotional reactions to sexual experiences, remains indirect. It has been established, however, that androgen causes the brains of male monkey fetuses to develop differently from female brains while they are in the womb. It is also known that the brains of men and women are organized differently, and these differences are probably caused by the organizing effects that androgens have on the developing male fetus.[12] The link between these sex differences in brain anatomy, and sex differences in sexual behavior and mate selection, is still hypothetical. But the sex differences we see in human sexuality and mate selection are consistent with the sex differences observed in hundreds of other species, and it is therefore likely that these same differences in humans are also mediated by sex differences in the brain.

Universality

A second means of testing the evolutionary view is to examine cross-cultural evidence. If we discover that the sex differences in question appear in all known societies, or in the overwhelming majority of societies, then we have not proved that these differences result from biology; however, the view that these differences are solely the result of social training becomes dubious. For example, universally men, more than women, tend to pay for sex. Whether it is a direct payment as in the case of prostitution, or a pledge of resources in marriage, sexual intercourse is something men want and are willing to pay for. Wherever prostitution exists, it exists to service men.[13] Homosexual prostitution is no exception. It might be argued that this sex difference is the result of unequal access to resources: in societies with prostitution men tend to have more financial resources than women, and when women have economic equality, this sex difference will disappear. Either prostitution will vanish altogether, or both men and women will make equal use of prostitutes.

This type of argument is specious. First, there are many women in these societies who already have more resources than the majority of men, yet these women do not find it necessary or desirable to engage in sexual acts with prostitutes. Second, we must ask why, when societies vary so greatly in other customs, is there no society where prostitutes primarily service women. If this sex difference were solely the result of social training, why is there not a single society where these sex roles are reversed? In fact, there is no society in which the men and women utilize prostitutes in equal rates, nor is there a single society with a significant market for prostitution that services women.

Although such evidence does not definitely prove that this sex difference results from biology, it is certainly consistent with such a view.

For the agricultural societies in Murdock's World Ethnographic Sample, in 83 cases women do most of the farm work; in 125 societies men do most of the farm work; in 133 societies men and women make equal contributions.[14] This variability suggests that if there are any biological factors influencing the sexual division of farm labor, their influence is not very strong. If men's and women's sexualities were entirely socially constructed, and there were no biological constraints influencing them, then sex differences in sexuality should show the same kind of variability that the division of farm labor does. But this is not the case. The pattern of sex differences we have examined appears to be universal.

Evidence for socialization

To assess the relative merits of the evolutionary view, we can also examine the evidence in favor of the sex-role approach. The idea that early childhood training determines sex differences so pervades works in social science that it now permeates public beliefs as well. In my interviews I repeatedly encountered the belief that little boys are encouraged to be more aggressive, to assert themselves more, and to express their sexuality more freely than girls, whereas little girls are encouraged to be more passive, nurturant, and restrained. This thesis is often encapsulated in the phrase "little boys are given trucks and G.I. Joe dolls to play with; little girls are given dolls." From these differences in early childhood training, all subsequent sex differences are supposed to spring. The evidence for this view is not convincing . The results of relevant studies are either ambiguous, and could be interpreted as indicating biological differences as well, or they are negative, indicating that differential training does not correlate with subsequent differences. In fact, research indicates that little boys are punished *more* for aggression because they aggress more.[15]

Social constructionists claim that women have been socialized to only accept sex with love, and that dolls, stories, and games orient girls' fantasy patterns toward marriage and family.[16] It is possible that factors like games and stories, parental advice, peer opinion, and sanctions and punishments produce basic sex differences, but the authors who claim this fail to present statistical evidence to support their claim. Instead, vague phrases and jargon like "traditional sex role socialization," "gender role identification," and "numerous and diffuse, subtle and unsubtle, experiences and relationships" are reified and turned into causes.[17]

Constructionists admit that homosexual men and women show the same sex differences in sexuality that heterosexuals exhibit: gay men stress youth and beauty in the choice of partners, desire casual relations with a variety of partners, are stimulated by visual materials, and emphasize the physical aspects of sex (genital stimulation and orgasm). Like heterosexual women, lesbians are not much interested in partner variety, uncommitted sex, visual materials, and youth and beauty are less important in their choice of partners than they are in men's. Constructionists claim that homosexuals show the same sex differences as heterosexuals because the same pattern of socialization remains in control. Again, however, constructionists offer no evidence to support this claim.[18]

Studies that have attempted to link basic sex differences to environmental factors like parental and peer socialization have consistently failed. In a national study of more than 1,100 college students, Graham Spanier found that factors social scientists normally assume determine people's sexual behavior did not actually correlate with people's sexual behavior. Spanier and his team examined nuclear family relationships, parental and peer attitudes, exposure to sexual materials, and religious and moral training. None of these factors seemed to have any effect on the students' current sexual behavior. College dating frequency, current religiosity, and a history of sexual assault for women, however, did correlate with their sexual behavior. In their detailed study of a stratified probability sample of Canadian adults, Edwards and Booth also concluded that childhood and adolescent socialization did not have lasting effects on sexual behavior. From their survey data and their review of the literature, LaPlante, McCormick, and Brannigan reached similar conclusions: "personality and attitudinal variables may have relatively little impact on people's actual sex-role and sexual behavior." To be convincing, constructionists must show that the sex differences in question co-vary with specific environmental factors both among and between the sexes. At present, this evidence is lacking.[19]

Special groups and individuals

Individuals and groups that have consciously repudiated traditional sex roles also provide test cases for evolutionary psychology's explanation of sex differences. If we find that these groups and individuals succeed in changing other aspects of traditional sex roles, but find it difficult or impossible to change these specific sex differences, then the evolutionary argument gains additional weight. The communes, utopian experiments, group marriages, and groups that advocated "free sex" we discussed earlier all invariably ended up showing precisely the patterns of behavior an evolutionary view predicts.

Sex differences in partner selection and sexuality are especially apparent among homosexuals. If the social-role view of sex differences were correct, we would expect these differences to be mitigated, eliminated, or even reversed among homosexual men and women because they have rejected so many aspects of normal sex roles—including the very basic aspects of heterosexual sexuality, marriage, and having children with their chosen partners. If, on the other hand, the evolutionary view is correct, we would expect these sex differences to be magnified among homosexuals. The logic of this argument runs as follows. In mating and sexuality, the sexes of any species have competing and often conflicting strategies: the sexual behavior that provides the greatest advantage for one sex operates to the disadvantage of the other. Mating between males and females thus involves a negotiation process with the possibility of a compromise that, though not optimal for either sex, is advantageous for both. This means that in mating, each sex's behavior is altered by the other sex's demands. In men and women this boils down to: if you do what pleases me, I'll do what pleases you.

Compared to heterosexual mating, sex between homosexuals does not involve the same compromises.[20] If men have fundamentally different desires than women, then they ought to be able to express these desires more freely with other men. Conversely, women should be able to express their basic sexual nature more freely with other women. Earlier we saw that the evidence strongly supports this argument. The same sex differences in sexuality and in the standards by which partners are chosen that we see among heterosexuals are exaggerated among lesbians and gay men.

The notion that sex differences are a result of unequal status and resources can also be assessed by examining the behavior of higher-status women. If sex differences are the result of differential income and resources, women with greater income and resources should show these sex differences to a lesser degree. Although their behavior might not be identical to that of men, they should show more of a male pattern than do women with lower status and income. This is not the case. In fact, women with high levels of income and education, provide strong evidence for an evolutionary view of sex differences because fundamental sex differences in mate selection and sexuality become more visible in these groups than among the mainstream population.[21]

The persistence and specificity of these particular emotions and behavior also support an evolutionary view. Some sex differences do appear to be parts of learned sex roles; these sex differences can be modified or eliminated rather easily. The sex differences we are discussing here are not easily modified, and attempts to eliminate or reverse them usually produce disappointing results. For example, in the 1980s the government in Singapore became concerned that an alarming percentage of young women were not marrying because they could not find husbands in their occupational bracket, and they refused to marry down.[22] In fact, the reluctance of educated women to marry down was so strong that educated women were producing only an average of 1.4 babies—a rate that would soon lead to extinction—but uneducated women had an average of 4.5 babies. The mayor, Li Guangyao, launched a campaign to convince young women that they should not be so picky, their standards were old-fashioned, and there were many advantages to marrying a loyal, industrious man even though he might have a working-class background. The government bombarded the newspapers, television, movie theaters, and the public address systems that stud the streets of Singapore with propaganda promoting such unions. The campaign was a miserable failure. Like women in the United States, Singapore women apparently prefer to stay single rather than marry down.

Women who have succeeded in high-status occupations that were previously closed to them have indeed rejected much of what was traditionally considered feminine. These women successfully compete with men in the workplace and in sports. Many report they were tomboys when they were growing up and had strong identifications with their fathers. They may place their careers above love and marriage for years or even indefinitely, and in their ambition and assertiveness they are equal or superior to most men in their professions. These women often enjoy competitive sports, drinking to excess, cursing, and sexual intercourse as much as any man. Yet, they continue to show the same pattern of sexual psychology that we see in more traditional women. We must ask ourselves why.

It is often claimed that although these specific sex differences persist, they are only statistical differences: men and women already overlap in their sexual behavior, and as women continue to increase their status and earning power relative to men, these differences will wane. This claim is both fallacious and misleading. It is fallacious because women's gaining status and earning power does not diminish these differences. On the contrary, we have seen that it causes them to become more obvious. It is misleading because the apparent overlap in behavior obscures fundamental differences in psychology. For example, there is considerable overlap in the number of sexual partners heterosexual men and women report they have had. Some women have had several times as many partners as some men, but there are always some men who have had several times as many partners as the women with the highest rate. This type of overlap could indicate that the basic sexual natures of men and women were identical and that, given equal opportunity and training, the distributions of men and women would be identical. Careful analysis, however, reveals that gross statistics of sexual behavior, like number of partners, mask qualitative differences in sexual arousal and experience. The man who has had one partner shares a basic male pattern of arousal, desire, and consummation with the man who has had 1,000 partners. The woman who has had 50 partners shares a basic female pattern with the woman who has had one. These male and female patterns differ in specific, identifiable, and demonstrable ways. These same patterns, and the differences between them, are also found in homosexual men and women. Different training, opportunities, and restrictions can and do mitigate sex differences in overt behavior, but the predicted differences persist in what men and women prefer, in their fantasies, and in their emotional reactions to sexual experiences and mate selection.[23] Social learning and opportunities cause considerable overlap in the behavior of the sexes, but different biologies account for the lack of overlap in basic arousal patterns, desires, and emotional reactions.

How Some Couples Stay Married

There are numerous books, magazines, therapists, and clerics telling people how to have successful marriages. Obviously, if their advice always worked, there would be very few divorces. I'm not sure that my advice will be any more effective, but my research did suggest some principles that might prove useful.

The grass isn't greener

A wealthy man in his seventies told me that people who got divorced were great believers in marriage. He explained that he had never bothered to get divorced—even though he had not lived with his wife for 25 years—because he had no desire to remarry, and a divorce would have been financially ruinous. Besides, his wealth continued to be part of his appeal to women, yet there was no way they could gain access to it, since his having remained married prevented remarriage. This old roué's arrangement might strike some as impractical or cynical, but it points up an important principle—most people who voluntarily divorce believe, consciously or unconsciously, that they can do better; that somewhere out there (or already waiting in the wings) is someone who does not have the faults of their current spouse—someone who is more exciting, loyal, sexy, loving, and caring. But most divorcees find that their new partners do have many of the same faults their old partners did, or they have different but equally serious flaws.

Women with financially successful husbands often complain that their husbands do not really communicate or spend quality time with them (willingness to invest). Women whose husbands are caring and available are more likely to complain that their husbands are not sufficiently successful or competent, and since they can not really respect them, they no longer find them sexually attractive (ability to invest). Although it is logical to expect that there might have to be tradeoffs among these traits—for instance, super successful careers may simply preclude large amounts of family time for men *and* for women—the human tendency is to want it all: financial success, true intimacy, passion, and security.

The urge to express basic sexual emotions and desires is strong—even when doing so seems irrational and imprudent. Many women I interviewed had reasonably satisfactory marriages and left them for the lure of superior emotional and material investments, only to find that the men they desired were unwilling to commit themselves to investment, or that they had much less to invest than the women had originally thought. For example, one woman I interviewed had left a young, successful lawyer who was reliable but "dull and boring," for a man who promised a glamorous life of sailing, travel, and affluence. This man turned out to be a dreamer who had deluded himself, and her, into thinking that he had the potential to become a great architect. He never became an architect, had a nowhere job, and ultimately depended on her ambition and income to attain a comfortable and secure standard of living. She divorced this man and is now 35 years old and on the dating-mating market. She regrets leaving her dull, boring, but devoted and stable first husband. Josie, a 30-year-old Mexican American, reports a similar experience.

Josie

My first husband was patient and considerate. I would come home tired from work and complain and put him down and he would just accept it. We shared all the household chores 50-50. I managed the budget and paid the bills. We hardly ever had disagreements. Our friends were shocked when we split up because they had thought we were the ideal couple. Anything I did was okay with him. I think I would have done better with someone more aggressive. He was too soft, too easy, too mellow; he didn't have the drive to go anywhere. He had gone to college but was satisfied to work the graveyard shift in a warehouse. I felt he could have done better.

The man I'm with now is very different. I met him in a club where he was playing in a band. He was very aggressive and persistent in trying to get me to go out with him. He acted very caring and affectionate at first. He was much more macho and sexy than my husband. But now that we're living together, he's not affectionate at all. He says he needs his space and I shouldn't bother him. We hardly ever do anything together. He's an artist and musician and wants to do his own thing, but he doesn't have a steady income. I feel pretty crummy about breaking up with my husband now. He didn't want to split up. He was good to me but I wasn't satisfied. Now he's got a girlfriend and is going to marry her, and I'm jealous. I made a mistake leaving him.

Joe was 32 when he began to have a "midlife crisis." He had three children, a loyal wife, and a stable marriage, but he felt that he was missing out on life. He had a fantasy of what singles life would be like: driving a sports car, dancing at discos, and meeting young, sexy women with whom he would have a string of torrid sexual experiences. He also thought that if he ever wanted to settle down again and get married, he could easily do so with someone more attractive and exciting than his wife. His fantasy did not materialize. Life in singles bars was bleak and unrewarding. The women whom he found really attractive rejected him. Even the women who were no more attractive than his wife did not make it easy for him to fulfill his fantasies. He missed his children and the security of homelife, and the divorce settlement and child-support payments would not leave him enough money to live the kind of life he had envisioned. When he finally was reconciled with his wife, he underwent a religious conversion and became deeply involved in Catholicism. He is now an exemplary family man and says that he is truly happy for the first time in his life.

During my research, I encountered numerous individuals who had left stable relationships, spent some time on the dating-mating market, and suffered from the rampant competition and situational morality they encountered. In some cases, the experience of being "burnt" caused a religious or moral transformation: they decided to no longer chase unrealistic fantasies but look for a good solid partner with whom they could establish a secure and comfortable life. Three of the married couples I interviewed had previously been separated or divorced and had gotten back together. In every case, their reconciliations were accompanied by religious transformations that involved the establishment of rules and understandings concerning marital duties and obligations. The men would be sexually faithful and make adequate and reliable emotional and material investments in their wives and children. As long as the men fulfilled this part of the bargain, their wives should be supportive and loving toward their husbands and resist temptations to seek superior investments from other men. The success of their new marriages seemed to depend on three factors: a rock-solid commitment to staying married; mutual agreement on their obligations to each other; and a more realistic appraisal of the benefits of their relationships and the probability of finding better partners.

Recognize sex differences in basic desires and goals and build them into your rules and expectations

This does not mean that people must accept their partners' acting out their fantasies. Few marriages would last if the wives tried to accept their husbands' infidelities because they had read somewhere that men are more inclined than women to desire a variety of sex partners. Most women today could not emotionally accept their husband's philandering, even if they rationally tried to so so, and their hurt and resentment would corrode the marital relationship. Men's womanizing would also undermine the marital bond indirectly because their lovers would eventually want more investment, resent the men's marriages, and pressure the men to invest more in them. For their part, few men can accept their wives seeking love and romance from other sources. So, recognizing basic sex differences in desires and effectively coping with them in marriage may entail agreeing on rules that *restrict* these desires rather than vent them.

One woman I talked to related that her husband was in sales and this required him to be out a lot drinking, having dinner, and networking with women colleagues and clients—many of whom were single or divorced and looking for husbands in his occupational category. She said she trusted her husband and wasn't paranoid, but she also accepted the ideas of temptation and human frailty. They were members of a conservative church, and they consulted the elders about her concerns. The elders recommended that the husband request assignments that allowed him to spend more time with his family, and he should only meet female clients and colleagues in their offices or with other people present. The elders said that they had confidence in the husband's ability to resist temptation, but that there was no point in rubbing his nose in it. Their view was pragmatic—it is easier for people to be right-eous if their opportunities for sin are limited. The husband accepted the elders' suggestions even though it meant taking a cut in pay. This couple still has a stable marriage—after 25 years.

As a society, we cannot and will not return to the days when sex outside marriage was unavailable to most people, and the sexes were inextricably, economically dependent on each other. Nor is it clear that such a return would be desirable even if it were possible. Effective contraception and mod-ern technology have irrevocably let the genie out of the bottle. Yet the free-doms we now enjoy entail risks. Millions of women and men are now freer than ever before to express their fundamental sexual desires: women's desire for romance, which is the quest for higher levels of emotional and material investment, and men's desire for sex with many attractive young women. We have more freedom to choose our partners and reject those we find unsatis-factory, but the partners we desire also have the freedom to reject us. Those who are clever, lucky, and attractive can make these freedoms work for them. Those who are less fortunate may feel these freedoms work against them. Fred's wife, for example, left her husband for the heir to a vast fortune. Her gamble was apparently successful. Her wealthy lover eventually married her and they now have several children. Some of the women we met, like Alison, Julie, and Betty, have not been as successful as Fred's wife in obtaining com-mitments from their lovers.

Among some conservative religious groups, the rules concerning the duties of husbands and wives explicitly recognize sex differences: wives should act as a support for their husbands, not compete with their husbands as primary breadwinners, and supervise the management of household and children. In return, men must avoid the lure of sexual variety, work hard to support their families, but also be loving and generous in spending time with their families. In erecting such rules, these groups are attempting to reaffirm the traditional economic and procreative bases of marriage.

Love is the result, not the cause

Americans are the most likely to believe that love is the basis of marriage; that it can conquer all obstacles; and that if you really love someone, all of your problems and conflicts can be solved. So when people explain why they decided to split up, they often say it was because they no longer loved their spouses. But studies of marital stability show that affectionate feelings for a partner are more a result than a cause. Women fall out of love because they no longer respect their husbands, or because their husbands hardly talk to them. Men fall out of love because they are dissatisfied sexually, or because they met someone at the office who was attractive and available. If couples work on satisfying both partners' desires—recognizing that doing so often involves compromising some of their own—they are more likely to have warm feelings for each other, and they are more likely to stay together.

In arranging marriages, most traditional peoples expect that if the families of the bride and bridegroom are well matched, and the couple were brought up well, they will be compatible because they have similar expectations about their roles and obligations, and in working together over the years to raise a family and meet life's trials, they should develop mutual esteem and affection. They do not expect marriage to be like a perpetual date—exciting and romantic. In expecting less, they may receive more.[24]

Recognize your own faults and that some of your partner's annoying traits are permanent

I talked with several couples who had been married more than 25 years. They all thought one of the most difficult things about living with someone was accepting the fact that that other person has his or her own perspective, opinions, and peculiar (from your viewpoint) habits, and that many of these traits are not going to change. They said that too often people marry with the idea that their partner is more or less okay but needs a little working on; that their partner will eventually see the light—How could they not?—and give up those annoying little habits. But very often the pet peeves that were there at the beginning of the relationship are still there 20 years later, only they are even more annoying because the romantic passion, naivete, and novelty of young relationships are not there to mask them. Even more difficult than accepting your partner for what he or she is, is recognizing your own faults and having the insight and humility to realize that your own quirks and habits are at least as peculiar and annoying to your partner as your partner's are to you. As a 50-year-old physician who had been married 25 years remarked:

> You know that line in the movie, "Loving someone is never having to say you're sorry"? Well, I think it's just the opposite. Really loving someone often means swallowing your pride and saying you're sorry even when you don't think you're wrong and don't want to apologize. Being married—or any long-term relationship for that matter—involves a lot of compromises. Both parties have to have a real commitment to making it work and that means being willing to give up a

lot of their own selfish desires. People who are only into satisfying their own needs, you know, the self-actualizing types that are into "growing" will never be content, and they sure as hell are going to have a hard time staying married.

Do things together

The most successful couples I met invariably had things that they really enjoyed doing together—sports, camping, reading, travel—and they took time to do fun things with their children. Couples who put money and work first usually had serious dissatisfactions, and there was little to hold them together when something happened that did challenge their relationship.

Accept that conflict is built in

Recognizing that these male-female differences are persistent and tenacious, and that a certain amount of conflict is inevitable, is a first step toward negotiating a compromise. I once talked to a couple who had just read my chapter on sex and marriage. The husband was amazed at how accurately my analysis matched their situation. He said that his wife just didn't understand that he really wanted sex, and he couldn't understand why she didn't want to do it. I asked the wife whether it was true that she did not understand that her husband wanted sex and that it was very important to him. She replied that she understood perfectly but that she didn't want to do it as often as he wanted. He found her attitude incomprehensible. Why wouldn't she just go ahead and do it? He really wanted it, it would make him feel good, and it wouldn't take very long. He did not understand that it was sometimes just as important to her *not* to have sex as it was to him to have it. As Claire said earlier, to enjoy sex a woman has to be in the mood, and it's not always easy for her to put herself in the mood. If her partner nudges and pushes, it usually makes it worse. Because men and women have different sexual strategies and psychologies, conflicts like this are virtually inevitable. At the age of 47, and after three marriages and a vast cross-cultural study of male-female relationships, Margaret Mead concluded that women's sexual desire was less regular, automatic, and insistent than men's and more dependent on "fitful moods."[25] As Alfred Kinsey observed, recognizing men's and women's different sexual interests and capacities is the first step in working out a healthy sexual adjustment.

Life is difficult

A final observation that some of my long-married couples made is that life itself entails difficulty and hardship, and one's love relationship is only one small part—although an important one—of the total scheme. Most of the time people are busy merely meeting the exigencies of survival—earning a living, combating illness, raising children, and making ends meet. If you have someone you can get along with most of the time while solving these problems, then you have made a good match and are lucky. Currently, about 50 percent of new marriages last. I believe they do so partly because the couples involved accept that some conflict and frustration are inevitable. But if you can tough out the rough periods while enjoying the good times, you can look forward to years of affectionate companionship. This is what the ancient Greeks called *agape* —the warm esteem and affection born of years of shared intimacy.

Notes

1. The methods of the interviews with medical students and highly sexually active college students are described in Townsend (1987, 1995) and Townsend et al. (1995). These interviews were coded and inter-rater reliability coefficients were computed (Cohen, 1960; Kvalseth, 1989). Along with various research assistants, I analyzed the open-ended interviews that were conducted with people in the community; inter-rater reliability coefficients were not computed for those interviews. Their use is purely illustrative.
2. See Townsend (1989, 1993, 1995, 1997); Townsend and Levy (1990a, 1990b); Townsend and Roberts (1993); Townsend et al. (1995).
3. On the argument that unequal resources and power produce sex differences in sexuality and mate selection, see the following: Wiederman and Allgeier (1992); Townsend (1987, 1989); Townsend and Roberts (1993); Kenrick and Keefe (1992); and Buss and Barnes (1986).
4. On eating disorders and standards for thinness in women, see Rodin et al. (1984); Mazur (1986); Rothenburg (1990).
5. Evolutionary psychologists accept that psychological and cultural factors affect sexual behavior and mate preferences, but they propose that the human brain contains elaborate programming that makes some behaviors easier to learn and more rewarding than others. They also believe that the evidence overwhelmingly supports the view that male and female brains are "programmed" differently—especially in those perceptual and emotional mechanisms that mediate sexual behavior and attraction. See Barkow et al. (1992); Tooby and Cosmides

(1992); Daly and Wilson (1983, 1988); Symons (1979, 1985, 1987, 1989); Townsend (1987, 1995); Buss (1989a, 1989b, 1995); Ellis and Symons (1990).

In contrast, most sex-role theorists believe that the emotions and sex differences discussed in this book are simply attitudes and beliefs, or parts of "scripts" that are socially constructed and learned through socialization (Blumstein and Schwartz, 1990; Laumann et al., 1994; Simon and Gagnon, 1986; Long Laws and Schwartz, 1977; Gagnon and Simon, 1973). The terms "role" and "script" are metaphors taken from drama. Just as an actor can learn a huge variety of roles, the concept of role in social science assumes that people can learn almost any role they are taught or wish to learn if they are given equal opportunity to learn and assume these roles. When applied to sex differences, the sex-role approach assumes that when men and women act differently, it is because they have been taught and encouraged to act differently. If boys and girls and men and women were given equal training and encouragement, the theory goes, these sex differences would disappear. Although male and female anatomy and physiology obviously differ in important ways, differences in *behavior* are assumed to result from different training. This view thus assumes that male and female brains are identical—blank tablets upon which the scripts for different or identical sex roles can be written.

The constructionist perspective assumes that the links between specific events and emotions are arbitrary and totally determined by one's culture. In this view parents could raise and then kill and eat their own children with relish, as long as their culture approved these activities. This sex-role constructionist perspective is the most diametrically opposed to an evolutionary/adaptationist approach. The idea of sex roles has been around for a long time, but recently it has been given a new spin with the influx of postmodern ideology into the humanities and social sciences. It has become the dominant, "politically correct" view of sex differences on most university campuses.

Evolutionary psychologists argue that although emotional reactions are learned, certain links between emotions and particular events are easier to forge than others. Some emotional reactions to particular events are therefore universal or nearly universal. This position is similar to earlier anthropologists' concept of a "developed human nature" (Brown, 1991). Although cultural customs and socialization may be able to make anything right, given human nature and certain universal needs, they have an easier time making some things right than others. Anthropologist Robert Redfield (1957) proposed, for example, that it would be easier to train mothers to cherish their children than to train them to cherish their children and then eat them. Male sexual jealousy is another example. In some societies, severe sanctions and punishments serve to control and suppress the violent reactions provoked by male sexual jealousy, but the emotions apparently occur in many individuals nevertheless, and some men express them violently despite the sanctions and punishments (Daly et al., 1982; Daly and Wilson, 1988).

CHAPTER ONE

1. Kinsey et al. (1948) covers male sexuality; Kinsey et al. (1953) compares male and female sexualities.

2. Clement et al. (1984) studied German university students and argued that sex differences had disappeared in some measures, e. g., age of first intercourse and number of sex partners. But Clement et al. acknowledged that young German women had intercourse earlier and more frequently than the young men because the women chose older males for sex partners rather than because the women were more sexually liberated than the men. Sex differences in some measures of sexual behavior and attitudes have declined in Western societies since the Kinsey studies (Alzate, 1984; Blumstein and Schwartz, 1983; Clement et al., 1984). But sex differences remain strong in masturbation rates, timing and causes of first arousal, motivations for intercourse, and the tendency to dissociate sexual relations from emotional involvement (Carroll et al., 1986; Clement et al., 1984; Knoth et al., 1988; Townsend, 1987; Useche et al., 1990; Wilson, 1981, 1987). Roche (1986) found college-age men were much more willing than women to condone and engage in intercourse "with no particular affection"; in fact, no women expressed this level of permissiveness. With higher levels of affection and monogamous commitment, however, the gap narrowed between the sexes' permissiveness. At the point where partners were in love and dating exclusively sex differences disappeared. On the persistence of Kinsey's basic sex differences, also see Blumstein and Schwartz (1983), Knoth et al. (1988), Townsend (1987, 1995), Townsend et al. (1995), Wilson (1981, 1987).

3. Hunt (1974); Hite (1976); Tavris and Sadd (1977) wrote up the Redbook survey; Blumstein and Schwartz (1983).

4. Laumann et al. (1994) are devout constructionists and argue that sex differences in sexuality are entirely caused by differential socialization. In fact, they believe that there is no biological basis for a "sex drive" because that is also a social construction that societies had to create in order to motivate their citizens to reproduce (Simon and Gagnon, 1986). Nevertheless, constructionists invariably identify the same sex differences that Kinsey found (Blumstein and Schwartz, 1983, 1990; Gagnon and Simon, 1973; Laumann et al., 1994; Long Laws and Schwartz, 1977). See Conclusion in this book for a critique of the sex-role/constructionist perspective. For reviews of studies using bio-evolutionary and social-psychological approaches, see Bailey et al. (1994), Feingold (1992), and Singer (1985a, b).

5. Lewin (1982) reports on Swedish adolescents. Knoth et al. (1988) interviewed high school and college students from a variety of geographic areas in the United States. Bailey et al. (1994) and Jankowiak et al. (1992) studied gay men and lesbians as well as heterosexuals.

6. On male visual arousal, see Symons (1979, 1987), Hill et al. (1987) and Bailey et al. (1994).

7. Flood (1981).

8. Knoth et al. (1988); also see discussion of Udry and Billy (1987) in Conclusion.

9. See Symons (1979, 1987), Hill et al. (1987) and Bailey et al. (1994).

10. Bailey et al. (1994); Singer (1985a, b); Ellis and Symons (1990); Symons (1987).

11. *U. S. News and World Report*, February 10, 1997.

12. Symons (1979, 1987); Ellis and Symons (1990).

13. Townsend (1987, 1995) and Townsend et al. (1995) contain good examples of men's tendency to renege on their promises, shirk, and spread their investments among several women.

14. On women's desire for cuddling, foreplay, and afterplay see Blumstein and Schwartz (1983), Denney et al. (1984), Townsend (1995), Long Laws and Schwartz (1977).

15. On heterosexual relations as compromises of male and female tendencies, see Symons (1979), Blumstein and Schwartz (1983), Denney et al. (1984), and Townsend (1987).

16. Denney et al. (1984).

17. See Hill, Rubin and Peplau (1979), Townsend (1987, 1995) and Townsend et al. (1995) on women's aversion to maintaining relationships that do not have any long-term potential.

18. Jules Henry (1963) coined the term *person bank* to describe adolescents' desperate need for popularity to prop up their perpetually precarious identities and self-esteem. Henry did not forsee that the fragility of adult relationships in the 1990s has extended this aspect of adolescence indefinitely. In their classic study *The Lonely Crowd*, Riesman et al. (1950) analyze how sexuality functions as entertainment and as reassurance of personal worth and likeability.

19. See Townsend (1987) on medical students and Townsend and Roberts (1993) on law students.

20. Bell and Weinberg (1978). Gay and heterosexual men express the same amount of desire for casual relations and multiple partners, but gay men have more casual relations than heterosexual men do presumably because other gay men have the same desires they do, whereas heterosexual men's desire for casual sex is constrained by women's desire for investment (Bailey et al. 1994).

21. Symons (1979) first pointed out that basic male and female sexual desires are more apparent in the behavior of homosexuals than among heterosexuals because heterosexuals must alter their behavior in order to accommodate their partners' desires amd capacities.

22. Social constructionists (Gagnon and Simon, 1974; Blumstein and Schwartz, 1983) as well as evolutionary psychologists (Symons, 1979; Bailey et al., 1994) have identified Kinsey's basic sex differences in the sexuality of both homosexual and heterosexual men and women.

23. Shilts (1987a, b).

24. On parental investment, sexual strategies, and emotions, see Symons (1979), Buss (1989b, 1993, 1995), Buss and Schmitt (1993), and Kenrick et al. (1990).

CHAPTER TWO

1. Coding categories for the interviews with medical students (Townsend, 1987) and highly sexually active undergraduates (Townsend, 1995; Townsend et al., 1995) were derived from theoretical literature (Symons 1979) and my own prior and current investigations (Townsend, 1987). One female and one male coder who were unaware of the hypotheses being tested coded the interviews.

Table 1
Medical Students' Sexual Behavior and Attitudes, By Gender

	Percentage	
	Males	Females
1. *Number of sex partners*		
None	0	20
1	0	25
2-4	45	25
5-7	20	25
8-11	10	0
12-16	10	0
17-25	5	5
over 25	10	0
2. *Age when subject first had sexual intercourse*		
15-17	35	10
18-19	50	25
20-21	15	30
21-24	0	15
Never	0	20
3. *Ideally, when would you like to marry?*		
3rd year of medical school	0	5
by end of 4th year	10	45

during residency	45	35
after residency	40	0
depends on various factors	0	15
not planning to marry	5	0

4. *Why would you prefer to marry at this time?*

more convenient (e.g., to obtain matched residencies with partner	15	30
prefer to start family by age 30	0	60
worry about increasing age reducing marital chances	0	45
being married to a medical student would be a strain on partner	10	0
not ready for marriage; fear rushing into such a serious commitment	45	0
will have more to offer partner after residency	20	0
prefer stability and support of marital relationship during residency	10	0
prefer not to marry	5	0

5. *What problems do you anticipate realizing these goals?*

will be harder to find suitable partner after graduation	5	50
opposite sex will not date professional peers	0	30
I only see classmates and prefer not to date them	15	0
no problems; I have a good relationship	25	10
dating someone in another city is difficult	5	20
prefer to avoid serious relationship at this time	20	0
chances of finding attractive partner increase as my status increases	15	0
concerned whether current relationship will last	10	30
finding acceptable partner may be a problem	5	0

6. *Would you like to have a serious relationship now—one that might lead to marriage?*

prefer to avoid serious relationships now	35	0
want serious relationship but not meeting right person	10	90
have good relationship now	25	10
want serious relationship but this is unlikely due to various reasons	55	0

20 males and 20 females. Total percentages exceed 100% in some cases because subjects gave more than one response to a question.

2. On emotions, sexual strategies, and mental mechanisms, see Tooby and Cosmides (1992); Daly and Wilson (1988); Daly et al. (1982); Nesse (1990); Buss (1989b, 1995); Buss et al. (1992); Buss and Schmitt (1993); Symons (1979, 1989). Anthropologist Donald Symons (1979) argued that women and men evolved different emotional reactions to certain types of sexual experience because throughout human history they faced different risks and opportunities in choosing partners for sex and marriage. Sex with little investment was more likely to increase men's reproductive success than women's, so men evolved a less selective sexual strategy. Although men usually invest heavily in their wives and children, they are also more inclined to engage in sexual relations with other partners that involve minimal investment.

Emotions are mental evaluations of experience: they tell us what makes us feel good and what makes us feel bad. The type of sex that served a man's reproductive interest often worked against a woman's, and what served the woman's best interest did not necessarily serve the man's. Because women can be impregnated and abandoned and men cannot, women's emotions evolved to evaluate the quality and reliability of male investment. These emotions act as an alarm system that urges women to test and evaluate investment and remedy deficiencies even when they try to be indifferent to investment.

3. Hill, Rubin, and Peplau (1979).
4. Laumann et al. (1994).
5. The results of these interviews appear in Townsend (1995) and Townsend et al. (1995). See Table 2 below.

Table 2
College Students' Sexual Behavior and Attitudes

	Percentage	
	Males	Females
1. *Number of sex partners*		
None	6	16
1-4	38	56

5-11	32	23
More than 11	24	5

2. *Age when subject first had sexual intercourse*

13-14	9	6
15-17	52	42
18-19	29	27
20-22	4	9
Never	6	16

3. *Have you ever had sex, and you knew before you had sex that you did not want to get emotionally involved with that person?*

yes	71	37
no	29	63

4. *If your answered "yes" to the previous question, was it difficult to control your feelings?*

easy	69	38
neutral	23	30
difficult	8	32

5. *I feel I should be emotionally involved with a woman/man before having sex with her/him.*

agree	32	78
ambivalent	28	15
disagree	40	7

6. *Even if I think I don't want to be emotionally involved with a person, if I have sex with her/him a few times, I begin to feel vulnerable and would at least like to know she/he cares about me.*

agree	38	74
undecided	35	16
disagree	27	10

7. *Even when I've first met a person, if I have sex with her/him, thoughts cross my mind like: "I wonder what it would be like being married to her/him; what would our wedding be like; what would our kids look like?"*

agree	32	45
undecided	16	23
disagree	52	32

8. *One of the reasons I would think twice about getting married is because I find the idea of having sex with only one person for the rest of my life depressing.*

agree	25	9
undecided	17	9
disagree	58	82

9. *I don't plan to be completely faithful forever to my wife/husband.*

agree	9	2
undecided	15	4
disagree	76	94

113 males and 175 females. Subjects recorded answers on 5-point, agree-disagree scales.

6. Townsend (1995) and Townsend et al. (1995).

7. Hill, Rubin, and Peplau (1979), Townsend (1987, 1995), and Townsend et al. (1995).

8. See Gilligan (1982), Townsend (1995), and Townsend et al. (1995). The sex differences in correlations between number of sex partners and sexual emotions were significant (Questions 2 through 4, Table 3 below).

Question 1 in Table 3 states, "I feel I should be emotionally involved with a person before having sex with him/her." Women were more likely than men to agree with this statement. Thi question correlated negatively for both sexes with number of sex partners; having sex with someone with whom they did not want to become emotionally involved, and the ease they experienced in avoiding emotional involvement with that person. Like very similar items in other surveys, this question is normative and attitudinal (Roche, 1986; Simpson and Gangestad, 1991b), whereas the questions concerning feelings of vulnerability and marital thoughts were designed to tap the actual feelings that occur when a subject engages in sexual intercourse. These results suggest that, compared to attitudinal or normative statements, women's responses to the questions concerning emotional vulnerability and investment thoughts covary less with other factors in their sex lives—i. e. they may be relatively constant, whereas this is less true of men. In other words, if these measures are valid, sexual intercourse elicits just as many (or more) feelings of bonding, desire for investment, and vulnerability in women who have had multiple partners as in women who have had one or two partners, whereas in men, greater numbers of partners correlate with increasing ease in detaching sex from emotional vulnerability and thoughts of investment.

Table 3
Correlations Between Total Number of Sex Partners and Emotions Questions for Undergraduates, By Sex of Subject

	Number of Sex Partners	
Question	Males	Females

1. *I feel I should be emotionally involved with a person before having sex with him/her.*

   $$.45 \qquad .29$$

2. *When I had sex with a person with whom I did not want to get emotionally involved, I found it easy-difficult to keep from getting emotionally involved with this person.*

   $$-.34 \qquad -.08$$

3. *Even if I don't want to be emotionally involved with someone, if I have sex with him/her, I begin to feel vulnerable and would at least like to know he/she cares.*

   $$.19 \qquad -.16$$

4. *Even when I've first met a person, if I have sex with her/him, afterwards, thoughts cross my mind like: "What would it be like being married to her/him; what would our wedding be like; what would our kids look like?"*

   $$.22 \qquad .00$$

113 males and 175 females. For Questions 2, 3 and 4 subjects who had never had these experiences were omitted from these computations.

9. On romance as women's quest for investment, see Ellis and Symons (1990), and Chapters 3, 4, and 7.
10. Schoof-Tams et al. (1976).
11. Bardwick (1971).

CHAPTER THREE

1. See Feingold (1992), Buss and Barnes (1986), and Townsend (1989, 1993) for reviews of sex differences in mate selection criteria. The following studies

demonstrate cross-cultural consistency of these sex differences: Buss l989a; Kenrick and Keefe (1992); Buss and Schmitt (1993). The following researchers found the same sex differences in mate preferences in personal advertisements: Davis (1990); Greenlees and McGrew (1994); Kenrick and Keefe, (1992); Smith et al. (1990). K. Davis (1985) discusses the problem of women's securing male investment in historical perspective. .

2. These results appeared in Townsend and Levy (1990a).

3. Graziano et al. (1993) analyze sex differences in the effects of peer opinion on judgments of attractiveness.

4. Lewin (1982) reports on Swedish adolescents; Clement et al. (1984) studied German university students. Both report females generally found older males more sexually attractive.

5. On the effects of increasing women's socioeconomic status on their standards for partners, see Lichter et al. (1995); Townsend (1989); Townsend and Roberts (1993); Wiederman and Allgeier (1992).

6. See Buss and Schmitt (1993), Buss (1989a), Kenrick and Keefe (1992), Townsend (1989, 1993).

7. Townsend and Roberts (1993) report on the mate preferences and sexuality of law students.

8. The results of the Preppy-Crunchy-Townie experiment appear in Townsend (1993). Students referred to one type of Townie as a "guido," a person sometimes, but not necessarily, of Italian ancestry, who is not part of the college subculture and is identifiable by dress, costume, hairstyle, speech mannerisms, and leisure activities. John Travolta's character in the film *Saturday Night Fever* was a 1970s guido. Michelle Pfeiffer's and Mercedes Ruehl's brilliant characterizations in *Married to the Mob* exemplify female "guidos," which some of the women research assistants facetiously termed "guidettes." These appelations are not anti-Italian. A high proportion of the students we polled in this study are Italian Americans and have friends and relatives whom they affectionately refer to as guidos. As they pointed out, "guido" is a social type rather than an ethnicity.

The descriptions in the experiment are stereotypical in the sense that probably no one individual consistently exhibits all of the characteristics depicted here, but there was virtual consensus among the students surveyed that these were actual social types, well known at least to students in the Northeast, and that these traits were associated with these types.

9. The three experiments on variability in ratings of attractiveness appear in Townsend and Wasserman (1997).

10. Remoff (1984) conducted ethnographic interviews with women from working-class, middle-class, and upper-middle-class backgrounds.

11. On the determinants of women's mate preferences, see Townsend (1989), Townsend and Roberts (1993), Lichter et al. (1995), Wiederman and Allgeier (1992), Blumstein and Schwartz (1983), Goldman et al. (1984). Acceptance of feminist ideology did not appear to correlate negatively with these female

responses (Townsend, 1989, 1993). In fact, some of the most outspoken advocates of feminist principles were the most explicit in describing their desires for strong, decisive, successful men (see Chapters 7, 8, and 9).

CHAPTER FOUR

1. See the following on overlap in male and female standards for marriage partners (Buss and Barnes, 1986; Buss, 1989a; Bixler, 1989; Kenrick and Keefe, 1992; N. Thornhill 1989; Townsend 1992, 1993; Townsend and Roberts, 1993). In responding to Townsend's comment (1992), Kenrick states explicitly that men desire two types of women: a sexy one for short-term relationships, and one more like them in age and personality characteristics for long-term, high-investment relationships like marriage (Kenrick and Keefe 1992). Kenrick argues that male and female criteria converge in Kenrick and Keefe (1989) and Kenrick et al. (1990). On the contrary, men are choosier about partners' looks for marriage than for casual relations because they have to invest so much more in marriage. Men do, however, consider other traits like social skills, class, and background important when they pick partners for marriage (Townsend, 1989, 1993; Townsend and Roberts, 1993).

2. On women's refusal to marry down, see Lichter et al. (1995), Townsend (1989), Townsend and Roberts (1993), Goldman et al. (1984).

3. The law student study appeared in Townsend and Roberts (1993).

4. Elder (1969).

5. Udry (1977).

6. Udry and Eckland (1984).

7. Trivers (1985) offers an excellent discussion of deception among humans and other species. Buss and Dedden (1990) report on derogation of female competitors' intelligence. Schmitt and Buss (1996) show that the types of insults differ depending on whether the insulter desires a short-term or long-term relationship.

8. See Townsend (1989, 1993), Townsend and Roberts (1993), and Chapter 7 for discussions of these issues.

9. The effects of increasing status on sexuality and standards for partners among medical students appear in Townsend (1987, 1989); among law students, in Townsend and Roberts (1993).

CHAPTER FIVE

1. Buss (1989a) presents the results of the 37 culture study. In choosing partners, men emphasize youth and beauty; women stress socioeconomic status. These sex differences appear in all studies of personal advertisements and actual marriage choices (Buss and Schmitt, 1993; Davis, 1990; Greenlees and McGrew, 1994; Kenrick and Keefe, 1992; Lichter et al., 1995; Smith et al., 1990; Sprecher et al.,

1994; Townsend and Roberts, 1993).

2. Murstein and Christy (1976) report on middle-aged couples. See Townsend and Roberts (1993) for a review of the literature.

3. Men's capacity for visual arousal is discussed in Chapter 1. See the following sources on men's capacity for visual sexual arousal and their criteria for choosing partners and maintaining relationships: Bailey et al. (1994); Kinsey et al. (1953); Symons (1985, 1987); Weinrich (1988).

4. Symons (1979, 1987) makes this point.

5. See the following sources on selection criteria and the marriage market: Buss (1994); Blumstein and Schwartz (1983); Goldman et al. (1984); Townsend and Roberts (1993).

6. Berscheid and Walster (1974) emphasized the arbitrary nature of attractiveness. The following studies indicate that some attributes of beauty are universal: Cunningham (1986); Cunningham et al. (1990); Symons (1979); Singh (1993, 1995).

7. Although Mazur (1986) stresses variability in standards of female beauty, his data are actually consistent with the views expressed in this chapter and with Singh (1993).

8. Mazur (1986) presents the mean measurements of Miss America contests from 1930 to 1983.

9. Fallon and Rozin (1985). Also see Smith et al. (1990).

10. Anderson et al. (1992) show that plumpness is considered a sign of health and wealth, and is therefore considered attractive, wherever food is scarce and female fertility is valued (e. g., in Third World countries).

11. Bell (1976).

12. For an excellent evolutionary explanation of the link between female fat and fertility, see Lancaster (1985). On cross-cultural standards of female attractiveness, see Anderson et al. (1992).

13. Singh (1993, 1995).

14. See Lancaster (1985), Buss (1989a), Symons (1979), and Singh (1993).

15. See Symons (1979, 1987).

16. Cunningham (1986) reports the study of the Miss Universe contestants. Langlois and Roggman (1990) argue that attractive faces are only average. Alley and Cunningham (1991) show that although average faces are attractive, the most attractive faces are not average. Instead, they embody certain features that correlate with health, sexual maturity, and masculinity and femininity. Some features, like high, wide cheekbones and wide-set eyes are attractive in both sexes.

17. Researchers have consistently reported these sex differences in mate preferences among gay men and lesbians: Bell and Weinberg (1978); Gagnon and Simon (1973); Blumstein and Schwartz (1983); Bailey et al. (1994); Sergios and Cody (1985).

CHAPTER SIX

1. Guttentag and Secord (1983).
2. Women's average life span is about ten years greater than men's, so a good part of the general surplus of women results from the fact that men are dying younger and leaving a large pool of women for which there are no men. But men's shorter life expectancy does not substantially reduce the number of available men until they are in their fifties. For example, by age forty only about one percent more women have survived than men. There is thus a huge shortage of men for women over 60, but this does not explain the problems facing single women in their thirties and forties: these women face a shortage of *suitable* men.
3. U. S. Bureau of the Census, Current Population Reports, series P-20, No. 445 through No. 49 Marital Status of the Population, by Sex and Age: 1989.
4. On men's preference for younger women, see the discussion of the marriage market in China in Chapter 10 and the following articles: Kenrick and Keefe (1992); Kogan and Mills (1992); Townsend (1992).
5. Goldman et al. (1984); also see Blumstein and Schwartz (1983).
6. Bernard (1979); Blumstein and Schwartz (1983).
7. van den Berghe (1979).
8. Daly and Wilson (1983) review the studies of polygyny threshold.
9. Dickemann (1979).
10. Lockard and Adams (1981).
11. Rossi (1985).
12. Bloom and Trussell (1984).
13. Bellah et al. (1985), p. 101–2, 8.
14. Blumstein and Schwartz (1983).

CHAPTER SEVEN

1. Ellis and Symons (1990) present an excellent discussion of this topic and an extensive bibliography. Also see Mussell (1984).
2. Money and Ehrhardt (1972).
3. For reviews and refutation of these predictions see the following: Buss and Barnes (1986); Buss and Schmitt (1993); Townsend (1987, 1989); Townsend and Roberts (1993); Wiederman and Allgeier (1992).
4. Jankowiak (1986).
5. See Townsend (1995) and Townsend et al. (1995).
6. Pat is definitely talking about romantic ravishment here and not rape, which all woman abhor. See Hazen (1983) and Faust (1980) on women's attitudes toward romantic ravishment.
7. Sadalla et al. (1987).

8. Buss (1995); Buss and Schmitt (1993); Sadalla et al. (1987).
9. Sadalla et al. (1987).
10. Townsend et al. (1995).
11. Benedict was a graduate student in political science at Northeastern University. His M. A. thesis, "Athletes and Rape: How Sport Culture Complicates the Establishment of Consent," was described in the *New York Times*, June 18, 1995, by Robert Lipsyte.
12. Buss and Schmitt (1993).
13. Townsend et al. (1995).

CHAPTER EIGHT

1. See van den Berghe (1979) and Daly and Wilson (1983) on brideprice and dowry.
2. Shorter (1975).
3. Kinsey et al. (1953).
4. Rhyne (1981).
5. Blumstein and Schwartz (1983).
6. *Family Circle*, June 11, 1985.
7. Kinsey et al. (1953).
8. Udry et al. (1982).
9. Murstein and Christy (1976).
10. Blumstein and Schwartz (1983).
11. See Rubin (1983) on women's need for intimacy.
12. On women's and men's motives for extramarital affairs, see Blumstein and Schwartz (1983) and Glass and Wright (1985).
13. Daly et al. (1982).
14. Buss et al. (1992) had men and women fantasize different scenarios of infidelity and measured their physiological reactions. The results supported the view that men's jealousy focuses on intercourse itself and this causes extreme emotional upset. Also see Harvard men's violent reactions to Thematic Apperception Tests in Gilligan (1982).
15. See Daly et al. (1982) and Daly and Wilson (1988).
16. Espenshade (1985).
17. Udry (1981).
18. The following authors all make this point: Bernard (1979); Norton and Glick (1979); Shorter (1975).

CHAPTER NINE

1. Harris (1981).
2. Strasser (1982).
3. See the following sources on women's power: Hofer (1974); Paul (1974); Tilly

(1978); James (1978); and Friedl (1967).

4. On the equal-partner marriage, see Keith and Schafer (1980); Chodorow (1978); and Scanzoni (1979, 1983).

5. On the effects of family background and sex-role attitudes on the division of domestic tasks, see the following: Atkinson and Boles (1984); Bailyn (1970); Bird et al. (1984); Blair and Lichter (1991); Model (1981); Scanzoni (1978, 1979); Yogev (1981).

6. On dual-career families and marital satisfaction, see the following sources: (Blumstein and Schwartz (1983); Hiller and Philliber (1982); Johnson and Johnson (1977); Keith and Schafer (1980); Scanzoni (1978, 1979); Yogev (1981).

7. Scanzoni (1979, p. 31).

8. Blumstein and Schwartz (1983).

9. Udry (1981).

10. See the following sources (Atkinson and Boles, 1984; Bird et al., 1984; Blumstein and Schwartz, 1983; Hiller and Philliber, 1982; Model, 1981; Scanzoni, 1978, 1979).

11. Johnson and Johnson (1977).

12. Weitzman (1985) and Blumberg (1985).

13. Chodorow (1978).

14. See Rossi (1977) on the biosocial basis of parenthood and (1985) for a critique of Chodorow and a review of sex differences in the organization of the brain.

15. Money (1961), p. 1392. Also see Money (1965). Symons (1979) gives an excellent review of this evidence.

16. Using magnetic resonance imaging, Sally Shaywitz (1995) and colleagues at the Yale University School of Medicine found clear evidence for a sex difference in the functional organization of the brain for language.

17. Rossi (1977, 1985) makes this point. See also Mead (1962) on fatherhood as a "social invention."

18. See Johnson and Johnson (1977); Townsend (1989); and Hakim (1995) on women adjusting career commitments to allow for family commitments.

19. See the following sources: Atkinson and Boles (1984); Bird et al. (1984); Hiller and Philliber (1982); Model, (1981); Scanzoni (1978, 1979).

20. Friedan (1981).

CHAPTER TEN

1. Buss (1989a), Buss and Schmitt (1993), Symons (1979), van den Berghe (1979), and Daly and Wilson (1983) offer good surveys of the cross-cultural evidence.

2. Betzig (1986), van den Berghe (1979), Dickemann (1979), and Stephens (1963) all indicate that men's control of women's behavior—especially sexual behavior—is more severe in agrarian kingdoms.

3. See Mead (1928), Marshall (1971) and Buss and Schmitt (1993).

4. Brown (1991) offers an excellent analysis of Mead's role in the nature-nurture controversy within anthropology.

5. See Freeman (1983), Brady et al. (1983), Holmes (1987), and Feinberg (1988).

6. The page numbers are from the original edition (Mead, 1928).

7. Mead (1928), pp. 157, 160, 201.

8. Mead (1928), p. 99.

9. Mead (1928), p. 104–05.

10. Mead (1928), p. 99.

11. Mead (1928), p. 155.

12. Mead (1928), p. 176–77.

13. Mead (1928), p. 181.

14. Mead (1928), p. 179–80.

15. Mead (1928), p. 92.

16. Mead (1928), pp. 37, 88, 99.

17. Marshall (1971).

18. Marshall (1971). p. 124.

19. Mead (1928) and Knoth et al. (1988).

20. Marshall (1971). pp. 128, 151.

21. Malinowski (1929).

22. Mead does present evidence of the "darker" side of Samoan life, although she did not emphasize this side because it did not fit her mentor's (Ruth Benedict's) notion of the dominant cultural configuration (Shore, 1983; Feinberg, 1988). In Appendix III Mead (1928) argued that Samoan culture was less flexible and dealt more harshly with deviance *before* the intrusion of western influence. Girls' deviations from chastity were formerly punished by a severe beating and a stigmatizing shaving of the head. Similarly, in former times the man who was head of the household had life and death powers over every individual under his roof, and young people who wanted to change their residence might have to flee a great distance to avoid being beaten to death. Mead concludes that the colonial prohibitions " . . . against blood revenge and violence have worked like a yeast in giving greater personal freedom." Traditional Samoa was in many respects more rigid and harsh in its punishment of deviance and its maintenance of a sexual double-standard than was Mead's colonized Samoa. Polynesian expert Bradd Shore points out that Polynesia has long held a special place in the minds of Westerners as representing an idyllic paradise where life was easy, violence and competition were absent, and sexuality was casual and uncomplicated. "[Mead's] portrait of Samoan ethos and life has remained fixed in the popular mythology of the South Seas, confirming our need to believe in a place free of the stresses that beset our own lives. The place that Polynesia in general and Samoa particularly have in that mythology has been dramatically confirmed in the various news-media accounts of Samoa. Rather than recognize the essential humanity of Samoans, the popular press has tended to explain away the contradictions between Mead's and Freeman's reports by placing the idyllic Samoa of Mead in

the past, and the darker, harsher Samoa of Freeman in the decadent, Western-saturated present. A myth has been virtually left intact with the aid of simplistic uses of history, to confirm the possibility of heaven on earth." (Shore, 1983).

23. Mead (1963), p. viii. Unfortunately, Mead never defines "temperament," but her principal topics are sex, aggression, and maternal tendencies, and she clearly claims that observable sex differences in these traits are the result of cultural conditioning and not biology (1963), p. 280.

24. Mead (1963), p. 280.

25. Haller (1963) discusses Nordicism, the eugenics movement in America, and Boas's role (and that of his students, Benedict and Mead) in combating these movements. He writes: "Among American anthropologists generally, Boas's influence and the understanding that comes through sympathetic study of diverse cultures were decisive in creating a climate unfavorable to racist dogmas. As a result, Americans who subscribed to these theories were seldom anthropologists and were forced to look to Europe for anthropological findings to buttress their case." (1963, p. 145).

Shore (1983) and Feinberg (1988) both point out the discrepancy between Mead's generalizations and observations, and that her attempt to use Ruth Benedict's theory of cultural configuration caused her to gloss over details and observations that did not fit into what she thought was the dominant configuration.

26. Mead (1939), pp. x–xi.

27. Mead (1962).

28. Mead (1962), p. 206.

29. Mead (1962), p. 202.

30. Whyte and Parish (1984).

31. Jankowiak (1993).

32. The personal interviews in this chapter are from Jankowiak's research from 1981 to 1983, and appeared in Townsend and Jankowiak (1986).

33. Jankowiak (1993, 1995).

34. *China Daily*, December 21, 1982, p. 5, on dipilatories; *China Daily*, August 8, 1983, p. 6. on cosmetic surgery.

35. This sex difference might be explained by the fact that men still tend to dominate the higher positions in China. But this fact alone seems an inadequate explanation of the observed sex difference because egalitarian policies have minimized inequality of career and educational opportunities among men and women, most urban Chinese women are employed, and there is a small gap between husbands' and wives' incomes (Whyte and Parish 1984, pp. 223–27).

36. See Buss and Schmitt (1993), Daly and Wilson (1983), Symons (1979).

37. Reviewed in Townsend and Jankowiak (1986).

38. See Shields (1983) and Thornhill and Thornhill (1983).

39. See Townsend and Jankowiak (1986) and Whyte and Parish (1984).

40. Croll (1981, 1983).

41. Xu Anqi (1994).

42. Zhang Huoshen (1991).
43. Chen Zaihua (1994).
44. Baxiaoshi Ziwai (1994).
45. Zhu Shuangxi (1992).
46. Wang Jinling (1992).
47. *China Youth,* 1987, no. 9, p. 27.
48. Huang Aili (1991).
49. Pan Suiming (1993).
50. Tong Xin (1993).
51. Given opportunity, communist ideologues show the same sexual tendencies we see in the West. Despite the sexually egalitarian, puritanical quality of Maoist thought, Mao himself was a devoted functional polygynyst who had multiple women brought to him for private sessions—often several young, beautiful women at a time. These private affairs were called "dancing parties," but as Mao's private physician testifies, everyone knew their purpose was sexual (Li Zhisui, 1994). See conclusion for more examples of utopian and communistic groups that evolved into polygynous patriarchies.

CONCLUSION

1. Brown (1991) provides a cogent demonstration of this point.
2. Goode (1963).
3. See Murstein (1980); Pellow (1986).
4. On out-of-wedlock births and single-parent households, see Davis (1985); Sheper (1981); Becker (1981); Harris (1981).
5. Rossi (1977, 1985); van den Berghe (1979).
6. Liebow (1967); Becker (1981); Espenshade (1985).
7. Levi (1982) discusses both Jonestown and Synanon. See also Wooden (1981) on Jones.
8. Mitchell et al. (1980).
9. See Sheper and Tiger (1983). Rossi (1985) offers a good discussion of this controversy, along with bibliographic references.
10. van den Berghe (1979).
11. See Udry and Billy (1987) for a literature review and bibliographic references.
12. See Halpern (1992); Durden-Smith and DeSimone (1983); and Shaywitz et al. (1995).
13. On prostitution, see Burley and Symanski (1981). For reviews of the cross-cultural evidence on sex differences in sexuality and mate preferences, see the following sources: Buss (1989a); Buss and Schmitt (1993); Kenrick and Keefe (1992); Symons (1979); Townsend (1995); Townsend et al. (1995).
14. See Stephens (1963) for a good cross-cultural overview of the sexual division of labor.
15. On the psychology of sex differences, see Maccoby and Jacklin (1974). See Daly and Wilson (1983), Townsend (1995), and Rossi (1985) for reviews.

16. Long Laws and Schwartz (1977).

17. Gagnon and Simon (1973). Laumann et al. (1994) also interpret their data from a constructionist perspective.

18. Gagnon and Simon (1973). Also see Blumstein and Schwartz (1983).

19. See the following studies: Spanier (1976); Edwards and Booth (1976); LaPlante et al. (1980); and Townsend (1995).

20. Symons (1979) first made this argument. For an update, see Bailey et al. (1994).

21. See Townsend (1987,1989); Townsend and Roberts,(1993); Wiederman and Allgeier (1992).

22. Report on CBS *60 Minutes*, January 7, 1990.

23. On fantasies, see Ellis and Symons (1990). On emotional reactions to casual sex, see Townsend (1987,1995) and Townsend et al. (1995).

24. Bohannan (1973) notes that couples in the United States use "love" as a rationalization for getting married, and when they divorce, they say they were no longer "in love," rather than recognizing the influence of economic factors, and sexual desires and dissatisfactions. On unrealistic expectations of marriage, see Bernard (1979); Norton and Glick (1979); Davis (1985); Symons (1985).

25. Mead (1962).

References

Alley, T. and Cunningham, M. 1991. Averaged faces are attractive, but very attractive faces are not average. *Psychological Science* 2: 123–25.

Alzate, H. 1984. Sexual behavior of unmarried Colombian University Students: A five-year follow-up. *Archives of Sexual Behavior* 13: 121–32.

Anderson, J., Crawford, C., Nadeau, J., and Lindberg, T. 1992. Was the Duchess of Windsor Right? A cross-cultural review of the socioecology of ideals of female body shape. *Ethology and Sociobiology* 13: 197–227.

Atkinson, M. & Boles, J. 1984. WASP: Wives as senior partners. *Journal of Marriage and the Family* 46: 861–70.

Bailey, J. M., Gaulin, S., Agyei, Y., & Gladue, B. A. 1994. Effects of gender and sexual orientation on evolutionarily relevant aspects of human mating psychology. *Journal of Personality and Social Psychology* 66: 1081–93.

Bailyn, L. 1970. Career and family orientations of husbands and wives in relation to marital happiness. *Human Relations* 23: 97–113.

Bardwick, J. 1971. *The Psychology of Women*. New York: Harper & Row.

Barkow, J. H., Cosmides, L., and Tooby, J. (eds.) 1992. *The Adapted Mind*. New York: Oxford University Press.

Baxiaoshi Ziwai, Tianjin. 1994. 1: 60.

Becker, G. 1981. *Treatise on the Family*. Cambridge, MA: Harvard University Press.

Bell, Q. 1976. *On Human Finery*. New York: Schocken Books.

Bell, A. P., & Weinberg, M.S. 1978. *Homosexualities*. New York: Simon and Schuster.

Bellah, R., Madsen, R., Sullivan, W., Swidler, A. and Tipton, S. 1985. *Habits of the Heart*. New York: Harper & Row.

Bernard, J. 1972. *The Future of Marriage*. New York: World.

Bernard, J. 1979. Foreword. In G. Levinger & O. Moles (eds.), *Divorce and Separation*. New York: Basic Books.

Berscheid, E., & Walster, E. 1974. Physical attractiveness. In L. Berkowitz (ed.), *Advances in Experimental Social Psychology*. New York: Academic Press.

Betzig, L. 1986. *Despotism and Differential Reproduction: A Darwinian View of History*. Hawthorne, New York: Aldine de Gruyter.

Bird, G., Bird, G., & Scruggs, M. 1984. Detrerminants of family task sharing. *Journal of Marriage and the Family* 46: 345–55.

Bixler, R. H. 1989 Diversity: A historical/comparative perspective. *Behavioral and Brain Sciences* 12: 15–16.

Blair, S., & Lichter, D. 1991. Measuring the divison of household labor. *Journal of Family Issues* 12: 91–113.

Bloom, D. & Trussell, J. 1984. What are the determinants of delayed childbearing and permanent childlessness in the United States? *Demography* 21: 591–611.

Blumberg, G. 1985. New models of marriage and divorce. In K. Davis (ed.), *Contemporary Marriage*. New York: Russell Sage Foundation.

Blumstein, P., & Schwartz, P. 1983. *American Couples*. New York: Morrow.

Blumstein, P., & Schwartz, P. 1990. Intimate relationships and the creation of sexuality. In D. P. McWhirter, S. A. Sanders, & J. M. Rheinisch (eds.), *Homosexuality/Heterosexuality: Concepts of Sexual Orientation*. New York: Oxford University Press.

Bohannan, P. 1973. Alienation in marriage. In L. Nader and T. Maretski (eds.), *Culture, Illness, and Health*. Washington, D.C.: American Anthropological Association.

Brown, D. 1991. *Human universals*. New York: McGraw Hill.

Burley, N., and Symanski, R. 1981. Women without: An evolutionary and cross-cultural perspective on prostitution. In R. Symanski (ed.), *The Immoral Landscape: Female Prostitution in Western Societies*. Toronto: Butterworths.

Buss, D. M. 1989a. Sex differences in human mate preferences: Evolutionary hypotheses tested in 37 cultures. *Behavioral and Brain Sciences* 12: 1–49.

Buss, D. M. 1989b. Conflict between the sexes: Strategic interference and the evocation of anger and upset. *Journal of Personality and Social Psychology* 56: 735–47.

Buss, D. M. 1994. Individual differences in mating strategies. *Behavioral and Brain Sciences* 17: 581–82

Buss, D. M. 1995. Evolutionary psychology: A new paradigm for psychological science. *Psychological Inquiry* 6: 1–30.

Buss, D. M., and Barnes, M. 1986. Preferences in human mate selection. *Journal of Personality and Social Psychology* 50: 559–70.

Buss, D. M., Larsen, R., Westen, D., and Semmelroth, J. 1992. Sex differences in jealousy: Evolution, physiology, and psychology. *Psychological Science* 3: 251–55.

Buss, D. M., & Schmitt, D. 1993. Sexual strategies theory: An evolutionary perspective on human mating. *Psychological Review* 100: 204–32.

Buss, D. M., & Dedden, D. 1990. Derogation of competitors. *Journal of Social and Personal Relationships* 7: 395–422.

Carroll, J. C., Volk, K. D., and Hyde, J. S. 1986. Differences in motives for engaging in sexual intercourse. *Archives of Sexual Behavior* 14: 131–43.

Chen Zaihua 1994. Beijing: Sui Aichao Nanzhu? (Who are the least marriageable in Beijing?) *Nuxing Yanjiu* (Women's Studies) 1: 14–16.

Clement, U., Schmidt, G., and Kruse, M. l984. Changes in sex differences in sexual behavior. *Archives of Sexual Behavior* 13: 99–120.

Cherlin, A. 1979. Work life and marital dissolution. In G. Levinger and O. Moles (eds.), *Divorce and Separation*. New York: Basic Books.

Chodorow, N. 1978. *The Reproduction of Mothering*. Berkeley CA: University of California Press.

Cohen, J. 1960. A coefficient of agreement for nominal scales. *Educational and Psychological Measurement* 20: 37–46.

Croll, E. 1981. *The Politics of Marriage in Contemporary China*. New York: Cambridge University Press.

Croll, E. 1983. *Chinese women since Mao*. Armonk, NY: M. E. Sharpe.

Cunningham, M. R. 1986. Measuring the physical in physical attractiveness: Quasi experiments in the sociobiology of female facial beauty. *Journal of Personality and Social Psychology* 50: 925–35.

Cunningham, M. , Barbee, A. P., and Pike, C. L. 1990. What do women want? Facialmetric assessment of multiple motives in the perception of male facial physical attractiveness. *Journal of Personality and Social Psychology* 59: 61–71.

Daly, M., & Wilson, M. 1983. *Sex, Evolution, and Behavior*. Boston, MA: PWS.

Daly, M., & Wilson, M. 1988. *Homicide*. Hawthorne, NY: Aldine de Gruyter.

Daly, M., Wilson, M., and Weghorst, S. 1982. Male sexual jealousy. *Ethology and Sociobiology* 3: 11–27.

Darwin, C. 1955. [1872.] *The Expression of Emotion in Man and Animals*. New York: Philosophical Library.

Davidson, R., Ekman, P., Saron, C., Senulis, J., and Friesen, W. 1990. Approach-withdrawl and cerebral asymmetry: Emotional expression and brain physiology I. *Journal of Personality and Social Psychology* 58: 330–41.

Davis, K. 1985. The future of marriage. In K. Davis (ed.), *Contemporary Marriage* New York: Russell Sage Foundation.

Davis, S. 1990. Men as success objects and women as sex objects: A study of personal advertisements. *Sex Roles* 23: 43–50.

DeLamater, J. 1991. Emotions and sexuality. In K. McKinney and S. Sprecher (eds.), *Sexuality in Close Relationships*. Hillsdale, NJ: Lawrence Erlbaum.

Denney, N. W., Field, J. K., and Quadagno, D. 1984. Sex differences in sexual needs and desires. *Archives of Sexual Behavior* 13: 233–45.

Dickemann, M. 1979. Female infanticide, reproductive strategies, and social-stratification. In *Evolutionary Biology and Human Social Behavior*. N. Chagnon & W. Irons (eds.), North Scituate, MA: Duxbury Press.

Durden-Smith, J. and DeSimone, D. 1983. *Sex and the Brain*. New York: Arbor House.

Edwards, J. and Booth, A. 1976. Sexual behavior in and out of marriage: An assessment of correlates. *Journal of Marriage and the Family* 38: 73–81.

Ekman, P., Levenson, R. W., and Friesen, W. V. 1983. Autonomic nervous system activity distinguishes among emotions. *Science* 221. 1208–10.

Elder, G. H. 1969. Appearance and education in marriage mobility. *American Sociological Review* 34: 519–32.

Ellis, B., and Symons, D. 1990. Sex differences in sexual fantasy: An evolutionary psychological approach. *Journal of Sex Research* 27: 527–55.

Espenshade, T. 1985. The recent decline of American marriage. In K. Davis (ed.), *Contemporary Marriage*. New York: Russell Sage Foundation.

Fallon, A., and Rozin, P. 1985. Sex differences in perceptions of desirable body shape. *Journal of Abnormal Psychology* 94: 102–05.

Faust, 1980. *Women, Sex, and Pornography*. New York: Macmillan.

Feinberg, R. 1988. Margaret Mead and Samoa: Coming of age in fact and fiction. *American Anthropologist* 90: 656–63.

Feingold, A. 1992. Gender differences in mate selection preferences: A test of the parental investment model. *Psychological Bulletin* 112: 125–39.

Fisher, H. 1987. The four year itch. *Natural History* 10: 22–29.

Flood, P. 1981. Body parts. *Esquire* (June): 35–43.

Friedan, B. 1981. *The Second Stage*. New York: Summit.

Friedl, E. 1967. The position of women: Appearance and reality. *Anthropological Quarterly* 40: 97–108.

Gagnon, J., and Simon, W. 1973. *Sexual Conduct*. Chicago: Aldine.

Gangestad, S. W. and Simpson, J. A. 1990. Toward an evolutionary history of female sociosexual variation. *Journal of Personality* 58: 69–96.

Gilligan, C. 1982. *In a Different Voice*. Cambridge, MA: Harvard University Press.

Glass, S. & Wright, T. 1985. Sex differences in type of extramarital involvement and marital dissatisfaction. *Sex Roles* 12: 1101–20.

Glenn, N. D. 1989. Intersocial variation in the mate preferences of males and females. *Behavioral and Brain Sciences* 12: 21–23.

Goldman, N., Westoff, C., and Hammerslough, C. 1984. Demography of the marriage market in the United States. *Population Index* 50: 5–25.

Goode, W. 1963. *World Revolution and Family Patterns*. New York: Free Press.

Graziano, W., Jensen-Campbell, L., Shebilske, L., and Lundgren, S. 1993. Social influence, sex differences, and judgments of beauty. *Journal of Personality and Social Psychology* 65: 522–31.

Greenlees, A. and McGrew, W. 1994. Sex and age differences in preferences and tactics of mate attraction. *Ethology and Sociobiolog,* 15: 59–72.

Gutentag, M. and Secord, P. 1983. *Too Many Women? The Sex Ratio Question.* Beverly Hills, CA: Sage.

Hakim, C. 1995. Five feminist myths about women's employment. *British Journal of Sociology* 46: 429–53.

Haller, M. 1963. *Eugenics: Hereditarian Attitudes in American Thought.* New Brunswick, NJ: Rutgers University Press.

Halpern, D. 1992. *Sex differences in cognitive abilities.* Hillsdale, NJ: Lawrence Erlbaum.

Harris, M. 1981. *America now: The Anthropology of a Changing Culture.* New York: Simon and Schuster.

Hazen, 1983. *Endless rapture: Rape, Romance, and the Female Imagination.* New York: Charles Scribner's Sons.

Hill C., Rubin, Z., and Peplau, L. 1979. Breakups before marriage: The end of 103 affairs. In G. Levinger & O. Moles (eds.), *Divorce and Separation* New York: Basic Books.

Hill, E., Nocks, E., and Gardner, L. 1987. Manipulation by physical and status displays. *Ethology and Sociobiology* 8: 43–154.

Hiller, D., & Philliber, W. 1982. Predicting marital and career success among dual-worker couples. *Journal of Marriage and the Family* 44: 53–62.

Hite, S. 1976. *The Hite Report.* New York: Macmillan.

Hofer, C. 1974. Madam Yoko: Ruler of the Kpa Mende confederacy. In S. Rosaldo and L. Lamphere (eds.), *Women, Culture, and Society.* Palo Alto, CA: Stanford University Press.

Holmes, L. 1987. *Quest for the Real Samoa: The Mead/Freeman Controversy and Beyond.* South Hadley, MA: Bergin & Garvey.

Huang Aili. 1991. Getihu shenghuo fangshi dui qi hunbian de yingxiang (Effects of private business owner's lifestyle on marital stability). *Shehuixue Yanjiu* (Sociological Research) 6: 41–49.

Hunt, M. 1974. *Sexual behavior in the 1970s.* Chicago: Playboy Press.

Irons, W. 1989. Mating preference surveys. *Behavioral and Brain Sciences* 12: 24.

James, W. 1978. Matrifocus on African women. In S. Ardener (ed.), *Defining Females.* New York: Wiley.

Jankowiak, W. 1986. Gender bewilderment: Sundays at 1364 1/2 Milford Manor. *California Anthropologist* 14: 16–30.

Jankowiak, W. 1993. *Sex, Death, and Hierarchy in a Chinese City.* New York: Columbia University Press.

Jankowiak, W. 1995. *Romantic Passion: The Universal Experience.* New York: Columbia University Press.

Jankowiak, W., Hill, E., and Donovan, J. 1992. The effects of sex and sexual orientation on attractiveness judgments. *Ethology and Sociobiology* 13: 73–85.

Johnson, F. and Johnson, C. 1977. Attitudes toward parenting in dual-career families. *American Journal of Psychiatry* 134: 391–95.

Keith, P. M., and Schaefer, R. B. 1980. Role strain and depression in two-job families. *Family Relations* 29: 483–88.

Kenrick, D. T., and Keefe, R. C. 1989. Time to integrate sociobiology and social psychology. *Behavioral and Brain Sciences* 12: 24–26.

Kenrick, D. and Keefe, R. 1992. Age preferences in mates reflect sex differences in reproductive strategies. *Behavioral and Brain Sciences* 15: 1–29.

Kenrick, D., Sadalla., E., Groth, G., and Trost, M. 1990. Evolution, traits, and the stages of human courtship: Qualifying the parental investment model. *Journal of Personality* 58: 97–116.

Kinsey, A., Pomeroy, W., and Martin, C. 1948. *Sexual behavior in the Human Male*. New York: W.B. Saunders.

Kinsey, A., Pomeroy, W., Martin, C., and Gebhard, P. 1953. *Sexual behavior in the human female*. New York: W.B. Saunders.

Knoth, R., Boyd, K., and Singer, B. 1988. Empirical tests of sexual selection theory. *Journal of Sex Research* 24: 74–89.

Kogan, N. and Mills, M. 1992. Gender influences on age cognitions and preferences. *Psychology and Aging* 7: 98–106.

Kvalseth, T. 1989 Note on Cohen's Kappa. *Psychological Reports* 65: 223–26.

Lancaster, J. B. 1985. Evolutionary perspectives on sex differences in the higher primates. In A. Rossi (ed.), *Gender and the Life Course*. New York: Aldine.

Langlois, J. and Roggman, L. 1990. Attractive faces are only average. *Psychological Science* 1: 115–21.

LaPlante, M., McCormick, N., and Brannigan, G. 1980. Living the sexual script. *Journal of Sex Research* 16: 338–55.

Laumann, E., Gagnon, J., Michael, R., and Michaels, S. 1994. *The social Organization of Sexuality*. Chicago: University of Chicago Press.

Levi, K. 1982. *Violence and Religious Commitment*. University Park, PA: Pennsylvania State University Press.

Lewin, B. 1982. The adolescent boy and girl: First and other early experiences with intercourse from a representative sample of Swedish school adolescents. *Archives of Sexual Behavior* 11: 417–28.

Lichter, D., Anderson, R., and Hayward, M. 1995. Marriage markets and marital choice. *Journal of Family Issues* 16: 412–31.

Liebow, E. 1967. *Tally's Corner*. Boston: Little, Brown.

Li, Z. 1994. *The Private Life of Chairman Mao*. New York: Random House.

Lockard, J., and Adams, R. 1981. Human serial polygyny: Demographic, reproductive, marital, and divorce data. *Ethology and Sociobiology* 2: 177–86.

Long Laws, J. and Schwartz, P. 1977. *Sexual Scripts: the Social Construction of Female Sexuality*. Hinsdale, IL: Dryden Press.

Maccoby, E. and Jacklin, C. 1974. *The Psychology of Sex Differences*. Palo Alto,

CA: Stanford University Press.

Malinowski, B. 1929. The sexual life of savages in north-western Melanesia. London: Routledge.

Mandler, G. 1984. *Mind and Body: Psychology of Emotion and Stress*. New York: W. W. Norton.

Marshall, D. 1971. Sexual behavior on Mangaia. In D. Marshall, and R. Suggs (eds.), *Human Sexual Behavior*. New York: Basic Books.

Mazur, A. 1986. U. S. trends in feminine beauty and overadaptation. *The Journal of Sex Research* 22: 281–303.

Mazur, A., Halpern, C. and Udry, R. 1994 Dominant looking male teenagers copulate earlier. *Ethology and Sociobiology* 15: 87–94.

Mead, M. 1928. *Coming of Age in Samoa*. New York: Morrow.

Mead, M. 1935. *Sex and Temperament in Three Primitive Societies*. New York: Morrow.

Mitchell, D., Mitchell, C., and Ofshe, R. 1980. *The Light on Synanon*. New York: Seaview.

Model, S. 1981. Housework by husbands: Determinants and implications. *Journal of Family Issues* 2: 225–37.

Money, J. 1961. Sex hormones and other variables in human eroticism. In W. Young and G. Corner (eds.), *Sex and Internal Secretions*. Vol. II. Baltimore: Williams and Wilkins.

Money, J. 1965. Influence of hormones on sexual behavior. *Annual Review of Medicine* 16: 67–82.

Money, J. and Ehrhardt, A. 1972. *Man and Woman: Boy and Girl*. Baltimore, The Johns Hopkins University Press.

Mueller, C. and Pope, H. 1980 Divorce and female remarriage mobility. *Social Forces* 58: 726–38.

Murstein, B. 1980. Mate selection in the 1970s. *Journal of Marriage and the Family* 42: 777–92.

Murstein, B. I., and Christy, P. 1976. Physical attractiveness and marriage adjustments in middle-aged couples. *Journal of Personality and Social Psychology* 34: 537–42.

Mussell, K. 1984 *Fantasy and Reconciliation: Contemporary Formulas of Women's Romance Fiction*. Westport, CT: Greenwood.

Norton, A. and Glick, P. 1979. Marital instability in America: Past, present, and future. In G. Levinger and O. Moles (eds.), *Divorce and Separation*. New York: Basic Books.

Pan Suiming 1993. Dangqian zhongguo de xing chunzai (Sex in contemporary China). *Shehuixue Yanjiu* (Sociological Research) 2: 106.

Paul, L. 1974. The mastery of work and the mystery of sex in a Guatemalan village. In S. Rosaldo and L. Lamphere (eds.), *Women, Culture, and Society*. Palo Alto, CA: Stanford University Press.

Pellow, D. 1986. *Ghana: Coping with uncertainty*. Boulder, CO: Westview.

Perusse, D. 1993 Cultural and reproductive success in industrial societies: Testing the relationship at the ultimate and proximate levels. *Behavioral and Brain Sciences 16*: 267–322.

Redfield, R. 1957. The universally human and the culturally variable. *Journal of General Education 10*: 150–60.

Remoff, H. 1984. *Sexual Choice*. New York: Dutton.

Rhyne, D. 1981. Bases of marital satisfaction among men and women. *Journal of Marriage and the Family 43*: 941–55.

Riesman, D., Glazer, N., and Denney, R. 1950. *The Lonely Crowd*. New Haven, CT: Yale University Press.

Roche, J. 1986. Premarital sex: attitudes and behavior by dating stage. *Adolescence 2*: 107–21.

Rodin, J., Silberstein, L., and Striegel-Moore, R. 1984. Women and weight: A normative discontent. *Nebraska Symposium on Motivation*: 267–307.

Rothenburg, A. 1990. Adolescence and eating disorder: The obsessive-compulsive syndrome. *Psychiatric Clinics of North America 13*: 469–88.

Rossi, A. 1977. A biosocial perspective on parenting. *Daedalus: Journal of the American Academy of Arts and Sciences 106*: 1–31.

Rossi, A. 1985. Gender and parenthood. In A. Rossi (ed.), *Gender and the life course*. New York: Aldine.

Rubin, L. 1983. *Intimate strangers*. New York: Harper & Row.

Sadalla, E., Kenrick, D., and Vershure, B. 1987. Dominance and heterosexual attraction. *Journal of Personality and Social Psychology 52*: 730–38.

Scanzoni, J. 1978. *Sex Roles, Women's Work, and Marital Conflict*. Lexington, MA: Heath.

Scanzoni, J. 1979. An historical perspective on husband-wife bargaining power and marital dissolution. In G. Levinger & O. Moles (eds.), *Divorce and Separation*. New York: Basic Books.

Scanzoni, J. 1983. *Shaping Tomorrow's Family*. Beverly Hills, CA: Sage.

Scheff, T. 1985. Universal expressive needs: A critique and theory. *Symbolic Interaction 8*: 241–62.

Schmitt, D. and Buss, D. 1996. Strategic self-promotion and competitor derogation. *Journal of Personality and Social Psychology 70*: 1185–1204.

Sergios, P .A., and Cody, J. 1985. Physical attractiveness and social assertiveness skills in male homosexual dating behavior and partner selection. *Journal of Social Psychology 125*: 505–14.

Shaywitz, B., Shaywitz, S., Pugh, K., Constable, R., Skudlarski, P., Fulbright, R., Bronen, R., Fletcher, J., Shankweller, D., Katz, L., Gore, J. 1995. Sex differences in the functional organization of the brain for language. *Nature 373*: 607–9.

Sheper, J. 1981. The matrifocal family—From anthrolpological curiosity to a world problem. In *International Conference on the Unity of Sciences: Absolute Values and the Search for the Peace of Mankind* (vol. 2):

999–1012. New York: International Cultural Foundation Press.

Sheper, J. and Tiger, M. 1983. Kibbutz and parental investment. In P. Hare, H. Blumberg, V. Kent, and M. Davies (eds.), *Small groups: Social-Psychological Processes, Social Action, and Living Together*. London: John Wiley & Sons.

Shields, W. and Shields, L. 1983. Forcible rape: An evolutionary perspective. *Ethology and Sociobiology* 4: 115–37.

Shilts, R. 1987a. Patient zero. *California Magazine* (October): 96 F.

Shilts, R. 1987b. *And the Band Played On: Politics, People, and the AIDS Epidemic*. New York: St. Martin's Press.

Shore, B. 1983. Paradox regained: Freeman's Margaret Mead and Samoa. *American Anthropologist* 85: 935–44.

Shorter, E. 1975. *The Making of the Modern Family*. New York: Basic Books.

Simon, W. and Gagnon, J. 1986. Sexual scripts: Permanence and change. *Archives of Sexual Behavior* 15: 97–120.

Simpson, J. 1987. The dissolution of romantic relationships: Factors involved in relationship stability and emotional distress. *Journal of Personality and Social Psychology* 53: 683–92.

Simpson, J., and Gangestad, S. 1991a. Individual differences in sociosexuality: Evidence for convergent and discriminant validity. *Journal of Personality and Social Psychology* 60: 870–83.

Simpson, J., and Gangestad, S. 1991b. Personality and sexuality: Empirical relations and an integrative theoretical model. In K. McKinney and S. Sprecher (eds.), *Sexuality in close relationships*. Hillsdale, NJ: Lawrence Erlbaum.

Simpson, J., and Gangestad, S. 1992. Sociosexuality and romantic partner choice. *Journal of Personality* 60: 31–51.

Singer, B. 1985a. A comparison of evolutionary and environmental theories of erotic response: Part I: Structural features. *The Journal of Sex Research* 21: 229–57.

Singer, B. 1985b. A comparison of evolutionary and environmental theories of erotic response: Part II: Empirical arenas. *The Journal of Sex Research* 21: 345–74.

Singh, D. 1993. Adaptive significance of female physical attractiveness: Role of waist-to-hip ratio. *Journal of Personality and Social Psychology* 65: 293–307.

Singh, D. 1995. Female judgment of male attractiveness and desirability for relationships: Role of waist-to-hip ratio and financial status. *Journal of Personality and Social Psychology* 69: 1089–1101.

Smith, J., Waldorf, V. A., and Trembath, D. 1990. "Single white male looking for thin, very attractive. . ." *Sex Roles* 23: 675–84.

Spanier, G. 1976. Formal and informal sex education as determinants of premarital sexual behavior. *Archives of Sexual Behavior* 5: 39–67.

Sprecher, S., Sullivan, Q., and Hatfield, E. 1994. Mate selection preferences:

Gender differences examined in a national sample. *Journal of Personality and Social Psychology 66*: 1074–80.

Stephens, W. 1963. *The Family in Cross-Cultural Perspective*. Washington, D.C.: University Press of America.

Stone, A. 1985. Emotional aspects of contemporary relations. In K. Davis (ed.), *Contemporary Marriage*. New York: Russell Sage Foundation.

Strasser, S. 1982. *Never Done: A History of American Housework*. New York: Pantheon.

Symons 1979. *Evolution of Human sexuality*. New York: Oxford University Press.

Symons, D. 1985. Darwinism and contemporary marriage. In K. Davis (ed.), *Contemporary marriage*. New York: Russell Sage Foundation.

Symons, D. 1987. The evolutionary approach: Can Darwin's view of life shed light on human sexuality? In J. Geer and W. O'Donohue (eds.), *Theories of Human Sexuality*. New York: Plenum Press.

Symons, D. 1989. A critique of Darwinian anthropology. *Ethology and Sociobiology 10*: 131–44.

Symons, D. 1992. What do men want? *Behavioral and Brain Sciences 15*: 115.

Tanfer, K., and Schoorl, J. 1992. Premarital sexual careers and partner change. *Archives of Sexual Behavior 21*: 45–68.

Tavris, C. and Sadd, S. 1977. *The* Redbook *Report on Female Sexuality*. New York: Delacorte.

Tennov, D. 1979. *Love and Limerance: The Experience of Being in Love*. New York: Stein and Day.

Thornhill, N. 1989. Characteristics of female desirability: facultative standards of beauty. *Behavioral and Brain Sciences 12*: 35–36.

Thornhill, R. and Thornhill, N. 1983. Human rape: An evolutionary perspective. *Ethology and Sociobiology 4*: 137–73.

Tilly, L. 1978. The social sciences and the study of women: A review article. *Comparative Studies in Society and History 20*: 163–73.

Tong, X. 1993. Woguo yinghui wuming de shehui weihai (Social harmfulness of obscene materials). *Shehuixue Yanjiu* (Sociological Research) *3*: 56.

Tooby, J., and Cosmides, L. 1992. The psychological foundations of culture. In J. H. Barkow, L. Cosmides, and J. Tooby (eds.), *The Adapted Mind*. New York: Oxford University Press.

Townsend, J. M. 1978. *Cultural Conceptions and Mental Illness*. Chicago: University of Chicago Press.

Townsend, J. M. 1987. Sex differences in sexuality among medical students: Effects of increasing socioeconomic status. *Archives of Sexual Behavior 16*: 427–46.

Townsend, J. M. 1989. Mate-selection criteria: A pilot study. *Ethology and Sociobiology 10*: 241–53.

Townsend, J. M. 1992. Measuring the magnitude of sex differences. *Behavioral and Brain Sciences 15*: 115.

Townsend, J. M. 1993. Sexuality and partner selection: Sex differences among college students. *Ethology and Sociobiology 14*: 305–30.

Townsend, J. M. 1995. "Racial, Ethnic, and Mental Illness Stereotypes: Cognitive Process and Behavioral Effects." In *Mental Health, Racism, and Sexism*, Charles V. Willie (Ed.). Baltimore: University of Pittsburgh Press, 1995, pp. 119–147.

Townsend, J. M. 1995. Sex without emotional involvement: An evolutionary interpretation of sex differences. *Archives of Sexual Behavior 24*: 171–204.

Townsend, J. M. 1996. *Race, status, and sexual attractiveness: An evolutionary interpretation of sex differences.* Paper presented at the Annual Meeting of the Society for the Scientific Study of Sexuality, Houston, Texas.

Townsend, J. M., and Jankowiak, W. 1986. Sex differences in mate choice and sexuality: A comparison of the United States and China. *Human Mosaic 20*: 9–76.

Townsend, J. M., and Levy, G.D. 1990a. Effects of potential partners' costume and physical attractiveness on sexuality and partner selection. *Journal of Psychology 124*: 371–89.

Townsend, J. M., and Levy, G.D. 1990b. Effects of potential partners' physical attractiveness and socioeconomic status on sexuality and partner selection: Sex differences in reported preferences of university students. *Archives of Sexual Behavior 19*: 149–64.

Townsend, J. M., & Roberts, L.W. 1993. Gender differences in mate preference among law students: Divergence and convergence of criteria. *Journal of Psychology 127*: 507–28.

Townsend, J. M., Kline, J. and Wasserman, T. 1995. Low-investment copulation: Sex differences in motivations and emotional reactions. *Ethology and Sociobiology 16*: 25–51.

Townsend, J. M. and Wasserman, T. 1997. The perception of sexual attractiveness: Sex differences in variability. *Archives of Sexual Behavior 19*: 243–68.

Trivers, R. 1985. *Social Evolution.* Palo Alto, CA: Benjamin Cummings Publishing Co.

Udry, J. R. 1977. The importance of being beautiful: A reexamination and racial comparison. *American Journal of Sociology 83*: 154–60.

Udry, J. R. 1981. Marital alternatives and marital disruption. *Journal of Marriage and the Family 43*: 889–97.

Udry, J. R., Deven, F., and Coleman, S. 1982. Cross-national comparison of the relative influence of male and female age on the frequency of marital inter-course. *Journal of Biosocial Science 14*: 1–6.

Udry, J. R., Billy, J., Morris, N., Groff, T., and Raj, M. 1985. Serum androgenic hormones motivate sexual behavior in adolescent boys. *Fertility and Sterility 43*: 90–94.

Udry, J. R., Talbert, L., and Morris, N. 1986. Biosocial foundations for adolescent female sexuality. *Demography* 23: 217–27.

Udry, J. R., and Billy, J. O. G. 1987. Initiation of coitus in early adolescence. *American Sociological Review* 52: 841–55.

Udry, J. R., and Eckland, B. K. 1984 Benefits of being attractive: Differential pay-offs for men and women. *Psychological Reports* 54: 47–56.

Useche, B., Villegas, M., and Alzate, H. 1990. Sexual behavior of Colombian high school students. *Adolesence* 25: 291–304.

Van den Berghe, P. 1979. *Human Family Systems.* New York: Elsevier.

Wang, J. 1992. Zhejiang nongmin yidi lianyin xintedian. (The new characteristics of peasants' marriage: Husband and wife from two different region. *Shehuixue Yanjiu* (Sociological Research) 4: 92–95.

Weinrich, J. 1988. The periodic table model of the gender transpositions: Part II. Limerant and lusty sexual attractions and the nature of bisexuality. *The Journal of Sex Research* 24: 113–29.

Weitzman, L. 1985. The divorce law revolution and the transformation of legal marriage. In K. Davis (ed.), *Contemporary Marriage.* New York: Russell Sage Foundation.

Whyte, M. and Parish, W. 1984. *Urban Life in Contemporary China.* Chicago: University of Chicago Press.

Wiederman, W. W., and Allgeier, E. R. 1992. Gender differences in mate selection criteria. *Ethology and Sociobiology* 13: 115–24.

Wilson, G. 1981. Cross-generational stability of gender differences in sexuality. *Personality and Individual Differences* 2: 254–62.

Wilson, G. 1987. Male-female differences in sexual activity, enjoyment, and fantasies. *Personality and Individual Differences* 8: 125–35.

Wooden, K. 1981. *The children of Jonestown.* New York: McGraw-Hill.

Xu, A. 1994. Zhongguo lihun xianzhuang, tedian jiqi qushi (Features and trends of divorce in China: The current situation). *Shanghai Shehui Kexueyuan Xueshu Jikan* (Quarterly Journal of the Shanghai Social Science Academy) 2: 156–65.

Yeh, B., and Lester, D. 1987. Statewide divorce rates and wives' participation in the labor market. *Journal of Divorce* 11: 107–14.

Yogev, S. 1981. Do professional women have egalitarian relationships? *Journal of Marriage and the Family* 43: 865–71.

Zhang, H. 1991. Lihun shijian zhong de "Xiufu Xianxiang" (The phenomenon of "husband dumping"). *Shehui* (Sociology Journal) 1: 35–36.

Zhao Zixing et al. 1992. "Zhongguo qi chensi qumin shenguo yishi yu laodong taidu yanjiu" (Report on perceptions of life and work in the seven cities of China). *Sheui Kexue Qikan* (Social Science Selection), (Shenyang) 2: 30–35.

Zhu S. 1992. Ziyouniao: Xiandai Ruzi Dusheng Xianxiang (Singlehood among modern women). *Shuhui* (Sociology Journal) 9: 42–44.

Index

Printed in the United States
37151LVS00002B/206